Advance praise for

THE PLACE BETWEEN OUR PAINS

"A gay man is obviously not the target audience of a memoir that revels in the memory of visiting a clothing-optional 'penis-free environment.' But K.J. Ramsey writes with soulful magic and witty, welcoming grace—and she creates belonging. She takes you places you never expected to go, shows you things you never thought you'd see, and stirs emotions you never imagined you'd feel. Banana slugs, very human bodies, marrow-level pain, soul-lifting marvel: This book is brave and beautiful."

—Jeff Chu, author of *Good Soil*

"The best writing is the most honest, and K.J. Ramsey has written a memoir that tells the whole truth with all its teeth and tenderness. *The Place Between Our Pains* is a searing and generous companion for anyone who's carried trauma, chronic illness, or the wreckage of bad religion in their body."

—David Gate, author of *A Rebellion of Care*

"What you need to know most about this book is that K.J. Ramsey could not have written it without going into the depths of her own being to pull out every sacred thread in order for us to come alongside her and quietly sew our own story together, too. In every essay there is an invitation into liminality and the complexity of being human while proclaiming that, as Ramsey writes [quoting Meredith from *Grey's Anatomy*], 'the sun still rises on my life.' I hope you'll accept the invitation she offers to go deeply into our stories and experiences, choosing to stay there just as she has, and to name presence even when it feels impossible to do so."

—Kaitlin B. Curtice, award-winning author of *Native* and *Everything Is a Story*

"This book is a harrowing account of a woman who has contended with serious illness for most of her adult life. It is also a witness to the hope that arises even in misery. 'We cannot heal our way out of being human,' she writes, but she insists that love and joy can uplift us in the spaces between our pains."

—Kathleen Norris, *New York Times* bestselling author of *The Cloister Walk*

"An antidote to cynicism and despair in the midst of suffering, K.J. Ramsey's latest book generously offers all of us a hard-won story of how to deepen our capacity for joy, even when nothing has turned out as advertised. As she writes, 'Hope is a team sport,' and after reading her book, I know that you will want Ramsey's wisdom, humor, and honesty on your team."

—SARAH BESSEY, bestselling author of *Field Notes for the Wilderness* and editor of *A Rhythm of Prayer*

"This book reads as a guide into the wild and natural worlds we exist within: the ones outside all around, and the ones inside that we embody. Ramsey reminds us that no matter how rugged, surprising, and full of mystery—it is our connection with them that invites us into a life full of beauty."

—HILLARY MCBRIDE, PHD, psychologist, author, and podcast host

"The body is fragile, the body endures. K.J. Ramsey takes us through the hope and hurt of a body enduring. When despair lurks, Ramsey finds the meaningful, the humorous shared looks of understanding, those moments of autonomy worth holding that hold us. From majestic mountainsides to the placement of a port to the challenges of physical therapy, Ramsey's memoir is alive with details, grand and small, of living with overwhelming pain and how the divine unexpectedly finds us in it. Here, you will find worth that stays in the hurt."

—J.S. PARK, BCC, hospital chaplain and author of *As Long as You Need: Permission to Grieve*

"K.J. Ramsey does it again in her new memoir, *The Place Between Our Pains*! She shares the ups and downs of living with chronic illness and pain, including the experiences we don't always know how to imagine. It is my privilege to endorse this beautiful book and to tell you that joy is always present if only we can be present to the joy."

—SUZANNE STABILE, co-author of *The Road Back to You,* author of *The Path Between Us* and *The Journey Toward Wholeness,* and host of *The Enneagram Journey* podcast

"There is a blessing that only the broken can hear, and K.J. Ramsey guides us to that blessing with sacred wit, beautiful grief, and surprising joy. . . . A literary oasis in our desert of despair."

—Scott Erickson, co-author of *In the Low* and author of *Honest Advent*

THE PLACE BETWEEN OUR PAINS

THE PLACE BETWEEN OUR PAINS

A MEMOIR OF WHAT JOY CAN SURVIVE

K.J. RAMSEY

CONVERGENT
New York

Convergent
An imprint of Random House
A division of Penguin Random House LLC
1745 Broadway, New York, NY 10019
convergentbooks.com
penguinrandomhouse.com

Grateful acknowledgment is made to Rosemerry Wahtola Trommer for permission to reprint "Safety Net" from *All the Honey* by Rosemerry Wahtola Trommer (Samara Press, 2023). Used by permission of the author.

Hardcover ISBN 978-0-593-72739-3
Ebook ISBN 978-0-593-72740-9

Printed in the United States of America

1st Printing

First Edition

Book Team: Production editor: Robert Siek • Managing editor: Allison Fox • Production manager: Sandra Sjursen • Copy editor: Scott Heim • Proofreaders: Robin Slutzky and Judy Kiviat

Book design by Debbie Glasserman

The authorized representative in the EU for product safety and compliance is Penguin Random House Ireland, Morrison Chambers, 32 Nassau Street, Dublin D02 YH68, Ireland. https://eu-contact.penguin.ie

TO RYAN,

WHO LOVED ME BACK TO LIFE.

AND FOR THOSE WHO ENDURE SICKNESS:

YOUR STORIES DESERVE TO BE TOLD

AND YOUR PERSEVERANCE

IS A MIRACLE.

Safety Net

This morning I woke
thinking of all the people I love
and all the people they love
and how big the net of lovers.
It felt so clear,
all those invisible ties
interwoven like silken threads
strong enough to make a mesh
that for thousands of years
has been woven and rewoven
to catch us all.
Sometimes we go on
as if we forget about it.
Believing only in the fall.
But the net is just as real.
Every day, with every small kindness,
with every generous act,
we strengthen it.
Notice, even now,
how as the whole world
seems to be falling,
the net is there for us
as we walk the day's tightrope.
Notice how every tie matters.

—ROSEMERRY WAHTOLA TROMMER[1]

1 Rosemerry Wahtola Trommer, *All the Honey: Poems* (n.p.: Samara Press, 2023), 26. Used with permission of the author.

CONTENTS

PART II

PART III

PART IV

AUTHOR'S NOTE

THIS IS A true story. The memoir you are about to read began as blank pages in empty journals, filled day after day in both delight and dread, daring myself to bless my existence as worthy of being witnessed, no matter how much my own story surprised me. To tell this story as true, viscerally honest, and accurate to what I lived and felt, I relied upon my journals, medical records, photos, memories, and conversations with eyewitnesses. By the time I began translating my journals into typed stories for this book, the story itself had untamed me. When you almost lose your life, you no longer want to waste any time being anything but whole. Tucked inside these pages is my most free and feral self. You are about to encounter words that were once washed right out of my mouth, a mind that processes reality through metaphor, a heart that holds as much humor as hurt, and a neurodivergent brain that can't build anything without excessive amounts of alliteration. Here I am! Don't say I didn't warn you.

To protect the innocent and damn the asses, the names of

most of my medical providers have been changed. You may recognize some names pulled from *Parks and Recreation*. One story has been condensed for brevity. Many more wonderful and horrible things happened during the span of time this book describes, but I'm not mean enough to make you read it all.

Finally, while I am a licensed professional counselor, please know that this book is not intended to provide medical or psychological advice. If you know or suspect you have a health condition or traumatic history that needs tending or find yourself feeling overwhelmed by the themes addressed in this book, please seek the care of a physician, therapist, or other professional support. You are utterly worthy of care.

INVITATION

You need not fear facing that which
you have already survived.

THAT'S WHAT I told myself before I put any words on these pages. For weeks—no, months—I feared the stack of journals beside my bed. They sat there benign as Easter eggs in their pastel hues, pale yellow and pink and lavender, holding memories I couldn't fully recall and wasn't sure I wanted to relive. I remembered enough about filling them over the past year to know there wasn't just candy inside.

The story you are about to read is the result of opening those pages. Both this book and I are among its main characters. And neither of us makes it to the last page unchanged.

This was supposed to be a book about joy, and it might still be. Years ago, I surveyed readers about what the word *joy* evokes in them, and nearly a thousand responses poured in within hours, mostly echoing the same thing: *joy feels elusive, unattainable, and triggering of guilt and shame.* Dozens upon dozens reported that joy didn't feel safe. Instead of sources of strength, imperative statements like "rejoice always," "choose joy," or "count it all joy" felt like swords aimed at their ache. It was clear: the concept of joy often feels more like a weapon than a welcome.

At the time, I was fresh out the door of what was then my hardest season, indignant that anyone I love would feel so crushed by disappointment or a lack of safe connection that they'd walk through life believing joy was something for other people, but not for them. In recovering from both complex post-traumatic stress disorder and my worst flare of chronic illness yet, I was surprised by the quiet joy that had met me, even in difficulty. Joy kept finding me, not in rising above sadness or anger but in reaching toward them—and through them, to others.

So many of us have been taught to rush past pain to get back to productivity, praise, or pleasantness, and in doing so, we sidestep the place where joy actually dwells.

"When we lose our tolerance for vulnerability," Brené Brown writes, "joy becomes foreboding."[2] When I set out to write this book, I ventured into the territory of my earliest vulnerabilities *and* joys. I had traced the trails of my childhood and adult trauma for years, both as a licensed professional counselor and as a client myself. I needed to look long and hard at the uglier parts of my life to no longer be bound by them. But I didn't want to focus on what was wrong anymore, as though my life were only a wasteland. I'd spent long enough looking backward for what was rotting. I wanted to forage through the forest of my family and faith to find what grew.

Finally feeling the best I'd felt in my adult life, I set off on the first of what was supposed to be many cross-country road trips to dare myself to discover that joy is more trustworthy than trauma. I planned a whole summer of revisiting national

2 Brené Brown, *Atlas of the Heart: Mapping Meaningful Connection and the Language of Human Experience* (New York: Random House, 2021), 215.

parks I'd first seen with my family—the places I first recall feeling joy. I drove off in hope that no matter how much trauma had shaped me or may scar me again, joy would always be my strength.

I came home to the hardest experiences of my life. If you ever want to write a book, let me be the first to warn you that your life will test its truth.

When I was a girl, stories were my safest place. I took refuge from reality in chapter books, each one a portal into a place where plots resolve and pain has purpose. Stories shielded me from shouts, usually in the solitude of my own curious and sensitive soul. But sometimes, on magical evenings, when stars surpassed cities in light and campfire corralled our family into a circle of warmth, stories would become a shared shelter.

Across the campgrounds of America, on more summers than not, Dad would read by the beam of a flashlight to me and my three siblings before he and Mom would tuck us into our motorhome beds for another day of exploring our national parks. His favorite stories were Patrick F. McManus's riotous tales of failed fishermen who sail ice-fishing shacks and bears that eat grandmas. We kids learned to love the land by laughing in the dark.

The following isn't the story I planned to tell, nor is it the story I would have preferred to live. But I decided to crack open the pages of my journals from the most beautiful and brutal year of my life, because in my best moments, I know I'm far from the only one carrying a load of pain through life from plotlines I never would have picked. If that's you, grab a seat.

Let me tell you a strange and sometimes hilarious story for the dark.

THE PLACE BETWEEN OUR PAINS

PART I

Even a wounded world is feeding us. Even a wounded world holds us, giving us moments of wonder and joy. I choose joy over despair. Not because I have my head in the sand, but because joy is what the earth gives me daily and I must return the gift.

ROBIN WALL KIMMERER,
Braiding Sweetgrass

SALT AND SKY

JUNE

I CAN HEAR the faint song of a stream outside the open mesh window of my rooftop tent. It's why we camped here, nestled between bald hills on the side of something so potholed it could only generously be called a road. I want this pilgrimage to begin with water.

I reach toward my toes to stretch my sore legs and sigh with contentment. I woke up before dawn to leave home in Colorado to make it to the Salt Lake City airport in time for my friend Sarah Southern's arrival from San Diego. Sarah lies beside me under a striped Pendleton blanket, raking her wavy brown hair into a messy bun. My eyes are bleary from the long drive, but I crack open the fresh yellow journal I bought to record this journey and write in the glow of a headlamp.

A warm breeze wafts the scent of wild sage through the tent window. The aromatic sagebrush matches what it feels like to be well enough to be here in the middle of Nowhere, Nevada, with one of my dearest writer friends, driving to national parks I haven't been to since long before my body ever broke. Pure. Sweet. Grounded. Perhaps even medicinal.

I spent the last month unpacking moving boxes, making Ryan's and my very first house a home. We had to move from Denver to Colorado Springs to afford it, but the joy of having a house far outweighs the sadness of leaving the city we've long called home. For the first thirteen years of our marriage, buying a house seemed impossible. Between the burden of my high healthcare needs and the ruin of leaving behind careers in abusive churches, a down payment seemed like a dream everyone else could see come true but us. But the dream did come true.

And it's funny to leave a place you just reached, especially after more than a decade of struggling to believe it was possible to get there. But I sense that to keep receiving joy and goodness as possible for *me,* not just everyone else, I need to explore the landscapes where I learned to look for them in the first place. In revisiting these national parks, I am returning to the roots of my resilience.

I can't stop smiling about the delight today held. When I finally reached Sarah, we were like giddy schoolgirls. We found a restaurant near the airport and shoveled down giant bites of chicken shawarma while plotting our plan for the night and spilling all the tea we could about the ridiculousness of the writing and publishing world. Then we drove-danced westward, our bodies crackling like lightning to the beats of Remi Wolf and the Doobie Brothers and Electric Light Orchestra's "Mr. Blue Sky," grinning and laughing at the good fortune of getting to go on this epic writing trip together. One year ago, this would not have been possible.

One year ago, I graduated from a program I never wanted to enter. I spent that spring in cardiac rehab beside people twice my age or more, training my body to walk again after spending months completely debilitated from a virus that tried to pit my heart and brain as enemies. Postural orthostatic tachycardia syndrome (POTS) was one of many new diagnoses I received that spring, on top of what was already challenging. Names of diseases and disorders I could barely pronounce kept stacking up beneath mine like a brick wall. The list was so large I could barely see over it to a life that could still be both long and good.

The day I started cardiac rehab, two minutes on the NuStep was all I could handle without collapsing in exhaustion. There were so many days when—as with the house I wasn't sure we would ever be able to buy—I also wasn't sure my body would ever feel like a home instead of a holding cell. Yet today I drove twelve hours, dancing in the driver's seat most of the way.

I'm trying to trust that this home will hold me. I drove westward not simply to explore places from my past, but to explore the possibility of joy that pain often obscures.

On the last stretch of our drive, roadside grass glowed fluorescent as light streamed through thick clouds in slants over the vast water of the Great Salt Lake. Right as the pale blue sky began shifting to amber and umber, the lake shone like a sea of crystals. We came upon the Bonneville Salt Flats without knowing they were there and pulled over. Sarah and I sprinted onto the salt, speechless in surprise at the beauty that just happened to be along our route. Waves of cotton-candy colors reflected in shallow pools of water over thick-grained salt stretching to the horizon, where massive mountains encircled the flats like a mother's outstretched arms.

It was as though we'd stumbled into a gift. We only expected to drive until dark to arrive at our free campsite for the night. Observing an orchestra playing across salt and sky was beyond what we had imagined for the day. But that's what joy does. Often, the most beautiful sights are the ones we didn't plan to find.

STRIPPED

SARAH AND I wake to sunlit warmth and unzip our tent to find verdant hills slathered with butter-yellow wildflowers, dripping color before a nearly cloudless azure sky. I wander off to find a secluded spot to pee and am met by patches of yellow bush lupine everywhere I look. Lupine, my favorite wildflower, greets me here at the beginning of a journey into my past. It is quiet, save for the chirping of birds and the gentle exhale of a warm breeze.

I didn't know Nevada could be so green. In my mind, this place was all desert.

After finishing the last sips of strong coffee, we pack up and decide to brave the bumpy road a little farther to a hot spring that supposedly sits at the end of the road. We come to a crossing, and instead of risking drowning Reepijeep—the ridiculous name my husband and I gave our Jeep Compass (shoutout to Narnia Nerds)—Sarah and I roll up our pants and wade to the other side of the fast creek.

Right in the cleft of two nearly neon-green hills, yellow arrowleaf balsamroot and purple penstemon flank the trail, leading us to the steaming water ahead. I set down my water bottle and phone next to some low-growing golden flowers and make a declaration. "There's no way I can be in a spot this stunning and this secluded and not strip!"

Sarah laughs and shakes her head at me—my skinny-dipping antics are clearly unsurprising. "That's fine," she says, "as long as you're fine with me keeping my suit *on*!"

I am learning that joy waits for our willingness to be stripped of societal expectations and norms. She nudges and tugs, asking us to be fully present to the magic of being *here*.

I smell sulfur and sage, and no one but Sarah is in sight. So I strip down to my skin and step into the steaming water, smiling bright with the memory of my younger self and her spark. I want to sense her defiance from head to toe. I want to channel her freedom. I want to remember what it is like to be naked and unafraid.

SCARS

WE DRIVE ALL day through the arid expanse of eastern Oregon and eventually wind our way into a thick forest. After a day in the desert, the sight of a waterfall is like a welcome mat. I pull to the side of the road, and we cross the vacant highway to take in the view.

For hours, Sarah and I have been talking about the freedom to take risks. From taking a road trip across America partly solo, to changing careers as an adult, I'm realizing that my own capacity to tolerate the fear of risk was forged in childhood. There are some risks I move toward like a dog to a bone because I was given free range to roam as a kid in a way that rarely happens today.

The forest surrounding my childhood home was my friend, with whom I played every day until Mom rang the dinner bell to call us kids home. I explored beneath the boughs of big ash trees, inspecting worms in the soil or resting my back against bark with a book in my hands. Across the dirt road at my grandpa's, I filled winters sledding down the steep, snowy hill, screaming in delight and swerving before hitting the frozen lake at the bottom.

The forest was also the place I was unsupervised and unprotected from my bully. I never knew when play would turn into pain, when walking through the woods would turn into being chased with a BB gun or sledding would end with my face shoved in the snow until I couldn't breathe. What I'm saying is, in my childhood, joy was often invaded by terror, and that volatility left invisible scars across my nervous system. For me, delight and danger are tangled.

This trip is more than an adventure—I'm on a pilgrimage into my past. I'm traveling to some of the national parks my parents brought me and my three siblings to as kids, so I can untangle trauma from love.

I don't remember vast stretches of my childhood, a hallmark of complex childhood trauma that I didn't recognize as dissociation until I was well into my studies to become a therapist. But I do remember many of our trips to the national parks. And I sense that revisiting the places where I most recall feeling wonder, joy, and safety as a child will help me hold the pain that remains in my adult life differently.

Complex trauma is not primarily living with a library of terrifying memories; it's living with the felt sense, held in our bodies, that at any moment love and goodness can and will hurt us.

And that we will end up alone with that ache.

Sometimes, I wonder how much of the pain of chronic illness is my child-self crying out for a witness. My screams and tears were not met with enough protection and presence, and that void taught me to shove vulnerability down deep beneath my skin. The places that pain still haunts me are the places I still need presence.

I'm taking this trip so I can re-experience the love that *did* exist in my childhood right in the midst of trauma—now that I have the internal resources to see it. I want to tell my younger self that *I* will never leave her alone with her pain.

I want to trust that joy is not a trick.

We are just hours from arriving at Crater Lake National Park. The roaring waterfall beside the empty state highway cools our skin as Sarah and I stand at its edge. Earlier, Sarah shared that she has never been to any of the national parks we're about to visit, nor was she given much room to explore on her own as a kid. I'm realizing that while my childhood held real chaos, it also fostered curiosity. And that curiosity has called out through the decades of my life just as much as my cries.

I am at home in the woods and safe in the shelter of mountains because the same parents who didn't hear some of my loudest cries did show me the wonder of rivers and trails and skies. Every skinned knee is part of my spirituality. I can risk being wrong. I can risk getting hurt. I can explore and question and stand in awe without answers because they let me play, because my parents showed me how to seek what is beautiful and good with my own eyes.

I crouch beside the steel guardrail separating me from the water far below. I trace a faint scar on my inner left calf as I take in the beauty of how this creek has cut the hill into falls. I'm beginning to recognize a pattern. Every scar is part of the story.

PLACES

AN APACHE MAN named Dudley tells a researcher:

> Wisdom sits in places. It's like water that never dries up. You need to drink water to stay alive, don't you? Well, you also need to drink from places. You must remember everything about them. You must learn their names. You must remember what happened at them long ago. You must think about it and keep on thinking about it. Then your mind will become smoother and smoother. Then you will see danger before it happens. You will walk a long way and live a long time. You will be wise.[1]

READ THE SIGNS

COOL AIR BLOWS through our open windows, giving me goosebumps. The air chills with every mile we ascend closer to Crater Lake. I close the windows. We curve through old growth forests, and the ground mists recent rain up into the most magical fog. The setting sun reaches toward us like God's two hands, fingers of light spreading through tall pines.

The farther we drive, the snowier it gets. By the time we near the caldera's edge and the brilliant water far below, the snowdrifts are at least twelve feet high.

1 Keith H. Basso, *Wisdom Sits in Places: Landscape and Language Among the Western Apache* (Albuquerque: University of New Mexico Press, 1996), 70.

I make a U-turn to grab the first parking spot I see, heart thumping with delight. I don't want to miss this moment. We rush to the trunk and stuff our bare arms into down jackets for the sudden thirty-degree temperature drop, slipping off our sandals and pulling on boots to crest the massive snowbank standing between us and the caldera. We scramble and then surrender, speechless.

Sapphire-blue water gleams hundreds of feet below, stretching into the largest circle I've ever seen, ringed by white-peaked mountains. The earth has collectively raised this singular spot, and stepping near her edges is like stepping into sky. Everything ugly recedes, not fading but bowing to a beauty that is infinite. This lake holds only rain and snow. A crater formed in the most violent of volcanic eruptions now holds some of the purest water on the continent.

We arrive just in time to see the sun wave goodnight over the lip of the mountain, hushed by a lullaby of amber light.

I look all around me at a world that's so *well,* so unmistakably alive though wildfires burn one state away and the water below becomes less pure each day. I look down at my legs with mirrored wonder to be well enough to be standing here, on the ledge of the deepest lake in this country. The caldera is a gaping mouth. Its jagged rim of teeth tells a story of eruption and genesis.

The sky ripens. Blueberry, tangerine, peach. I'm breathing deeper than I have in weeks, in months, in over a year. The frigid air stings my cheeks and clears my lungs. It smells of pine and dirt. At the corner of my eye, I glimpse a sign sticking out of the snowbank, almost completely buried. The reflex to read it is strong.

A national park is a memory castle. A sign locates not just a place but my purest memories. I swear Dad made us stop to read every sign we ever saw in a national park, an annoyance to us kids that is now entirely endearing. Dad was determined not just to show us the sights, but to teach us their stories.[2]

I sigh into the expanse, breath meeting breeze, grateful to have been given a learned impulse to revere a place by respecting its stories. Sarah perches beside me, her face transcendent. The sky's symphony sounds through us.

"This is holier than any church I've been in," Sarah says.

"I agree."

HOLD MUSIC

WE TURN BACK as the light fades. Plan A for tonight's campsite is covered in ten feet of snow that the park website definitely didn't mention, so we head to Plan B—a parking lot sanctuary from the snow, at a slightly lower elevation.

The sky drips like peach ice cream down the hand of a child who can't lick fast enough. I pull over at the first stop sign, eager to savor every drop. From my phone, I play *Recomposed by Max Richter: Vivaldi, The Four Seasons*.

For as long as I can remember, I've consumed music like a child who will only eat chicken nuggets—that is, I usually want the same one or two albums, on repeat, for months on end. I'm sure it's a pleasure to everyone in earshot.

Recomposed is my latest aural special interest. I came across it in the early stages of planning this trip, while reading Terry Tempest Williams's *The Hour of Land: A Personal Topography of Amer-*

2 At least, the ones the United States government deemed worthy of sharing.

ica's National Parks.[3] Near the end of the book, Tempest Williams drives through Yellowstone on her way to Livingston, Montana—a drive I've made many times on my way back to my parents' home just west of Livingston. She listens to *Recomposed,* letting the metaphor of how the music was made meet her desire to see public lands return to being places of sacred refuge.

The only time I can recall hearing *The Four Seasons* before reading *The Hour of Land* was on hold with one of my many doctors' offices. The thrum and build reminded me of long waits, awful symptoms, and feeling more like a number than a person with a name.

As soon as I finished Williams's book, I began googling and spent the rest of my waking hours that day enthralled, reading and watching Max Richter respond to questions about why he reimagined one of the most famous pieces of classical music in history.

In the eighteenth century, Vivaldi's *The Four Seasons* was the first of its kind—inventive and even radical in painting polyphonic pictures of scenes that tell a story. Violas become barking dogs. Violins mimic fierce wind and chattering teeth.[4] But somewhere in the last century, the distinctive sounds of *The Four Seasons* became filler. The story was split apart into sound bites to sell us BMWs and banking. The more Max Richter heard Vivaldi commodified into a sound to sell products or to soothe us on elevators waiting to get to where we really want to be, the less he could hear the music's original goodness.[5]

This is how I feel about Christianity. This is how I feel about the human body.

3 Terry Tempest Williams, *The Hour of Land: A Personal Topography of America's National Parks* (New York: Sarah Crichton Books/Farrar, Straus and Giroux, 2016).

4 "A Journey Through *The Four Seasons,*" Vivaldi's *Four Seasons* app, 2018.

5 "Max Richter Interview on *Recomposed,*" Star Sessions YouTube video: https://youtu.be/txG40u0MI18?si=amNrg02aB46DPG8b.

Richter decided to recompose the concertos so he could rediscover their beauty. "It's like if you make the same drive through a beautiful landscape every day to your office," Richter says. "You don't see the landscape after a while. And this was my problem. So I've taken a detour through this landscape to try to find a new way through it, to try to rediscover it."

FACT OR FICTION

THIS MORNING, WE walked along what seemed more like a tunnel of snow than a closed road. It's early June and, yet, this place still wears the clothes of winter.

Sarah laughed and grinned as I took a video of her walking alongside the towering berm with her outstretched hand snaking the snow. The plowed windrow was over twice as tall as I am.

We're currently taking a break from hiking, resting on a long dry log, journaling in near silence. Many meters of snow and a handful of pine and scrubby fir trees sit between us and the shining water far below. In the glare of the sun, Crater Lake gleams ultramarine, resting smooth as a plate of glass.

Sarah and I have both been surprised and delighted by how much snow is here. But I—I'm stunned at it, because the story I most remember about this place seems to match what I am seeing.

I know all too well that the story our body remembers is not always the story that is believed or documented as true. In my early years of suffering with chronic pain, doctors often dismissed my distress because my bloodwork did not yet match my symptoms. Specialists shrugged and made snide comments, invalidating the scary story I was experiencing in my sensations. I knew that a woman in her early twenties shouldn't feel as awful as I did. But the disbelief of doctors often made me feel crazy, as though I had made up my misery or brought it upon myself.

The only way out of a life of debilitating pain was dignifying my own perception of that pain as real and worthy of a response of care. I had to believe myself before any doctor believed me. I had to fight for help before most doctors saw the evidence that I needed it.

Both childhood and medical trauma erode our trust in ourselves as reliable narrators of our own lives. And that is what brought me here, to the site of one of my few clear memories from childhood. Every time I've told others about the memories I need to revisit on this trip—friends, my agent, my editor—I've told them about my older brother and me getting lost at Crater Lake. And inside, I wonder if the story I remember is actually true.

That summer morning decades ago, the two of us pedaled away from our parents at the campsite and ditched our bikes before descending through thick woods into a snowy ravine. Exploring was great until we realized we hadn't brought any water. We were just kids, with no food and no water, and in our panic, we lost the path we'd been following. We listened closely to get our bearings, and when we heard the gentle gurgle of a stream, we decided to trace its edge, hoping it would lead us to safety. Eventually, we spotted a ridge that seemed familiar far above us, but the only way to get there was to cross the creek, and with all the snowmelt, it was too deep. Farther down, almost out of eyeshot, thick snow formed a bridge over the creek, like a page pulled from a fairy tale. I could barely believe it even then.

We stepped as lightly as we could over the snow bridge and came to a steep rockslide leading to the ridge. The only way back was through. My brother trailed beneath me as we scurried up the rockslide so the rocks would fall on him instead of me. One sharp rock scraped my left calf as I climbed, and the scar is still there. But we made it back safe.

It's the one memory I have of my older brother helping me. And I've always feared it was fiction.

SURVEYING

THE WIND SHIFTS, and I pull a navy wool fleece over my bare arms. A giant thundercloud crouches over the remote eastern edge of the lake. I don't want us getting stuck exposed in a storm.

We cut our hike short and hustle toward the parking lot, fast-walking the whole two miles back. Cold wind whips against our faces, carrying a fresh, slightly charged scent—ozone. I keep scanning through the trees, checking on the dark clouds amassing like a crowd on the horizon over the lake. I hold a healthy fear of the power of wild places and shifting weather.

The first people to look at this lake knew it was a place of power, naming it *Giiwas,* "a sacred place."[6] At 8,157 feet tall, Mount Mazama holds the depths of Crater Lake like a gem at its core. I recently learned that the white man who named this mountain dubbed it after his hiking club, choosing an obsolete

6 "Origin Stories of the Lake: The History of Crater Lake," Crater Lake Institute, https://www.craterlakeinstitute.com/smith-chronological-history-of-crater-lake/sources-and-articles-of-interest/orgin-stories-of-the-lake/.

word for mountain goat—a species that doesn't even live in this area.[7] The Klamath Tribes who have long called this region home already had given this mountain a name—*Tum-sum-ne,* "Mountain with the Top Cut Off."[8] They considered it a place so powerful that only those who were spiritually, physically, and mentally prepared should step near its shores.

We reach the parking lot long before the rain. The lake that was sapphire is now steel, grayed and rippled with wind. We grab two tall Corona Lights out of the cooler in our trunk and sit on a log at the caldera's edge, watching the slow-growing storm.

Many myths surround this mountain, and the stories that get told over time are not always the whole truth. White settlers claimed the Indigenous peoples of southwestern Oregon were so afraid of Crater Lake they avoided it.[9] But respect for a place is not the same thing as avoidance.

Terry Tempest Williams reminds us that the "creation of America's national parks has been the creation of myths."[10] As in Yellowstone, America's first national park, Crater Lake was treated like some shiny stone Indigenous peoples had been too superstitious to touch. What white settlers perceived as fear was respect for the power and danger of a place whose volcanic memory lives in their stories and blood. This was not an unexplored or ignored place; it was and remains a place of reverence.

I think back to all the ranger talks I attended and park visitor centers I wandered as a kid, eager to earn every junior ranger badge I could, including here. I have no memory of

7 Stephen R. Mark, "Mount Mazama," Oregon Encyclopedia, https://www.oregonencyclopedia.org/articles/mt_mazama/#:~:text=Still%2C%20its%20seemingly%20bucolic%20state,on%20Mount%20Hood%20in%201894.

8 "Crater Lake and the Klamath," Oregon History Project, https://www.oregonhistoryproject.org/articles/historical-records/crater-lake-and-the-klamath/.

9 Douglas Deur, "A Most Sacred Place: The Significance of Crater Lake Among the Indians of Southern Oregon," *Oregon Historical Quarterly* 24 (2002).

10 Tempest Williams, *Hour of Land,* 11.

learning that the stunning places families like mine flock to each summer for entertainment and amazement were not uninhabited nor unused before the federal government named them national parks. I was never taught that the establishment of America's national parks was concurrent with the removal of Indigenous peoples from their ancestral lands to reservations aimed at absorbing and annihilating their ancient cultures into American supremacy.[11] So I sit now, staring at *Giiwas* in solemn acknowledgment of silenced stories and stolen land.

A robin cleans herself in a puddle of snowmelt under a fir tree that is so wind-whipped it looks half-dressed. Through the contrast of its shorn, moss-covered branches, the abyss below shimmers even more. I close my eyes, surveying every inch of my body from my toes to my scalp, revering this somatic geography whose depths hold secrets and whose stories have been scorned. This place—this human body—still holds power not only to entertain or please, but to erupt, change, and heal.

THE PARTS WE'D RATHER SKIP

WHEN WE'RE TOO cold to sit outside any longer, Sarah and I get back in Reepijeep. Before I pull away, I start Richter's *Recomposed* again. It plays from where we left off last night at the very end of "Summer 3," with its anguished, roaring storm and a violin solo that sounds like a mourner's cry. Its solemnity matches mine.

We listen to the next movement before pulling away, enjoy-

11 Ibid.

ing the cadence and frivolity that seem straight out of a ballroom. "Autumn 2" comes on shortly after. In it, a harpsichord practically haunts the other instruments away with a sleepy, eerie sound that is far from my favorite.

I used to skip this song. Lately though, I've started to listen to *Recomposed* all the way through, to practice learning to love the whole of what someone else made with such intention. I want to grow in being able to hear something as good, even when my initial reaction is repulsion.

As we wind down *Tum-sum-ne* one last time, listening to sounds I'd rather skip, I can sense how much is being recomposed in me—in my relationship with my story, my family, the land, and maybe even my future. Like the song, the parts I'd rather skip might be the parts I need to revisit the most.

NOTE TO SELF

RIGHT BEFORE WE leave the park's borders, we cross a creek—Annie Creek. Last night, it was too dark to really see it. The snow is so deep, and I almost shudder in recognition.

This is what the land looked like when we were lost. This might be the creek my brother and I crossed to safety.

And I finally know for sure: the myth of that day decades ago, when my brother brought us home over a snow bridge and up a rockslide, matches this matter. It wasn't a fairy tale. I didn't make it up.

As I turn toward our next destination, I tell myself: *Remember this. You can believe your own version of events. Your self-perception is a story you can trust.*

CLOTHING OPTIONAL

IT'S SARAH'S TURN to drive, so I'm in the passenger seat, searching for the best place for us to stay tonight between Crater Lake and the Redwoods. We're tired and, I'll be honest, a little stinky.

"I know where we're gonna stay tonight." I smirk while I hold up the phone so Sarah can glance at the page while still seeing the road. "LADIES SOAK NIGHT," the website reads. "Honoring the Divine Feminine. Sacred Soaking in a Penis-Free Environment."

Sarah's body instantly tenses, shoulders sharp at the suggestion.

"Look," I say, holding up my free hand like a stop sign. "It's a campground *and a hot spring. And* it happens to be *ladies' night. Tonight.* On the very night we are passing through, directly along our route, when we both need a shower and a place to stay." I pause. *"AND IT'S A PENIS-FREE ENVIRONMENT."*[12]

I emphasize this key point, wagging my left eyebrow up and down like a clown, half because I know Sarah needs convincing and half because I'm twelve years old inside and will not pass up the chance to say "penis" in casual conversation.

Sarah shrugs her tight shoulders and somehow agrees to stay at the hot springs. I make the reservation from my phone and plug the destination into Google Maps while I start reassuring her that no, she does not have to get naked, even if I'm naked. And no, I will not judge her one bit, naked or not.

Once we're off the highway, we pull into a dirt driveway fringed by flowering trees and tall grass and hand-lettered signs

12 For the record, I'm not shitting on schlongs. I'm just stating what's *on* the website! Pretty sure they just didn't want a bunch of straight cis men junking up our goddess gunk.

with messages like "Save the Soil" and "We Recycle" and "Goddess Temple." I start nodding at our surroundings with a smirk. *Mmm-hmm, this is sufficiently culty.*

Before we get out of the car, I promise Sarah that if we check in and it's just way too creepy, we can find somewhere else to stay. That's the beauty of a rooftop tent. Your bed travels with you.

We walk inside and are greeted by the scents of palo santo and patchouli and the sight of little statues above altars of pinecones and crystals. There's a sign-in process involving our driver's licenses, and there are no men in sight, so we give each other a look that says we both feel safe enough to stay.

Once we're setting up our site a safe distance from the hippies, we laugh hard at how this is definitely a place that our younger selves would have prayed over and maybe even anointed with holy oil before promptly leaving. Who am I trying to fool? We probably wouldn't have dared to check it out at all.

We park beneath the branches of a giant maple and eat a simple dinner of brats and veggies. After, we rinse off the dirt of the last few days in the showers and step across grippy rubber mats toward the pools. I'm wearing nothing but a towel and a smile, and Sarah is wrapped in a towel over her black one-piece. A sulfuric scent hangs in the air, and when I see the water, the knot between my shoulder blades softens.

One large pool spreads before us, reflecting the fading light of the day in purple and periwinkle. In the corner, a smaller pool steams up against a cedar privacy fence butted by a hill so forested and alive it's practically chartreuse. Baskets overflowing with bright flowers hang about every five feet on the fence in between block-lettered signs of inspirational maxims and one large statue of the elephant-faced Ganesha, the Hindu god of new beginnings and remover of obstacles.

We wander to the pool in the corner, and I slip into the steaming water as naked as I came into this world. Sarah slinks in beside me. The water is hot and welcoming. We're surrounded by women, mostly nude, leaning back against the concrete pool edge, tits up and unashamed. I've never seen so many bushes in one place in my life.

When we entered the pool area, we saw laminated signs marked "Clothing Optional." There was no expectation of exposure, just a welcome to come as you are comfortable, and, maybe, to let the confines of comfort stretch past inherited body shame.

Floating and lounging and sitting around us are women of every age—from pubescent to post-menopausal. Many chat and laugh. Some sit in silence. One older woman cannonballs into the big pool with big joy, sagging skin bouncing as she leaps.

Sarah cools off in the larger pool, and I notice a cluster of women next to me who appear to be family—a mom and teenage daughter, aunts, and a grandmother, in all states of undress. I can't think of a time I've seen more than my mother naked, and it inspires me—even fills me with hope—that our bodies are not obstacles to overcome, but sources of connection. *Imagine a world where women regularly gather naked and safe in the steam to sweat away the shame society has stuck on us. Imagine a family where aging is seen instead of hidden or mocked. Imagine a life where other women's bodies silently show you that you are free.*

I glance at the other pool and see that Sarah has stepped out of her suit. Earlier, she confessed that in her whole adult life, only her gynecologist and husband have seen her naked. Sarah steps slowly through the shallow end, arms covering her breasts. She dives under the water and emerges drenched, arms wide, face gleaming. It's the holiest baptism I've ever seen.

THE SOUND OF BELONGING

LATER, SHOWERED AND tucked away up high in our tent, we open our notebooks to make sense of what we just experienced. A camp light hangs between us, giving off just enough glow to scratch out the start of the poem I'm sure is going to be technically awful but emotionally a delight.

I punctuate the poem with laughter, giggling every ten or twenty seconds, searching for synonyms for the shapes and freedom we just saw.

"Sarah," I speak up through another laugh I can't suppress. "Let me read this to you."

CLOTHING OPTIONAL
It was ladies' night.
"A penis-free zone,"
the website said.

Pinecones and patchouli
greeted us. Along with
every shape of boob.

Traffic-coned,
tea-cupped, mounded,
skin sagged into scarves.

Every wrinkle wrote
a new story on our skin
where every shape of body belongs.

It turns out
"clothing optional" means
"belonging unconditional."

We laugh so hard at the traffic cones I almost pee my pajamas. Our bodies shake with irrepressible cackling as we search for the best similes for our own shapes, landing on *cantalouped* and, maybe, sort of, *tennis-balled*. We can't stop laughing. And the laughter is an echo of the hot springs. The sound of safety stripping away shame, of belonging in a new way than when we arrived.

WILD LILAC

WE'VE BEEN DRIVING all morning and have finally made it to Redwood Highway. The pavement is like a slash of permanent marker through the middle of the thick forest. We pull into a turnout to see our first giants up close.

I open the door into a dense understory of fern and brush. The air is earthy, and it feels like stepping into a cedar closet, but better. Nearly blooming rhododendrons peek out pink through green branches like novice ballerinas about to step onstage. I only take three steps into the beauty before I notice bark carrying the marks of past fire. I stand there a long time, hushed beneath the scars.

Something lavender catches my eye. A shrub sits at the base of the scarred giant. Its lacy, pale purple clusters and serrated green leaves sway ever so slightly in the air. *Is this lilac?* I've only seen it cultivated, not wild. I tear away a couple of fragrant sprigs to take back to the car, where my wildflower guide rests on the dashboard.

It *is* wild lilac—deer brush.

I'm one singular person holding one fistful of blooms, but this plant's power extends to an ecosystem. She is food for deer, seeds for quail, soap for skin, and nectar for butterflies, birds, and bees. But she is also an alchemist. Wild lilac is nitrogen-fixing. She transmutes nitrogen from the atmosphere into a form that aids flourishing, rebuilding the scorched soil beneath her blooms so much that every plant in her orbit better thrives. She is one of the first to rise from the ruins of wildfire.

I think of how I've needed help when my body couldn't produce its own chemical chain of nourishment in extreme stress. In addition to Ankylosing Spondylitis, primary immunodeficiency,[13] and several other conditions that all require regular injections and long infusions, I live with adrenal insufficiency. Each morning and afternoon, I swallow steroids to replace the cortisol my adrenal glands are unable to make. If I get an infection or get into an accident, I need an emergency steroid shot to prevent a life-threatening adrenal crisis. That vague threat became real a few months ago, when I got a stomach bug while in Nashville on a business trip. Now I don't just carry my wallet and phone everywhere like most people. I have to carry a vial of Solu-Cortef and an intramuscular syringe everywhere I go.

Yesterday, we were parked outside a ranger station overlooking Crater Lake when I realized I hadn't yet shown Sarah how to use my steroid shot in an emergency. I pulled out a pouch from my backpack to show her the vial and syringe. Beyond the car windshield, the lake shimmered like a sapphire. I felt nauseous sitting between the juxtaposition of that beauty and such a brutal need.

I explained to Sarah that if I'm in an accident or suddenly can't keep liquids or food down, I'll need someone—probably

13 My body doesn't make all the antibodies I need to fight infections. Before learning about my immunodeficiency, I spent five months of most years in adulthood fighting infection after infection. What would take most adults one or two weeks to fight would take me months and many rounds of antibiotics and steroids. Diagnosing and treating my immunodeficiency changed my life. You can learn more about primary immunodeficiency through the Immune Deficiency Foundation: primaryimmune.org.

her—to give me the shot. I lifted each part, demonstrating how it works. *Push the yellow button on the top of the vial to mix the powder and water. Take the syringe and pull back all the way to get air inside. Remove the lid from the vial and inject the syringe into the top . . .*

I looked over at Sarah. Her face had gone pale. Her body was a board, focusing hard to internalize every word.

"Don't worry." I met her eyes. "I'll write it all down."

I continued my personal paramedic lesson, listing off each step in detail, including that if we use the shot, we'll need to head to an ER. I heaved a sigh as I finished. "I hate that being my friend includes knowing how to save my life."

Sarah touched the vial and syringe on my lap. "This is not a burden." She looked up at me with tears in her eyes and thanked me for letting her cross the threshold into knowing this part of me, the medically fragile part of me.

Now I sit in Reepijeep alone while Sarah takes photos of the redwoods outside. I hold the wild lilac back up to my face, breathing in both her scent and my safety. The soil of my life is seeded with love. I may not have all I need on my own, but I am not all that is growing here.

SALTY

BEFORE WE FIND our campground, we take a short hike to the beach. The sky over the Pacific is moody. Wind shakes the stems of purple lupines and orange poppies. I stand at the edge of the sea, open my mouth, close my eyes, and taste salt. The last time I stood on the California coast was five years ago, maybe five *mes* ago.

My husband Ryan—my gentle, kind husband—was an assistant pastor in a fairly conservative nondenominational church. He spent his days caring for congregants in crisis or transition, leading groups for those struggling with their marriages or addictions, and training others to do the same. But in our church, speaking from a stage was far more valued than sitting with people in pain. And when other congregants and staff started confiding in us about how they also felt demeaned by senior leaders, we started asking questions about whether the church's theology and norms tended or trampled the terrain of the soul.

During that season, Ryan and I were part of a two-year spiritual formation program that met quarterly in Southern California with other pastors and their wives. (Yes, *wives*. Women were not allowed to be pastors in this church network.) We quickly realized that the program existed because the same domineering and controlling dynamics we were noticing among our church's leaders existed in these other leaders and their churches, too. We were in a network of churches where leaders cared more about maintaining their own power than caring for actual people. More than what we learned in the teaching sessions, what we observed in California helped clarify what we needed.

The last time I opened my mouth to this ocean, I closed my heart to the hope that our church could change. I was hopesick, grace-laced, forgiveness-fragmented. Our empathy was the ecstasy that kept our pastors on stages. Our willingness to be gracious enabled their bad behavior. We were done being a drug, done with divinity that didn't see every face as grace, done with dismissing our own internal ache. We could no longer silence the story our sensations were telling us about the lack of safety and true love in our faith community. We watched too many people get squashed by our leaders, heard too many raised voices behind closed doors, felt too much tension in our bodies to keep saying that this spirituality actually led to life.

We confronted the wrong we saw. And no one in power believed us or cared.

We lost our paycheck, our health insurance, our home, and our community in a matter of months.

I can still taste the salt.

Today, I stand among survivors. I see sitka spruce with half-bare limbs on the bluff, standing strong despite the harshness of the sea. Yellow constellations of wild parsnip reach up from the earth. Huckleberry bushes bank the trees. Each plant protects the redwoods over the ridge from the Pacific's salt shear.

I used to worship inside walls, sat in pews where my physicality prohibited my preaching, tithed my time and money and truth to support a system that didn't support a free and thriving soul. And now I lick my lips to taste and bless the salt that showed me a sanctuary I could carry out the door.

BURNED

INVITING SARAH ON this trip was one of my better ideas. Before we left, we decided together that anytime either of us needed or wanted to pause to write, we would. Most friends would be annoyed at stopping this much, but Sarah loves to write just as much as I do. Our goal isn't to get to every sight but to let what we see alter *how we see* the stories we carried here with us.

We're parked on the shoulder of a quiet stretch of Redwood Highway. I can't stop thinking of the charred bark of the first stand of redwoods we saw today. I came to this particular forest to find the younger me who once stood amid this beauty with her family, amazed. But I also came because bearing witness to what is brutal in my life has changed how I see. My vision has been altered by allowing ache and amazement to exist in the same breath.

The redwoods also hold the memory of both. In 1969, just one year after the establishment of Redwoods National Park, the then–vice president of the Sierra Club, Edgar Wayburn, outlined the near extinction of primeval redwood forests. At the time, almost 90 of every 100 acres of redwoods had been logged. Only 4 percent had been set aside in protected public ownership. Just as recently as 1830, coastal redwood forests had covered around two *million* acres of Northern California like a thick green coat over the coast.[14]

Today, the remaining coastal redwoods are practically clinging to the cliff of California. Only 5 percent of old growth coastal redwood forests remain, standing sentinel in small pockets of land like guards against climate catastrophe.[15] I am here because I want to see the beauty that remains.

Yesterday was my thirteenth wedding anniversary. Ryan is back home in Colorado, working, while I camp across America. And while we would have loved to spend our anniversary together, he gets that this trip is one I *needed* to take.

Trauma in my childhood burned up my trust in others to protect, love, and stand by me no matter what. I spent the first years of my marriage on high alert for abandonment, always afraid that I was too damaged, too anxious, and mostly *too much*

14 Edgar Wayburn, "Publisher's Note," *The Last Redwoods and the Parkland of Redwood Creek* (San Francisco: Ballantine Books, Sierra Club, 1969), 11.

15 "Why Protect Redwoods?" Save the Redwoods League, accessed May 29, 2024, https://www.savetheredwoods.org/redwoods/why-redwoods/.

to love. I got sick a year before we got married, and chronic illness continuously confronted my tendency to believe I had to be perfect to be loved. I'd pick fights, not even knowing why, because stress was the love language I knew best. It took years—and lots of trauma therapy—to learn to trust that Ryan's steady, calm love wasn't going anywhere.

We have learned that almost nothing—not church, not money, not work—is as important as protecting the place between us.

Today I stood beneath scars, charcoal black wounds stretched tall up the trunks of mighty redwood trees. High above, huge branches full of healthy, green needles spread out like hands into the air, a silent benediction that after fire, life can grow.

CHERRY PIE

WE SIT FIRESIDE at our campsite under a canopy of leafy maples and second-growth redwoods. At our feet, the understory is a sprawling crowd of sword ferns, their green fronds reaching toward one another in every direction.

I've never seen so many shades of green in one place. A bigleaf maple shelters our already tall tent, its moss-robed branches draped like lacy curtains. From inside the tent on the car's roof, it feels like you're part of the trees and approximately nine years old, discovering a treehouse in a forest that's been there far longer than you.

This place shrinks you down to child size. When we arrived at the campsite, I opened the door to a redwood stump that was larger than my Jeep. I took a photo of Sarah next to it for scale. Her head is like a mouse beside a lion.

For dinner, I seared a large ribeye and shishito peppers on a cast-iron skillet over open flames with foil-packed potatoes in the embers below. We are satiated and small. Coals crackle between us. Mill Creek trickles to my left, just beyond a handful of trees and hundreds of ferns. I swipe butter over bread. A grin spreads across my face. With just a pie iron, butter, bread, and cherry pie filling, I can transport Sarah to the brightest edge of my childhood.

When the hobo pies cool enough to hold to our mouths, we sprinkle them with powdered sugar and take huge bites. Cherry filling bubbles at the brims of our mouths. This is the flavor of my childhood. This is who I am.

Sarah points out my smile. She's granted herself the role of my unofficial documentarian for this trip. Everywhere we go, she's been snapping photos without me realizing it. She says that in every photo she's taken of me, my face is lit with pure joy. My outsides must be matching my insides, because that is how I feel. This whole trip, I've been awash in uninhibited wonder and pure joy.

Tonight, we've been trading stories of our families across the embers. Brothers who struggle. Tensions that separate. Unbelief that sparks suspicion. With the residue of cherry pie filling still on the corners of our mouths, we both swallow a sadness we each have tasted since we were small.

The sweetness in my mouth subdues the salt of these stories. I am a woman who grieves what wasn't and can't be, but I'm also a woman who stands in awe of redwoods and makes my friends hobo pies—because my parents took the time to show me how.

Mom and Dad brought us to the national parks every summer during the formative years of my childhood. Dad worked extra hard all year to make those trips possible. All school year long, he left for work before the sun to get to jobsites heaving concrete forms, pouring basement walls, and managing his large team of employees. Somehow, he often made it home for dinner or to coach both of my brothers' hockey teams at the ice rink. Concrete was the commodity that made it possible, and hard work was the ethic we all were taught to prize by example. For one month during most summers—and two months during the year we drove to Alaska—Dad and Mom carved out time for wonder with us.

There's so much from my childhood that still stings, but I'm beginning to sense there may be even more that sings.

A new truth is starting to shade my story: Who I am is not despite my family. It is *with* them. It is, in so many hallowed ways, *because* of their love that I love.

It's too easy to cast aside every weight as we age and change. But in throwing off the weight of pain and shame, we too easily also shed the weight of glory.

EATING DEATH

LAST NIGHT, SARAH and I went for a walk around the campground. We wandered through quiet campsites, stopping to marvel at giant redwood stumps, most of which were ten or even twenty times the size of us. This place was once logged, and that memory looms. All but 200 acres of the 25,000-acre temperate rainforest surrounding this campground was harvested. And after the logging, too many trees were planted too close together, reforesting for future harvesting, not future flourishing.[16] The trees here struggle with one another for enough light, water, and space to stretch up and out. The redwoods in this forest haven't been given enough room to thrive.[17]

Sarah and I wandered around stumps and stumbled into pews, stepping into an unexpected cathedral of trees. Instead of walls, there were woods. The ceiling was a fresco of emerald needles, ruddy branches, and steel-blue sky where an opening had been cleared in the forest for groups to gather. The campground's amphitheater was empty, so I lay in the center of a split log bench. The sun slanting through the trees warmed my face. As a kid, I'd visited similar amphitheaters with my family for countless ranger talks, learning the names of flora and fauna. And on most summer Sundays, the amphitheaters served as sanctuaries, where we worshipped the maker of it all.

I haven't stepped inside a church in months, in part because I've seen too many beautiful souls get cut down inside the walls of her forest. So I lay on my back, eyes resting on branches, breaths as deep as prayers, and wondered what rewilding the forest of my faith could look like.

On the way back to our campsite, we spotted a downed log in the distance, its length flecked with white. I rushed ahead and kneeled at the altar of the dead log, amazed to recognize the life rising from her decay. Oyster mushrooms. *Pleurotus ostreatus.* Mushrooms I've hunted back home, but more abun-

16 "Mill Creek Habitat Restoration," Smith River Alliance, accessed June 6, 2024, https://smithriveralliance.org/millcreek/#:~:text=Overview,for%20protection%20in%20the%201920s.

17 "Mill Creek Restoration," Save the Redwoods League, accessed June 6, 2024, https://www.savetheredwoods.org/project/mill-creek-restoration/#:~:text=Our%20restoration%20efforts%20are%20focused,filled%20streams%20and%20abundant%20wildlife.

dant than I've ever found before. Oyster mushrooms digest pollution and death into something delicious.[18]

I took my trusty wood-handled Opinel knife out of my pocket and popped off a few for our breakfast. I scooped them into my T-shirt, a makeshift basket, and tucked them safe under my fleece in case a ranger questioned us or some nosy stranger asked if we knew mushrooms can be poisonous. I knew what I found. And I wanted to feast.

I slept and dreamed so hard last night, sung to sleep by the drip-drop lullaby of rain. I dreamed of eating death, seated at a long table in a forest like this, among some of my dearest friends. Each person present had known the pain of being disinvited from tables where they once had a seat, losing their place, whether because of sickness or standing up for wholeness. Together we traded story after story of how we've been shamed and how we've grown strong. And the stories we shared became our sustenance, turning from sentences into supper.

I woke to birdsong and dangled my wool-socked feet out the window of our tent, high above the ground, marveling at how the rain had hypersaturated the green of the trees and ferns. Now I stand at a picnic table, slicing our cache of oyster mushrooms into a breakfast sauté of sausage, leftover potatoes, and eggs. Maybe the feasts we most long for will be found among what has fallen.

18 Nahid Akhtar and M. Amin-ul Mannan, "Mycoremediation: Expunging environmental pollutants," *Biotechnology Reports* 26 (2020). https://doi.org/10.1016/j.btre.2020.e00452.

WASTE

THE BIOLOGIST MERLIN Sheldrake says that mushrooms thrive on the mess that humans make.[19] Oyster mushrooms, like the ones in our breakfast, usually grow on decaying wood, but can also grow on "a diet of used diapers."[20] Researchers have even trained oyster mushrooms to digest one of the most disposed items in the world, cigarette butts, whose toxins sometimes can take a decade to decompose. The mushrooms have always held the metabolic pathways they need to transform toxins into nourishment. They simply needed nudging to remember what their genomes had held dormant for generations.[21]

Father Richard Rohr has written, "If we do not transform our pain, we will most assuredly transmit it."[22]

Maybe, like mushrooms, all our wasted years and wasted hopes are simply the start of something truly satiating. Maybe there is no waste or wound that cannot be metabolized into goodness. Maybe we simply need to remember what our bones already hold. What is wasted? Maybe—I hope—nothing.

19 Merlin Sheldrake, *Entangled Life: How Fungi Make Our Worlds, Change Our Minds & Shape Our Futures* (New York: Random House, 2020), 180.

20 Sheldrake, *Entangled Life*, 181.

21 Sheldrake, 182.

22 Richard Rohr, "Transforming Pain," Center for Action and Contemplation, October 17, 2018, accessed June 4, 2024, https://cac.org/daily-meditations/transforming-pain-2018-10-17/.

STARFISH

WE DRIVE DOWN the coast to a trail while morning mist lingers in the trees. I can't help but stop at almost every overlook. I pull into a parking lot at a cove. We step out to explore tide pools in the gentle lapping of low tide's waves.

Fog hangs over the water and the distant trees beyond the highway. I stretch out my arms in wonder. This world. This world is so beautiful. I am amazed to get to be standing here, on my own two legs, in a body that could handle the 1,600-mile drive.

I step toward black rocks covered with burgundy seaweed and parakeet-green algae. Shallow pools of water rest between rocks over nearly obsidian sand. The first creature I spot is a bright orange starfish sprawled on a rock. I step closer, slack-jawed.

My friend Sarah Harrison has been calling me Starfish for years. It started when she first saw how sick I can get, and that somehow, I am always able to grow back into safety and strength in my body and life. Sarah loves to point out that like a starfish who has lost an arm, being sick in body or soul never seems to stop the substance in me that holds the capacity to grow back strong.

The first time the nickname shows up in our texts was one year ago, just weeks before my graduation from cardiac rehab. I was just beginning to breathe again—to *be* again. Sarah and I were texting back and forth about a dinner we were going to host in her and her husband Pat's backyard to celebrate the publication of my second book, *The Lord Is My Courage*. I wanted to feast with the friends who survived that story with me and Ryan—our story of reckoning with spiritual abuse and religious trauma. It was one of the most beautiful nights of my life, a night when love was made more real than loss. Now that I think of it, that was essentially the table I dreamed of last night.

This is my first time seeing a starfish in the wild. I absorb every detail in awe: white dots over spiny tangerine skin, arms swirled over black and white sand, resting cool on a large charcoal rock. I close my eyes and wrap my arms around my body, a silent assent to the substance my friend sees, even when I can't.

REWILDING

WE TURN RIGHT into the parking lot of Fern Canyon. Apparently, you can hike between fifty-foot-high fern-covered walls here, which sounds magical. I've had this hike saved on a list for months.

A man who appears to be a ranger greets us before we park. Sarah rolls down the window. A jovial smile stretches across the man's bearded face. The lapel of his khaki uniform bears a gold "You Are on Native Land" pin.

"Do you two know what's happening here today?"

I lean over Sarah in the passenger seat to see him better. "No idea!"

"I'm with Redwoods Rising," the man says, as he opens a pamphlet. "Today we are rerouting a trail that's impeding a creek, so the trail is currently closed. I'm Griff Griffith, by the way." He shakes both of our hands.

I grin. My dad's name is Mark Markovich, and the whole Name on a Name situation has always made me smirk with secret joy.

Griff asks us about what brought us to the Redwoods and if it's our first time visiting. My dad's never met a stranger, and when I'm in the right mood, I'm the same way. So I share that my parents brought me here as a kid but that I haven't returned to the Redwoods since, and that I'm here working on a book, exploring the roots of the wonder and joy that have sustained me in devastation.

Griff lights up. "I'm here because of my family, too," he says. "I'm a direct descendant of Irish immigrants who clear-cut the Redwoods. I view it as my life's mission to restore what my own family ruined."

Griff explains that he has been working as a conservationist in the Redwoods his entire adult life. He unfolds the Redwoods Rising pamphlet again, pointing at how they work to restore forests that were previously logged and damaged in ways that can't be restored without collective action. Griff tells us about a nearby restoration site where they cleared a creek that a logging road had been cutting through. Just six days after rerouting the road and cleaning the creek of debris, salmon started spawning there again.

"Six days?" I ask.

He nods, standing a little taller.

"That's . . . magical." I'm stunned just as much by that as I am by Griff's choice to devote his life to this place's restoration.

I know from my junior ranger days that salmon and redwoods live in symbiosis. Each shelters and strengthens the other. Making room for that relationship to thrive sounds like more than a good reason to not be able to see the magical Fern Canyon. Instead, we stumbled into a different kind of magic, the magic of a man who sees his life as connected to all the lives that came before him, who knows he can carry peace where others brought a saw.

CROWN SHYNESS

SINCE WE COULDN'T see Fern Canyon, we've spent the day meandering through the Lady Bird Johnson Grove. My joints are hurting from hiking, so Sarah and I rest on the forest floor. We sit with our legs outstretched and our backs against a pair of redwoods so large, even with our wingspans combined we wouldn't be able to wrap our arms around them. Fog hangs in the air like the thinnest of cloaks, covering every tree in a darkness that somehow makes every green deeper, every gray warmer, every red russet. We just ate squished PB&Js from our packs and made a batch of French-pressed coffee with care on a jet boil. *I was listening, Smokey Bear. I am not going to be the person who starts a forest fire here or anywhere.*

Sarah and I sit a body's length apart in silence, save for the whisper of wind rustling through leaves, the trill of birds calling to one another, and the scratch of our pens against the open pages of our journals. Everywhere I look is fog and fern, fir and giants. I sip my black coffee, watching my friend for a few moments. Sarah wears a steel-blue down jacket and olive-green pants with gray Blundstone boots over light gray wool socks. She writes steady as quiet rain, saturating the page.

On our drives, Sarah has described the painful work of rediscovering her voice after decades of being told by conservative Christians that her perspective as a woman was less worthy of space and respect than a man's. Earlier, she said that this is the most she has journaled in years, maybe ever. Something holy happens in the hidden confines of a journal. Empty pages, filled in private, grant us space to say whatever we need to say without fear of judgment or pressure to be perfect. Sarah sips from a brown ceramic mug and takes a hushed, deep breath, looking up at the trees in awe before she begins filling another page.

I smile at our shared silence, at our two solitudes protecting the peace we each need to let our souls speak. I journal, too, reexperiencing the wonder I first felt here in the Redwoods as a little girl with my family.

I'm stirred from my recollections by the sound of some hikers in the distance. It's a family, hiking back to the trailhead. I overhear the dad explaining the environment to his barely listening family—just like mine—and laugh.

"There's this thing called crown shyness." The dad points upward. "The crowns of the trees won't touch each other."

Yes. I smile. These trees give each other space so they each can catch the light.

EVERLASTING

WE'VE BEEN SLOWLY moving through the grove, pausing to write and, a couple of times, to lie down on the duff to take in the lofty crowns of the trees more fully. I've been following the National Park Service's trail guide, learning about the ecosystem along the way.

Sequoia sempervirens. The scientific name for the coast redwoods means "everlasting." These trees live longer than almost anything else on our planet.

In my hardest moments, physical and spiritual pain appear pointless. I've seen friendships, trust, and old beliefs burn and die. I want to know that there is something that will outlive all the pain.

Fire is a necessary part of the process of the redwoods' regeneration. At the base of many redwoods, and even far up into the canopy, massive, knobby, wartlike growths called burls hold reservoirs of unsprouted bud tissue. Under the stress of the largest storms and fires, redwoods shift their energy to their burls, releasing sprouts previously held dormant. Sprouted from scorching, these new trees are genetic clones of their parents and are sustained by sugars made from the sunlight of decades and even centuries before.[23]

All that the tree has held dormant ensures its survival. *Everliving*. Even the death of a redwood is not death.

Each day, a single redwood breathes out more moisture than is in an hour-long shower, collectively creating the cooling fog greeting us today.[24] With limbs like lungs, their trunks tall spines, these gentle giants stand in meditation. Their towering presence absorbs and stores more carbon than any other kind of forest on earth.[25] In an age of climate disruption of our own making, with climbing levels of carbon dioxide overheating the earth, the redwoods hold what we cannot and create what we most need to survive. They breathe a better world into being.

Earlier, I stood beneath a hollowed-out living redwood. Twenty people could have stood in the space beneath her scars. Forest fire scorched through her outer bark and into her heartwood, no doubt also releasing life that had been dormant.

What was damaged decayed. But what decayed became a

23 Kelly Andersson, "Redwoods Are Sprouting 1000-Year-Old Buds," *Wildfire Today*, December 8, 2023, accessed June 10, 2024, https://wildfiretoday.com/2023/12/08/redwoods-are-sprouting-1000-year-old-buds/.

24 "Survivors Through Time," California State Parks, accessed June 8, 2024, https://www.parks.ca.gov/?page_id=24728#:~:text=A%20single%20redwood%20can%20transpire,in%20an%20hour%20long%20shower!.

25 "Resilient Redwoods," Sempervirens Fund, accessed June 8, 2024, https://sempervirens.org/learn/climate-action-plan/#:~:text=Studies%20show%20that%20coast%20redwoods,into%20the%20oxygen%20we%20breathe.

domicile. Hollowed-out trees like that provide a home to bats and birds and bears.[26]

Fire does not only burn. It builds.

UPSTREAM

MY FISHERMAN FATHER taught me that wild salmon swim from the sea to the streams of their birth to spawn new life before they die. Against the velocity of water rushing down snow-covered mountainsides, over rapids and past bears forty times their size, salmon return to the place that originally nourished and sheltered them until they grew strong enough for the sea. So strong is the pull toward home. Strong enough to turn a river red.

Sarah and I just stopped at a visitor center at Stone Lagoon, Chah-pekw O' Ket'-toh, a place our conservationist friend Griff said we had to visit. A dark-haired woman greeted us from behind the counter, as well as a sign declaring, "This is Yurok Land." Above the sign was a quote from the Yurok Tribe's constitution: "Our people have always lived on this sacred and wondrous land along the Pacific Coast and inland on the Klamath River, since the Spirit People made things ready for us and Creator placed us here . . ."

The signs stand as a counter-story to the myth of discovery projected onto most of the American West. As I've heard Griff say in an interview, "There was *no wilderness* in California." When western-minded people arrived here, they saw the land

26 "Tall Trees Walking Tour Stop 7," National Park Service, accessed June 8, 2024, https://www.nps.gov/places/tall-trees-walking-tour-stop-7.htm.

through their own culturally conditioned John Locke lens of utility and landownership. They saw this as a place Native Americans were not *using,* when in truth, they were not *using it up*. "Every square inch of this land had a relationship with people," Griff has said, "and it needs to have that again—but with healthy people."[27]

This is the first tribally operated visitor center in California's state parks, and it's only been open one year, telling the oft-forgotten and essential history of this place and its people. Its existence is its own return, a small restoration of the role of the Yurok people as the stewards of this place.

Before we left, I spoke with the Yurok woman overseeing the visitor center. "I know there's so much history and wisdom on these walls, but what do *you* wish visitors knew?"

The woman looked up from her hands, finely braiding bear grass into earrings. "That's hard." After a long pause, she replied, "That we still use this land."

Sarah and I are driving farther down the coast to our next campsite, and I can't stop thinking about the woman's wish and the relationship beneath it. I think of the Klamath River that we crossed earlier today, which the Yurok see as a life-source of their people. The majority of their food swims in those waters, including ney-puy, salmon.[28] To the Yurok, salmon are not simply a food source, but relatives to revere.[29]

What would this world look like if we revered the rhythms of

27 Griff Griffith, podcast interview with Michelle Fullner, "Redwoods Trees with Griff Griffith," *Golden State Naturalist,* September 21, 2023, https://open.spotify.com/episode/25pRrBXBlQM4Aceygje3Bo?si=cJqo6owVSyOMZpDQjXUQJg.

28 "Yurok Tribe History," The Yurok Tribe, accessed June 10, 2024, https://www.yuroktribe.org/our-history.

29 Brook Thompson, "The Familial Bond Between the Klamath River and the Yurok People," *High Country News,* August 24, 2021, accessed June 10, 2024, https://www.hcn.org/issues/53-9/indigenous-affairs-klamath-basin-the-familial-bond-between-the-klamath-river-and-the-yurok-people/.

salmon? What would happen if we practiced emulating an indigenous posture of relationship with—rather than management of—land? And what if we treated our bodies the same way?

Perhaps, we might start to see our singular stories of struggle as an upstream movement, a collective force of return and regeneration stronger than the river itself.

Perhaps more rivers would again run red.

UNCOVERED

OUR CAMPSITE AT Sue-meg State Park is tucked behind rows of trees and tents right at the edge of the forest and sea. An opening between pines reveals a trail, which we follow, passing a few hikers speaking in German along with wild iris in pale purple, tall grasses, and pockets of mushrooms and ferns. A singular Monterey cypress stands like a living statue before the trail sharply descends to the sea. Near the bottom, sea lions loll on boulders in the misty air, and I watch as they bask and then plunge into the churning water.

A sudden urge to submerge myself in the ocean overcomes me. I want to be as wild as them, washed in water that cools and cleans even as it stings.

It's too dangerous to swim here, not to mention crowded with people, so I search online for a safer spot nearby. We drive down backroads to the cove, wowed when we see houses with redwoods right in their yards, waving our arms out open windows in the warm wind while the women of First Aid Kit sing us into shaking every bit our mamas gave us.

We pass over a single-lane bridge on our way, and I see

MISH spray-painted on the side of the wood beams. I stop and snap a picture through the open window. It's fitting to find my best friend's name here, over a thousand miles from home, as though pulsing all around me are waves and winks from the women who have taught me to dance and endure and thrive.[30] At the parking lot, Sarah and I are greeted by a patch of forget-me-nots, their pale blue clusters like fountains spouting from olive-green leaves. I am here for me, but I am also stepping toward the sea holding honor for every woman in my life who wants to be well and free.

We walk down an empty trail between conifers, surrounded by sword ferns and thimbleberry shrubs with leaves larger than our hands. The trail plunges seaward, and we hold on to roots and rocks to avoid falling, stopping every few feet to stare at the green-gray water calling out through the jade and brown of the trees.

On the beach I glance around, open-mouthed. A house-sized rock roofed by a smattering of trees and thick moss stands at the edge of the cove where the forest meets sand and waves. Black whale-sized rocks jut from the water in the distance. The cove is quiet and calm and, somehow, completely secluded.

We walk toward the rocky barrier of the cove and find a giant redwood stump covered in smooth stacked stones. Cairns. Every inch of the red-and-gray gnarled stump has been covered, rock upon rock. I wonder about the hands that placed them. I wonder what they carried with them to this water. What hopes, what happiness, what grief. What joy.

We step beyond the cairns and find a hidden opening in the rocky cove. Setting down my backpack, I untie my boots and wriggle off my wool socks. "I'm going in!"

30 By the way, my best friend's name is pronounced *Meesh*.

I hastily peel back layers of fleece and leggings, down to my bare skin, and wade knee-deep into the water of the cove so I can see a little farther beyond the opening. *Wow, that's cold.* I can't tell how rocky the bottom is, so I step back toward Sarah and the wider expanse of tan sand to protect my bare feet.

I set my towel and phone on a large piece of driftwood and then step toward the water, cellulite and confidence showing. I fling my arms wide in the air to feel my aliveness. Long dark brown hair hangs over my shoulders, dancing in the light wind. I lick my lips to taste the brine and look back toward Sarah, fixed like a pillar of salt on the sand.

"Do you wanna come? We can get in together."

And she does. Sarah strips off her clothes and stands by my side.

We run arm in arm into the sea.

WE GLIMPSE A GALAXY

I EMERGE DRENCHED. Drenched and dripping with delight.

This body has been broken. Bent down on the ground. Pushed. Pinned. Plundered.

This body has been brave. Shouted syllables of pain. Rested. Risked. Risen.

For some reason I don't yet know, I *need* to see myself soaked and shimmering with delight. Something in me hungers to see my whole body bare before the ocean, like looking back on land I was supposed to forget, the object and reason for some god's great wrath. A deep and tidal part of me, perhaps as primal and ancient as the Pacific herself, calls out for corroboration. I need to see my face bright from the freezing water, hair dripping down my bare chest, standing where I have chosen to be.

Sarah snaps a few photos of me as I stand there before the ocean, wet from the water and now my own tears, arms hugging myself, holding and memorizing this joy. *This is my body. This is my body. This is my body.*

"KJ, do you see that?"

I open my eyes. "See what?"

"There are starfish all over the rocks next to where we ran in."

I whip around. We both stare at the family of starfish spread over the craggy, giant wall of charcoal rock. The name for a family of starfish is a galaxy. I read their presence like yet another sign, like a constellation that can guide me home.

We shiver and hurry to pull on our clothes and get back to our warm car. And though I did not set stones on the stump to mark what I carried to this place, I know what I am carrying away. I greeted a whole galaxy in that water, a baptism of my own seeking. *This body is and always will be beloved.*

DETRITIVORES

IT IS OUR final morning in the Redwoods. Camp is packed, and I start the car, but I decide to step toward the forest one more time. There is one more thing I want to see.

On each morning of this trip, today included, I've stepped away in solitude to set an intention before beginning the day. Each time, I've stood before tall trees and sensed the four corners of my feet, elongating and straightening my spine in alignment with the trees. I breathe deep, close my eyes, and imagine that my feet have roots that reach the trees' and the mycelium that connect them. I swallow a capsule of crushed mushrooms, a microdose of psilocybin, and consider that we all share one source. And from that sense of kinship, I ask my soul what we need. I name it aloud like a wild woman—or maybe more like a child at play—a soliloquy of the soul.

Yesterday, I set an intention to see the little girl in me who felt so unseen and to bless the forest for holding her wonder. Later that afternoon, while Sarah and I sat trailside in the duff, writing, a little girl scampered off from her family and ran up to us. "Isn't this *aaaaaammmmaaaaazing*?" she exclaimed. Her family apologized for her interruption, not realizing she had just given me a glimpse of my younger self's pure joy.

Today, I want one more glimpse, this time of one of the creatures I most loved here as a girl. Last Christmas, my mom's present to my dad was digitizing all our home videos. We stayed up late that night drinking hot chocolate and eating sugar cookies, watching birthdays and Christmas mornings unfold like a flip-book before our eyes. And then, we were in the trees: on our family trip to the Redwoods in the nineties. Dad held the video camera, tilting it up to capture their soaring height, narrating everything he saw with both factoids and astonishment. Then the camera panned to me.

I was around seven years old, with big bangs and lime-green overall shorts, and the look on my face was exactly like it's been in every photo Sarah has taken of me this week. I lifted my little hands to the camera. "Look at this banana slug! Isn't it *amazing*?!" I held the yellow creature so gently in my palm.

I marveled at the smallest of things among some of the world's largest trees, and all I wanted was to share the wonder. It's all I've ever really wanted.

I stand at the edge of the forest and close my eyes in open-hearted prayer. Just as I open my eyes, I notice something slimy and yellow on the fallen log in front of me. A mustard-colored banana slug rests there, chewing a tiny bite of moss. Tears fill my eyes. I can't deny the delight that the love pulsing through the earth hears our hearts, holds our hopes, and conspires to meet us with what we need.

I step over the mossy log to observe the hermaphroditic slug from every side—their four tentacles like periscopes to see and sense, their nearly invisible razor tongue of 25,000 teeth, the mucus that lets them travel without getting stuck.

Banana slugs are detritivores. Great decomposers, slowly unwriting the score of strength and weakness in the forest. They digest the death of trees, plants, and animals, recycling their matter into nutrient-dense material that enriches the soil. They chomp on the plants that compete with redwoods for shade but refuse to bite redwood saplings. Banana slugs protect and nourish the life that shelters and shades them. Though they are small, they are essential.

I watch the slug, its keel glistening in the humid air, as it crawls across the cut log. And I am seven again yet thirty-four, transfixed by a delight that has never fully departed.

And I know it might be silly to have prayed to see a slug, but sometimes we need substance to reveal what's invisible and much harder to imagine. And right now, I can see it: Suffering has never been able to stop my sense of wonder nor kill my desire to share it with others. The truth is that no pain can change the core of who I am. Delight has always decomposed discouragement. And it always will. Before I turn to leave, I spot one more banana slug traveling across the serrated frond of giant sword fern. This trip has planted hope within me that there will always be more wonder to see.

SOURDOUGH

WE LEAVE THE campsite and turn toward the ocean, aquamarine and shimmering with small waves. Sea stacks guard the small harbor. At the end of a steep street, a white pier darts from the coast beside a rocky, lichen-covered promontory with trees like a thick head of hair capping its heights. Nestled in its shadow is a tiny hole-in-the-wall diner with sourdough hotcakes that Griff said we *had* to try, made with starter that is well over a hundred years old. Griff had no idea that sourdough is somewhat of a spiritual discipline of Sarah's—a ritual she would almost assuredly want me to tell you started long before the pandemic momentarily prompted millions to reach for flour and a starter, desperate to see something rise. *Touché.*

Inside the restaurant, we're greeted by friendly smiles and the scents of strong coffee and bacon sizzling from the back. A server seats us right away. All the booths between us and the door are clearly filled with locals, and in the center is the apparent ringleader, a weathered woman with glasses low on her nose, one hand on a cup of black coffee and the other slung over the back of the booth, holding court with her neighbors. I eavesdrop while we wait to order. I love that this woman is all up in everyone's business. I love that these people clearly come here all the time. I love that there are still pockets of places where people are not islands.

The last time I tried sourdough was around four years ago, after multiple people said many people like me who can't digest gluten can tolerate sourdough. I bought a two-pack of loaves from Costco, because *why not,* and while I savored every bite, I did not savor spending the rest of the night doubled over in the bathroom, wishing I hadn't been so stupid. Sarah, being an actual baker, has explained to me that mass-produced bread like that isn't the same as hers, and that the longer sourdough ferments, the more gluten breaks down, so this might be my best chance to indulge.

We ask our server about their sourdough and learn it ferments well over twenty-four hours—often much longer—and that their starter came down the coast from Alaska, where it was born during the Klondike Gold Rush around 1898.

This starter was gifted to a local deep-sea fisherman who seasonally fished off the coast of Alaska. When his favorite café there closed, he couldn't stand that their sourdough pancakes would die with it and brought some back to Trinidad.[31]

Sarah's eyes double in size as she listens to the server. Thoroughly reassured, we each order a hotcake, eggs, hash browns, and bacon. While we wait for our breakfast, I give my body a tiny pep talk in the bathroom mirror: *We can try this. I trust you. We can risk discomfort for this. Now is not last time.* Sarah promised me earlier that she'll take today's seven-hour drive if anything goes wrong, even though it'll be our final stretch of the trip together before I drop her off at the Portland airport tomorrow afternoon. I'm sad to say goodbye, but it feels right to end our time together taking one last risk, this time to share in one of Sarah's favorite joys.

Our hot buttered pancakes arrive, and we take each bite like it's a sacrament. *Holy holy holy mother of God* the tangy sweetpiness fills my whole mouth, my whole body, with warmth so piquant I don't even care what comes next. I watch Sarah savoring the sweetness. Every hour she's spent kneading her own dough

31 Janine Volkmar, "The Story of the Mother Dough from Alaska's Mother Lode and How It Lives On Today in Trinidad," *Mad River Union*, February 26, 2018, https://www.madriverunion.com/articles/seascapes-sourdough-centennial/.

is welcoming her into even greater wonder, and I know she's marveling at the story of the starter as much as its tang. Every bite blooms with flavor from strains of microbes passed down from their mother lode—a good that has kept rising because person after person kept feeding it.

We leave with plates empty and bellies full.

And, no, thankyouverymuch, I didn't get diarrhea.

MOTHER

SEATTLE'S SKYSCRAPERS POKE through low misty clouds like the tines of a notched comb. My sun-flowered wildflower guide rests on the dash, reflecting against the raindrop-flecked windshield. I've never been to this city, only through.

I dropped off Sarah yesterday afternoon, after spending the morning together hiking to waterfalls with some Portland writer friends. I drove north this morning to the sound of The Highwomen, listening to their album on repeat to memorize most of the lyrics before I see them perform at The Gorge in a couple of days with Mish and our dear friends Rachel and Amy.

I exit the highway, winding past several bridges and locks that stitch the skin of Seattle together. When Natalie Hemby's "My Only Child" comes on, some dam inside me bursts. Natalie sings to her daughter, her only child, acknowledging the grief of wanting a larger family than they have. I have barely let myself long for a larger family than I have.

I married Ryan at twenty-one, after being adamant for as long as I can remember that I wanted to be "more than a wife and mother." Young love found me while I was busy looking for something else, studying my way into a career in community economic development in places my parents considered "unsafe." I've always loved my mother, but I've never wanted her life. She chose to be a stay-at-home mom and fought to be able to have us four kids, even though she had severe endometriosis. We were her dream and her prayer. More than rejecting *her,* I was resisting a conservative religious system that seemed to want me to believe that being a woman was mostly about making good use of my womb.

As I got older, autoimmune disease creeped into my cells, and my body kept begging me to be honest about my resistance to the responsibility of being a mom. I was and still am resisting the shriveled social imagination that sees bright, bold women as aberrations to corral. But I also was noticing needs—meltdowns that brought me to the brink of self-hatred, sudden surges of disease symptoms after holiday visits to my family where the person who abused me as a kid was present, sensitivity to noise and textures and stress that I felt secretly ashamed of beside my calm and cool peers.

Enter: therapy.

It wasn't until I was well into my own training to be a therapist that I began to flirt with the truth that so much of how I see and move through the world is a response to early childhood trauma. As I allowed my supervisors and therapists to see behind my strong, sharp-minded facade, I came into contact with a kid who needed more from her parents than they could give. They gave and continue to give me so much. *And* they were so busy fighting the fires of one of my siblings' explosive behaviors that they didn't realize how much I kept getting burned. I silenced my own cries without even knowing I was, determined instead to be as good and self-sufficient as I could—to be the kid who brought them sunshine instead of pain.[32]

When I backstitch the thread of my story, I can see my mom felt a similar need to silence her own childhood stress. The longer I have bent my ear to the girl in me who still needs to grieve, the more I begin to imagine the possibility of being a parent without passing on so much of our intergenerational pain.

But every time I have turned the knob on the door to the quiet dream of having kids, my doctors have said I wasn't healthy enough to walk through it. And if I'm honest, I have calluses on my hands, not from gripping the knob, but from holding a shield over the part of my heart that could *want* children but has barely dared to dream.

Late this winter, Ryan and I had the talk again—first, together, then with my immunologist and rheumatologist—and I started the process of weaning off the weekly chemotherapy injections I've been on for fourteen years—a neon-yellow medicine whose side effects include both a weekly bout of debilitating nausea and being abortifacient. I'm finally well enough to try. I want to say "try to start a family of our own," but the truth is, we already are a family. And we've already made a home where even the most childlike parts of ourselves feel safe enough to belong.

I guess what I'm trying to tell you is that today I'm singing in a way I've never sung before. Singing this song, in the tenor of my grief, is like setting down a shield and picking up a key to unlock a long-bolted entrance. I'm stepping through the door of my desire, even though the lights aren't on and I can't see what all is inside. And, God, it's wild to *want*.

32 Hi, my legal name is Katie Jo, and I was nearly named Sunshine for actual real; lovingly sung to sleep by *You are my sunshine, my only sunshine;* and, in the way only a precious little neurospicy kid could, took the nickname as a literal role to fulfill.

GIVE ME COMPLIMENTS

WE JUST FINISHED a walking tour of Seattle's underground, which, I gotta say, was surprising and stinky. After I arrived at our Airbnb this afternoon, I tried to access my veins on my own for the first time, since I was due to infuse my dose of a medicine that's supposed to stop my overactive complement system from cascading the rest of my body into chaos. It's a disease called Type 3 Hereditary Angioedema (HAE), and my immunologist wants me infusing the medicine weekly, on top of any time I have an attack.

I kid you not—this medicine is purified in the milk of genetically modified rabbits. My deal with my doctor was that I could go on this trip *if* I learned to inject the rabbit-milk elixir directly into my own veins so I wouldn't miss a dose.

Before I started supplementing my diet with mutant rabbit's milk, I didn't even know I *had* a complement system, and when I learned that mine doesn't function right, I told Ryan that maybe if he had given me more compliments all these years, I wouldn't need such weird-ass medicine. Shocking, I know, but that only elicited a polite chuckle from him.

Please imagine me, fresh from the forest, having just tried poking my own arms with a butterfly needle for half an hour, deciding my blooming bruises would just have to be my fashion statement for the evening, arriving with three dear friends into a parking garage in downtown Seattle, still woozy, and nearly—thank God, only *nearly*—stepping into a fresh puddle of pee right outside the car door. We proceeded to be led into even smellier lows beneath the city's streets by a bleach-haired femme tour guide whose jokes evoked much more than a chuckle. I could *not* stop snort-laughing, much to my friends' chagrin.

We're now driving back to our Airbnb in Ballard, and my

friends are all discussing some sort of molten lava cake they *must* try. But all I can think about is trying to breathe the butterflies in my stomach into some semblance of sleep so I can attempt to access my veins again.

Mish and Rachel are chatting nonstop up front. But Amy notices that I've gone quiet and am downing as much water as I can to hydrate my veins.

She leans over and whispers, "Are you okay?"

I swallow back tears and nod.

Amy knows what it's like to be in a body that aches and needs more than others can see. After a skiing accident in her twenties, multiple unsuccessful knee surgeries left her with permanent pain. And multiple deaths in her family have left her permanently tender to grief that doesn't go away.

Amy squeezes my knee, acknowledging the ache I have to carry, even on a fun girls' trip. There is an unspoken solidarity between people who are suffering. An invisible but inextricable thread ties us together, helping us feel a little less alone.

We park, and Mish and Rachel leave to find their lava cake. But Amy stays by my side.

ACCESS

THE TWO OF us hobble up the stairs to the apartment, looking more like eighty-year-olds than thirtysomethings thanks to the walking tour and our mutually arthritic joints. Amy washes her hands after I scrub mine and helps me stretch out my medical supplies over the kitchen table.

It's absurd how many plastic vial covers and syringes and

tubing and butterfly needles and bottles of sterile water it takes to get one *five-minute* infusion into my body.

I sit at the table, trying to breathe away my shakiness, steadying my hand to tie a tourniquet around my arm. I find a juicy-looking vein, and before I can overthink it, I pierce my skin for the fifth time today. I've reconstituted the medicine from white powder in two vials to clear liquid in a large syringe. Now, I'm committed.

A trainer from the pharmaceutical company flew to Colorado last month to teach me how to reconstitute the medicine—only that, not even how to administer it; that was a whole different training. The trainer said that once the medicine has been reconstituted, it must be used within eight hours. Each vial costs around $8,600 without insurance and co-pay assistance, so the pressure is officially on.

I think I've got it. I start pushing the syringe just like my nurse taught me. Little pushes, every thirty seconds. But before I reach a minute, I notice the skin near the needle is swelling.

The vein has burst. The medicine is making a miniature kiddie pool under the surface of my skin.

We hear voices from the stairs, and Mish and Rachel fling open the door, their arms full of bags of dessert, laughing and talking up a storm. This weekend is a precious chance to be together, and I don't want to miss a moment of the fun.

But I also don't want to waste this medicine or the help it could give me for the final leg of this road trip. They pull their cakes out on the other side of the table and start digging in, while I try my damnedest to focus my fingers, digging again and again at veins that pop up, only to hide or roll as soon as a new needle pricks my skin.

When I practiced accessing my veins in front of my nurse, I got it on my first try. I felt like a badass bitch who could handle what others faint at, a woman with the courage and skills to give her body precisely what she needs. And now, all jokes about milking the tits of mutant rabbits and my incessant need for compliments aside, this is no longer funny. I want to be on the other side of the table eating cake, not filling my arms with bruises and my body with fear.

Fuck.

I'm giving up. I'll have to hope for the best and just ask for more help once I get home next week.

BIOGEOGRAPHIC BARRIERS

I'VE TRIED FOR years to live like my body is not a barrier to belonging. When I first got sick fourteen years ago, I felt like my body had betrayed me. I was a junior in college, and seemingly overnight, I went from running and rock climbing between classes to spending every day in bed. I'd sink into my twin XL, hands clawed with the heat of inflammation, back burning in pain, and shame myself for not being as strong as everyone else. All my peers were getting to start their lives while I was stuck searching for both relief and a reason for why I was so sick.

I feared my body was becoming a prison.

The only way I've found to part the bars of pain is to listen to my body like I would listen to my best friend.

Yesterday we saw The Highwomen perform at The Gorge, and today I'm joining Amy at Mount Rainier National Park,[33] where she's spending a few days supporting her staff in her role

33 The true name of Mount Rainier—the name the Puyallup Tribe is lobbying to reclaim and return—is *Tahoma,* which means the "mother of waters."

as co–executive director of A Christian Ministry in the National Parks (ACMNP). Amy's nonprofit leads the worship services in the parks that my parents so often took us to as kids, and I couldn't pass up the brief chance to see a park through her eyes.

I hike beside Amy and two of her coworkers. In the distance, a waterfall echoes through the thick mossy forest of Doug fir, western hemlock, and cedar to climb down, down, down to where the water shouts. We reach a set of steep, wet stairs. Amy waits at the top, protecting her knees. I keep going.

I scramble over boulders and stand in the spray, arms wide as wings. My whole body vibrates from the roar of the falls. It's the pitch of purification, the sound of a stream cleaning herself on her long journey to the sea.

Scientists sometimes refer to waterfalls as biogeographic barriers, natural filters that promote biodiversity through what appears like fragmentation.[34] A break in the earth, a current leading to a cliff, a place of pressure that purifies.

I bask beneath the waterfall, reciting its roar, so that the next time my body falls into a flare of disease, I might better remember the true function of a fall.

By the time I reach the top of the stairs again, my sacroiliac joints are shouting in pain, begging me to slow down. Amy's coworkers dash ahead, but we limp our way back together, pausing every few minutes to rest on downed logs.

"I'm so glad we get to share this place together," Amy pauses, cradling a trinity of merlot petals, an aging western trillium. "I don't often get to hike with people who go the same speed as me. Usually, I have to push myself harder than I should just to keep up."

34 Murilo S. Dias, Jean-François Cornu, Thierry Oberdorff, Carlos A. Lasso, and Pablo A. Tedesco, "Natural Fragmentation in River Networks as a Driver of Speciation for Freshwater Fishes," *Ecography* 36 (2013): 683–689.

"I know, right? It's nice to not be the only one stopping constantly for once." *It's nice to belong.*

PRESERVED

THE NEXT MORNING, I wake with the sun and climb down the tent's ladder to a cherry-blossom sky, the pale pink light like petals about to fall. Last night, I slept at the base of the sleeping snow-covered giant, and this morning, the mountain is showing her face again. The next three days mark the last leg of this trip. While I don't want it to end, I do need to get home for my next treatment of intravenous immunoglobulin (IVIG) and to figure out how to safely infuse my HAE medication. Today I'll drive to Bozeman, Montana—or at least as far as my body will let me—to see my parents in person before I head home to Colorado. It wasn't my original plan, but after all I've encountered, I *have* to look them in the eyes and say thank you.

Our national parks are meant "to preserve the natural and cultural resources" of this land for current and future generations,[35] and now I see, as unmistakably clear as this mountain, that the time my parents spent bringing our family to national parks preserved something pure in me. They taught me the skill that has most counterbalanced continuous suffering: amazement. This land, like all the national parks of the United States, bears the memory of atrocities and loss, and so does the land of my life, but the glory of both endures.

35 "About Us," U.S. National Park Service, accessed June 28, 2024, https://www.nps.gov/aboutus/index.htm#:~:text=this%20page%20helpful?-,Our%20Mission,of%20this%20and%20future%20generations.

Before I leave, I meet Amy for coffee. We sit outside the historic Paradise Inn in the cool shadow of the mountain. Gray jays whoop-whistle from the bare branches of nearby trees. I tell Amy about my newfound gratitude for my parents and ask how the national parks became such a fulcrum of her life, too.

"I often tell my team," Amy begins, "if you could only see: every person who comes to the parks comes with a story, seeking to soothe some pain."

Amy shares that she was an ACMNP staffer in Olympic National Park the summer after her freshman year of college. Her dad had died a few years beforehand, and that summer in Olympic finally gave her space to grieve. There, among the salt of the ocean and the rain of the forest, she felt safe enough to release her tears.

In the years since, Amy has lost her mom, a best friend, and in one car accident two sisters and a nephew. Other than her husband, she has one living family member left. All these years and griefs later, the land still offers her solace. She tells me that she sees her mom in a flash of a fox crossing the road. She hears her dad's voice as she hikes through forests. Here, in the parks, their memories are alive.

The parks have done something similar for me. When I was growing up, my fundamentalist Christian school superglued belief in God to escaping a world that was just going to burn. But it was in the open-air amphitheaters of the national parks—in worship services led by young adults from ACMNP—that I first experienced that flowers and forests are not a distraction from faith but friends in it.

I no longer trust that the four walls of a church building will always protect or preserve what is good, but the forest has held my faith for me. Nature reveals the holiness of now while preserving the purity of the love we received in the past. Heaven, perhaps, is already here, even when veiled by pain in sightings of hell.

LIKE LUPINES

FOR SO LONG, I've stood at a necessary distance from my family. For years, I've had to moderate my visits and calls to limit my exposure to a climate of stress they can't seem to acknowledge or change. Like a burnt redwood, I couldn't reach toward my family with new limbs until I had tended the wounds at my core. For years, I've had to send all my energy to my own cambium and bark—through therapy, in setting boundaries, in learning new ways to cope with stress. I'm finally feeling strong enough in myself to receive my family's love in a new way. In talking with my parents today, I'm realizing that they have been healing, too. Today, Mom shared over coffee about painful boundaries she and Dad are setting to protect themselves and the rest of us—boundaries I never thought they'd choose, boundaries that make it safer for me to be closer to them. The pain in our past doesn't have to keep us from enjoying each other now.

High in the Bozeman Pass, the tall grass along my parents' driveway is fluorescent. It's my favorite time of year to visit, when the snow has finally receded and color returns to the earth. Each summer, wildflowers quilt their land in color.

As soon as I park at their log house, I notice purple and yellow sweeping over the hills. I duck under wire fencing, eager to see the wildflowers up close. Mom and my sister Kenzie come, too. We stand together on top of a small bluff as the sun sprints toward the snowcapped Bridgers to the west. Beneath us, the pasture is a sea of purple blooms.

I've never seen so much lupine in one place in my life. Periwinkle, violet, and indigo blend in tall spikes of petals whose tiny mouths tip toward the sky. At their base, long silver-edged leaves fan their arms outward. They wave in the warm breeze, stretching over nearly every foot of the slope down to the horse corral.

They're superblooming.

Some plants hold their seeds dormant during dry years, safeguarding the precious start of life in the soil until enough rain can come. I've loved the lupines on this land for over a decade, but I've never seen them bloom like this. There were more underground waiting to grow here than I could have imagined.

The three of us wander through the field, admiring the flowers. I hug my mom and sister tight. Billowing clouds roll toward the mountains like farmer's market trays bursting with cherries and peaches. I watch the lupines dance in the fading light like I am watching my family come to life.

BEST PICTURE

THE NEXT MORNING, I drive home to Colorado with my hopes sitting like a passenger in the seat beside me. All day long, hope tells me stories of what is possible. All day, the hurt inside of me hears her out. The two recognize each other, long-lost twins both mothered by the patient hands of honesty. There's room in my internal family for both hurt and hope.

I reach the border of Colorado and Wyoming. Storm clouds form in the distance as I pass the large brown "Welcome to Colorful Colorado" sign. I watch the shifting sky as though it's a giant silver screen.

I start to smile at the story rolling through me like summer storms in the afternoon, predictable and essential. All those summers in my childhood, we traveled the arteries of America, our motorhome a metal cell streaming through the blue blood of the body of this country. I didn't realize how much our time on the road would circulate and conserve what is true and alive in my own body.

We kids would park ourselves in the back bedroom of our forty-foot-long rolling home, begging Mom to put *Forrest Gump* or *The Truman Show* in the VCR again and again. And Dad would call out from the driver's seat: "Why do you kids need another movie? You can watch the best movie in the world right through these windows!"

We'd roll our eyes, and Mom would eventually cave. But at some point, I listened. At some point, I started to look. And I'm realizing now that the willingness *to look* is what has most sustained me through the pain in my life.

I have more of these national park trips planned for the rest of the summer, but even this first trip has shown me that love has always been the net beneath my life, even when I could not see it. In returning to the places where I first encountered wonder, I have found a place inside myself from which I can always rise, ready to look for the goodness that is already present.

I am beginning to see joy not as a task but as a thread. Joy is always there, weaving us to love. And I sense the thread of joy most when I participate in the present moment, watching for wonder and beauty, kindness and kinship, grace and the generous pattern hidden in both soil and souls that death is always antecedent to more life.

I am returning home with renewed hope that the net of love will hold me whenever I fall.

PART II

But what happens if joy is not separate from pain? What if joy and pain are fundamentally tangled up with one another? Or even more to the point, what if joy is not only entangled with pain, or suffering, or sorrow, but is also what emerges from how we care for each other through those things? What if joy, instead of refuge or relief from heartbreak, is what effloresces from us as we help each other carry our heartbreaks?

ROSS GAY,
Inciting Joy

MYCORRHIZAL

I HOLD OUT my arm and wince as my nurse twists the IV, digging under my skin to get a vein to flow. The tiny infusion room holds a faint antiseptic scent, wiped down and cleaned after the patient who sat here yesterday. Warm light slants over my body through half-opened blinds. I breathe in and slowly exhale, knowing that if I stay calm, the vein *might* cooperate.

My nurse—a young male who appears to spend as much time working out as he does working—keeps palpating and then pokes and digs again, trying vein after vein. I mention how much trouble I had accessing my veins a little over a week ago, back in Seattle.

"Well, that tracks." He tightens the tourniquet again. "If I don't get this one to work, we'll have to call it."

I've lost count of the attempts. Six? Eight? I glance down and finally see a flash of blood at the tip of the catheter. *Whew.* I immediately feel relief that my struggle in Seattle wasn't because of my IV skills. If it's this hard for a nurse to access my veins, no wonder it was nearly impossible for me.

The nurse hangs a big bag of saline on the pole beside me and places a box full of giant vials of IVIG on the side table. "Most patients who think they need a port really don't. But *you* do. Your veins are gnarled."

The words sink inside me like a heavy stone. For years, nurses have mentioned that I might need a port, but I've brushed it off. *Maybe it's time.* I make a mental note to bring it up with my immunologist the next time I see him and slump into my recliner. Sadness ripples from my center. A thirty-four-year-old's veins should not be *gnarled.*

Big clear drops of IVIG drip into a pump, glinting in the light as they travel down plastic tubing into my left arm. As a college student, I donated plasma a few times in dingy donation centers in Chattanooga for a little extra cash. I had no idea then that I was helping make what would sustain me now.

Every three weeks for nine hours, I become a small city of health. The rivers of my veins carry the boats of others' better health to land that would otherwise languish. Healthy antibodies gathered from 10,000 to 100,000 human donors replace the antibodies my body cannot make while flushing out the ones she makes that only make more trouble. All day long, me becomes we.

If you held a vein finder to my arms, you would see rivers and roads. They splinter and stretch under the surface of my skin just like mycelium connects plants and trees beneath the ground we see.

When I went on my first foray with my mycological society[1] last year, I followed a climate scientist around the forest like a lost puppy. He showed me fungi shaped like tiny bird's nests on branches, lifted red russulas so I could learn their shrimpy scent, pointed out phallic purple cortinarius, and kneeled down before brown hawk's wings in their edible prime. When we returned to the parking lot, a scientist from the Denver Botanic Gardens was gathering up our goods on a large tarp, lifting

1 For the uninitiated, that's a mushroom nerd club for adults.

specimen after specimen before our little group of geeks, introducing each one like a new friend to love.

"Look at these pines." The scientist motioned to the forest we had just walked through. "None of these trees would be taller than your kneecaps if mycorrhizal fungal networks were not nourishing them from below."

We, too, are trees in a forest who can only flourish by the life others send our way.

MF.

I HOLD A heating pad to my arm and try to breathe. I was *just* wrapping my mind around the strong probability that I need a port. How did *maybe* become *must* so fast?

I try to sort out what just happened. About thirty minutes ago, I had gotten up to go to the bathroom for something like the sixth time of the day. IVIG is such a high volume of liquids that I basically have to pee all day long. I dragged my IV pole to the sink to wash my hands, and when I glanced up at the mirror, my left arm was roughly the size of a small child's torso.

I rushed out the door with wet hands, yelling. "Someone! Help me! I don't know what's happening!"

My favorite nurse, Sadie, rushed to my side, inspecting my arm. Her eyes went wide and her jaw dropped. "It's a vein blowout," Sadie said. "A really bad one. How did you not feel this happening?!"

I reached for a chair, nearly falling from shock. I'm pretty sure I told my macho nurse earlier that my arm was hurting a little and felt strange, but he shrugged it off. Sometimes the only veins we can get to flow end up stinging and aching all day, and I've gotten too used to swallowing back the pain.

The small room whirled like a spinning top while the nurse stopped the IV and wrapped my arm in a large heating pad. A physician's assistant named Heather hurried in and crouched in front of my recliner. I struggled to take in her words. It's starting to make sense now. Heather said that it's too dangerous to continue future infusion treatment unless I get a port placed. Someone from the hospital nearest my house will be calling me, and I'll probably be having surgery in less than a week.

I can't go back to living with immune deficiency without IVIG. It's too dangerous. It's too hard.

Maybe it's shock or maybe it's pure stubbornness, but I've decided to carry on with today's treatment. These infusions protect me from infections but also keep my diseases under control, and if I'm having a port placed soon, I want my body to go into surgery as strong as she can. Sadie somehow, thankfully, found another functional vein. She just left the room, keeping the door slid open, probably so the team outside can keep an eye on me.

I see my nurse—the male nurse—charting at the desk outside the door, and I speak up like I'm reaching for a rope to find my way through a blizzard.

"I can't believe we were *just* talking about me maybe needing a port and then my vein blew out so bad," I tell him. "I can't believe I *have to* get a port."

He barely looks up from his computer. "Well, that's life. Life is hard."

Motherfucker. Did he really just say that?

He's not the one who has to have surgery.

I am *this close* to barring this asshat from my room and asking that he never be my nurse again.

The only reason I'm not is that my friend Meredith is on her way to sit with me. Thank God. Meredith lives in North Carolina, but she just happens to be in Denver this week for a conference, and of all the days I might need a companion at IVIG, it's today.

FORCE OF NATURE

MEREDITH SITS IN the corner in a bright floral maxi skirt and black shirt, leaning against the pale yellow wall, reading to me from a book bent open in her hands.

"To sing means to use the soul-voice . . ."

I relax into my recliner and stop checking the IV in my right arm for signs of another blown vein, finally settling down to the dulcet sound of her voice.

"It means to say on the breath the truth of one's power and one's need, to breathe soul over the thing that is ailing or in need of restoration."

Meredith is reading from Clarissa Pinkola Estés's classic, *Women Who Run with the Wolves,* but it feels like she is breathing soul over me.

"This is done," she reads, "by descending into the deepest mood of great love and feeling, till one's desire for relationship with the wildish Self overflows, then to speak one's soul from that frame of mind. That is singing over the bones."[2]

I can't help but think of the weird old prophet Ezekiel from the bible stories I learned as a kid. My mind swirls with his vi-

2 Clarissa Pinkola Estés, *Women Who Run with the Wolves: Myths and Stories of the Wild Woman Archetype* (London: Rider, 2008), 24.

sion of a valley of dry, dead bones, and the breath that enters them, bringing their bodies back to life.

Sadie peeks in the door. "A tornado is coming through this area. Look." She holds out her phone. "It took out my entire fence!"

Sadie's yard looks like a giant sprinted through it—a force of nature bigger than imagination—and we're amazed her house is okay. Meredith and I catch each other's eyes, hushed. We've always connected most deeply on the plane of metaphor, so I sense what we both are thinking without needing any words. It's like the tornado in my body today is mirrored by the storm outside.

We learn that the tornado is still distant and will probably miss us by a few miles. But just to be safe, Meredith decides to drive back to the church holding her conference so she won't get stuck in the storm.

She hugs me gently and presses her book into my hands to keep. I know her well enough to know it's a gesture of guidance—that she's inviting me to sing over the wildest forces within me, trusting that my own voice in this descent will bring what seems dead back to life.

TWIRL

I'VE LONG SUBSCRIBED to the script that not every shitty story has to be experienced as *traumatic*. In the trauma therapy world, we talk about hard experiences with big hopes. I want to believe that when we build support around our bodies through intention, regulation, and connection that even horrifying things don't have to thrust us into post-traumatic stress.

I've been practicing therapy for nearly a decade. I needed a career that afforded flexibility around chronic illness, which I've found running my own practice. But the profession I chose out of pragmatism became a vocation of joy. Body-centered therapy modalities have widened my capacity for connection, tolerance of pain, and access to delight. In being helped to heal from my own history of trauma (childhood, sexual, spiritual, and medical), I have specialized in offering clients room to heal from their own—often complex—trauma through partnering with the body as a wise witness and regulating resource.

In less than a week, I'll have a port placed in my chest that will be there for many years to come. It doesn't have to be a big deal, but it is a departure from my expectations. I'm determined to take this frustrating turn of events and make it meaningful. I'm determined to face the next five days as a friend to my body.

I just came outside to journal in the sun, and from the back deck, I saw a bucket and giant bubble wand that I'd gotten out to play with our friends' kids a couple of days ago.

I set down my journal and stood up, the sadness inside me surging into stubborn mischief: I wanted to dance before I grieved. I stepped barefoot onto our thick green grass and twirled bubbles the size of my body into a circle of light. My red spaghetti-strapped dress fluttered out as the sun kissed my bare arms and uncut upper chest.

I danced in defiance of disappointment. I basked in the goodness of my body. I twirled to tell her she is good.

MAKE IT MYSTICAL

WHEN WE BOUGHT our house a couple of months ago, the first thing I did the night our offer was accepted was purchase a membership to the local mycological society. Today is the group's first foray of the summer, and I'm here because I don't know how long it'll be before I'm well enough to forage again.

I follow our group's leader through a field flashing with purple and indigo penstemon, stretching into a thicker stand of ponderosa pines. He forks left and kneels in a patch of green plants, plucks one, and pops it in his mouth. "Wild onion," he says, handing me a tiny white bulb on a long green stalk. I chew and immediately love the taste—bright and sharp with a hint of grass. He shows us how to pluck it ourselves, pointing out the light purple fireworks of flowers at the top of the plant, the telltale sign of what's below.

We walk through warm yellow light slanting through the pines and start finding little brown mushrooms, but not much else. It's still too dry for the lobster mushrooms I was hoping to see for the first time. Someone finds a shriveled but hefty bolete and passes it around our group for closer inspection. Each face is bright with delight. I often forage alone, but I love when I get to see others as entranced in the forest as I am.

"The beauty of this earth," Simone Weil once wrote, "is the tender smile of Christ through matter."[3] These days, I'm noticing that beauty requires attention, which the French philosopher and mystic wrote of like prayer. To Weil, "Attention is the rarest and purest form of generosity."[4] When I first read Weil's

3 Simone Weil, *Waiting for God*, Routledge Revivals (New York: Routledge, 2009), 60.

4 Simone Weil, "Letter to Joë Bousquet," April 13, 1942, quoted in Simone Pétrement, *Simone Weil: A Life* (New York: Pantheon Books, 1976), 462.

work years ago, I found the two most consistent jolts of my attention confirmed and revered. To her, there are two things piercing enough to penetrate our lives with the love of God: beauty and affliction.[5]

All day, I've seen this forest as more vivid than any time I've visited before. I've cherished every step and taste and scent because I am carrying affliction with me.

Simone, I think. *I'll name my port Simone.*

SCARS

I STAND OVER steaming water, drawing the last bath I'll take before my body changes.

I've filled every open hour this week with intention—seeing my therapist, journaling, and accessing somatic resources for releasing stress. I've been connecting the dots between horrors in my childhood and the sense that parts of me are terrified to be held down again, even on an operating table, to be powerless in a way I haven't been since I was a little girl.

In trauma recovery work, we talk about trauma as anything that is too much, too fast, or too soon for the nervous system to handle. My own trauma recovery and the work of witnessing the courage of my clients tells me that the body does not simply keep the score; the body carries the story. And I don't want my body to have to carry this sudden and unwanted circumstance around like a millstone. I don't want to shove down this or any

5 Simone Weil, "The Love of God and Affliction," in *Simone Weil: Late Philosophical Writings,* ed. Eric O. Springsted (Maryknoll, NY: Orbis, 1998), 41–71.

past story. Perhaps by listening well to my body now, I can prevent future pain.

I light two candles and flick off the lights before pouring some CBD forest bathing salts into the water. I want the earthy sweetness of the forest to shelter me for the procedure tomorrow. I queue up a healing sound bath playlist on Spotify and get in.

I need to let my body speak.

The body's speech, the body's first language—learned long before words—is sensation. Tears, and the urge to be rocked and held. I sink in the hot water as though there is no clock, letting the water hold me. I wrap my arms around myself and sway.

This is a wordless dialogue—sensation and movement speaking back and forth—and having been soothed in this quiet reconnection to my body, I begin to speak. I hold out my arms and trace every vein that my nurses have accessed over the years, thanking each one for helping me get the medicine I need. *Thank you. Thank you. Thank you.* Then I hold my hands over my chest where the scalpel will cut and the port will be placed, and I cry while thanking my body for receiving this thing that we need.

I pray, consenting to the change I wouldn't have chosen.

And then, I hear a voice I cannot explain, but sense as Christ, as God:

By my wounds you are healed.

My scars are sacred, and yours are too.

I heave sobs, heavy with indistinguishable sorrow and relief. And when there is no longer any separation between the steam and my tears, I hear one more thing:

You won't be less whole tomorrow.

CUT

WHEN THE SURGICAL nurse arrives to wheel me away, those words meet me in my mind, calming my fear like a weighted blanket.

I lie on the table in the cold, sterile operating room under layers of thin blankets, clutching a tiny wooden cross. Capped and gloved and masked bodies swirl around me in preparation. The words hold me still.

This wound won't make you less whole.

INFORMED CONSENT

JULY

THE SURGEON SAID I should feel better in a couple of days, but it's been five days, and this pain is fearsome. The whole right side of my chest hasn't stopped aching. The area around and beneath my port burns, hot and deep and sore. This week, I called the nurse line at interventional radiology, desperate for relief, and I learned they had to cut deeper than I thought to place the port well. Afterward, I called my mother-in-law, Suzanne, who was a charge nurse in a short-stay surgical unit for almost forty years. She said she's been present for many port surgeries. "They tug and tug at your body to position the port. *Of course* you still feel sore."

Why did they downplay how much this would hurt? Why would they lead me to believe this was no big deal? *You'll be back to work in a couple of days, my ass.*

Before surgery, a nurse placed a plastic dummy chest on my lap, skin made of silicone, anatomy like a man's, a chest without a body. "Place your fingers here. Feel that bump? That's what your port will feel like."

She handed me a fake curved Huber needle and showed me where to poke. She warned me to never let anyone who isn't trained in accessing ports touch my port, but she didn't say how far they would cut. She didn't say I would feel like my body was in a car wreck. She just handed me a consent form, and the surgeon's assistant came in to witness me sign.

But I am not a chest without a body. And that was not informed consent.

FIREWORKS

OUTSIDE OUR BEDROOM windows, light flashes in the sky above the ridge. *Fireworks.*

It's the Fourth of July. But I feel like a moonless sky. It is dark inside me. The therapist in me knows this dark is but a thick blanket thrown over my body by old memories of being brutalized. But the body doesn't always know the difference between past and present, between childhood cruelty and adult healthcare.

I lie in bed with an ice pack clutched to my chest, observing and interrogating the dark. *Why did no one screen me before surgery for post-traumatic stress?*

I know the hopelessness hanging heavy on my body is a response to realities I lived long before this year. I know this is a sustained emotional flashback to being held down against my will as a girl, powerless to fight, and too small to squirm away. I sense that my time on that operating table activated ancient memories. But that doesn't make it less dark.

The fantasy novelist Ursula K. Le Guin wrote, "Light is the left hand of darkness and darkness the right hand of light."[6] I hold a sprig of lupine in my hand that I picked earlier when Ryan—concerned about my despair—made me get out of bed to stand in the sun for a few minutes at the park. I want to trust that this dark is the right hand of coming light.

BONE COLLECTOR

AFTER A WEEK in bed recovering from surgery, I find it both strange and good to get away from home and get outside. The sun shines hot on my shoulders, and I cool my feet and calves from a camp chair in the cold, clean water of the Arkansas River. Pinkish-brown granite walls rise from the river, dotted green with juniper. Behind me, the rocks spire like a cathedral against an azure sky and the distant giant Collegiate Peaks.

White-water rafters keep floating by, waving and laughing, and I sit quietly with my yellow notebook open on my knees, along with the copy of *Women Who Run with the Wolves* that Meredith gave me, trying to open my heart to accept the object tunneled under my skin as part of me now. I place my hand over my port. *Simone, please calm down.*

I'm probably too sick to be here, camping for two nights at Browns Canyon National Monument with Mish and Ryan for

6 Ursula K. Le Guin, *The Left Hand of Darkness: 50th Anniversary Edition* (New York: Berkley, 1969), 232.

Kish Camp,[7] the cutesy name my best friend and I have dubbed our annual tradition of low-key camping—complete with naps and crafts—which we squeeze into each summer like lime. Earlier, we embroidered matching bandanas, stitching shapes to match how we each feel about the season we are in.

We've had this site reserved for months, but I didn't think I'd make it to Kish Camp this year. Ryan and I drove here straight from the hospital yesterday, where an interventional radiologist checked my surgical incision and prescribed a strong antibiotic, Bactrim, in case an infection is the reason I'm just not recovering. I'm in so much pain, but I'm here anyway, because I need nature to nourish me.

I'm enthralled by the words in this book about the wise woman inside each of us, singing over dead bones, and I write out some quotes.[8]

"This is our meditation practice as women, calling back the dead and dismembered aspects of ourselves, calling back the dead and dismembered aspects of life itself."[9]

The sand at my feet glints gold, and a gentle breeze wraps my skin in warmth. I close my eyes and let the sound of the river calm my fears. In the dark of my eyelids, I see stars.

I jot down lines, the start of something that might be a poem.

The stars and river sing
a creation hymn
over my bones,
over every riven thing.[10]

7 KJ + Mish = Kish. Kish Camp!

8 Estés, *Women Who Run with the Wolves*, 26–27.

9 Ibid., 30.

10 I definitely was influenced here by Christian Wiman's poem "Every Riven Thing," though I was not aware of it in the moment.

Last night, Ryan and I slept with our tent open to the sky. The whole right side of my chest burned like hydrogen squeezed at the core, but we watched the stars dance long into the night, our heads cradled together in equilibrium.

This is why I want to be alive, I thought, eyes dazzled by the sky, *because though there is ache, there is also amazement.*

I bask in the sun, holding my hand over the jagged, bruised dash on my chest, still scabbing and throbbing with pain. I breathe the scent of water and mud deep in my lungs. I will call back the dismembered parts of myself. I will.

I write down one more quote before I walk back to our campsite.

"Today the old one inside you is collecting bones. What is she re-making?"[11]

THE CARE AND FEEDING OF SIMONE

MY FRIEND ILA texted yesterday to ask what I ended up naming my port. Ila lives with chronic illnesses, too, and she used to have a different kind of central line, so she knows more than others how big of a change this is for me.

"Simone," I texted back, "for Simone Weil. She suffered with migraines every single day, even during her deepest times of joy and mystical visions . . . I figured I could use some Simone energy in my body. (Minus the part where she died young. ☠😂)"

Ila replied a few minutes later with a strong-arm emoji and said, "And now infusions can be your time to feed Simone 😉"

11 Estés, 34.

"Gah!! YES!" I texted right back.

While I know the real Simone isn't actually alive in the device in my chest, I also want to relate to my port like a person with a story and a soul. I don't want to be at war with the thing I need to get the medicine that keeps me well. I want to look at my port like an icon, a portal into prayer and presence rather than a pain I have to put up with because of my body's many problems.

An on-demand nurse just came to my house to access Simone for the first time and administer my weekly IV medicine for HAE. I was in no mood to tell the nurse I just met that the medicine she's giving me is made from mutant rabbit's milk nor that I've weirdly chosen to name my port after a dead philosopher. Having a needle pierced into the silicone and plastic device implanted under my skin is science fiction enough.

"Remember this acronym for accessing your port," the nurse explained. "SASH. Saline. Administration. Saline. Heparin. SASH."

She pointed at the expanse of medical supplies sprawled over the end of our bed, showing me the syringes of saline and heparin I'd need to flush the port and the tubing and catheters to connect everything. She demonstrated each step carefully, because eventually, even soon, I'll be doing this all on my own. I watched, blinking back tears. *How did my home suddenly become a little hospital?*

I sat in the armchair at the foot of our bed, with the nurse sitting on the footstool in front of me. After the pinch of the needle into my still-unhealed skin, I tasted pennies on my tongue and gripped the sides of the chair tightly, trying hard to not freak out about the fact that medicine was entering my bloodstream from a catheter at the internal jugular vein, straight into my heart.

After the nurse left and the room stopped spinning, I took

my copy of Simone Weil's *Waiting for God* down to the living room, where I now sit, curled up on a chaise lounge. I figure, if I'm going to have to live with Simone and feed Simone, I might as well spend some time with her words. And I sure as hell am going to have some words for her if she doesn't start to calm the fuck down.

In all my previous time with Simone Weil's words, I somehow always skipped over the introductions that set her writing in the context of her life. Midway through Leslie A. Fiedler's introduction to *Waiting for God,* I learn that Simone essentially starved herself to death.

What the fuck? How did I not know this before I named my port Simone?

I knew Simone was French, born into a Jewish family, and had written while World War II raged through her homeland, but I did not know that Simone had starved herself in solidarity with her fellow French citizens who were oppressed by the occupying Nazis. My jaw drops as I read that "on August 24th in 1943, she succeeded at last in dying, completing the process of 'de-creation' at which she had aimed all her life."[12]

I wonder if all the Christians who *love* to sound cultured quoting Simone Weil realize that she died by suicide.

I sit there a long time, stupefied, and then grab my phone to text Ila.

"Tell me you already knew that Simone Weil died by starving herself. Because now I really can't stop laughing about 'feeding Simone.'"

12 Leslie A. Fiedler, introduction to *Waiting for God* by Simone Weil, xxvi.

TERRA INCOGNITA

I'M WRAPPED IN two blankets, one of which Amy sent in a care package for my surgery recovery. After all her knee surgeries, Amy knew I'd need to wrap myself in something soft. It's the fluffiest pink blanket I've ever seen.

A pack of frozen peas rests on my chest, calming the pain leaching from my port. I open my notebook to turn this pain to speech.

Yesterday, Simone and I made it through our first long feeding. And by that I mean: yesterday I had my first IVIG treatment through my port. It was not easy. And, we did it.

I advocated for myself when I arrived at the clinic so I wouldn't be stuck all day with that dismissive male nurse hovering over my still-healing port that he didn't think was a big deal to get. *Ass.*

I feel like I've arrived in an unknown land. I'm disoriented by the customs and language surrounding my new port. *SASH. Access. Huber needle.* I'm on guard, easily spooked by the smallest things. The sensation of saline entering my chest instead of my arms is strange. I haven't known Simone long enough to trust that she won't hurt me . . . or even kill me . . . without meaning to, of course.

I did glimpse good things in this new land yesterday. IVIG is definitely more comfortable through my port. Even with the site still so tender, my infusion felt better flowing there than through my battered veins.

I am going to be okay in the new landscape of my life.

This morning, I listened to my friend Suzanne's interview on Glennon Doyle's podcast. Her wisdom was like light to my dark. "We're not going to get anywhere if we can't tell the truth,"

Suzanne said, "and we're not going to get anywhere if we can't tell the truth shamelessly."[13]

I am not ashamed of my trauma responses. I did not make a wrong turn or deliberately sabotage my strength.

This season is simply inviting me to shed and to shift. To shed over-functioning. To shift back into the solitude of a spirituality that can soothe the most aching parts of me. Shedding and shifting are active processes. Healing has been worlds harder than I was led to expect. *And* I am giving my body gentleness. I am softening my way into strength. I will keep moving my pen across this page to participate in the truer life that is mine to receive. This is *doing* that supports *being*.

Living in a body that shows me a different face daily has shaped me to see softly. Uncertainty is the only certainty. Whether a day holds difficulty or ease, I can be okay. I do not yet know what is happening within me in this shadowed season in a new, stranger country of sickness. But I trust the goodness intended for me will emerge. It always does.

I write a note to myself, instructions for the posture I most want to take:

"I echo Julian of Norwich: *All shall be well. All shall be well.*[14]

It's a reality that runs deeper than my shifting breath.

Hope lives in my bones."

13 Suzanne Stabile, "Enneagram: Why You Are the Way You Are with Suzanne Stabile," *We Can Do Hard Things* podcast, episode 226, https://momastery.com/blog/we-can-do-hard-things-ep-226/.

14 Julian of Norwich, *The Showings of Julian of Norwich: A New Translation*, trans. Mirabai Starr (Charlottesville, VA: Hampton Roads Publishing, 2013), 27.

RESCUE

THE NEXT MORNING, I wake in searing pain. I swallow my morning dose of steroids but rush to the bathroom, where the pills come right back up. I crawl back to bed to grab my phone to text Ryan. He's on the other side of Colorado on the next trip of what I thought this book would be about, exploring Mesa Verde National Park with dear friends. I sent him there without me, because I've been in too much pain to drive that far from home.

The sensations I'm feeling are frighteningly familiar to those from a few months ago, when I had an adrenal crisis in Nashville while there to meet my new editor. That day, my literary agent saved my life. Alex rescued me from the airport when I couldn't stop vomiting before my flight home and rushed me to a doctor for an emergency steroid shot right before I lost consciousness. It was something I knew technically *could* happen, since I have adrenal insufficiency, but I never thought it actually would. And I don't want to relive it. I text Ryan what's happening and tell him I'm stress-dosing my steroids.

But I can't keep the pills down. I'm shaking too hard to safely get downstairs to get my emergency steroid shot from my purse. Mish happens to be on her way down from Denver to hang out for the day.

"I think I'm in an adrenal crisis. You're going to have to give me my emergency steroid shot. Here's what you'll need to do." I copy and paste the instructions I wrote in my Notes app for Sarah a few weeks ago into a text to Mish.

I hear Mish opening the front door just after I've retched up my pills again. She finds the pouch with my Solu-Cortef vial and syringe in the kitchen and runs upstairs to help me. Her hands shake drawing up the liquid into the syringe, but she sticks me like a total pro.

Ten minutes later, I'm still convulsing, so we drive to the urgent care one street over. Mish holds my body up, dragging me inside, and I stand there, white as a ghost, shaking so hard I have to clutch the counter to keep from falling. The woman behind the front desk glares at us and looks past me to Mish.

"Miss," she says, glowering. "We are not an emergency room. We can't do anything."

We don't even have time to bitch about her bitchiness. We stumble back to Mish's Subaru.

"Turn . . . right," I slur, so quiet. Forming words is taking everything I have. "The hospital where I got my port is five minutes up the road."

IVERMECTIN

THE TRIAGE NURSE gets me into a room fast, and then everything slows. For hours, I shake under layers of scratchy blankets, chattering my teeth as though this is the Arctic and I am unclothed. My D-dimer comes back high, which I know could indicate a blood clot, since I have a clotting disorder and have had a small pulmonary embolism.

Mish and I are coping with the chaos how we normally do, making fun of each other. She pulls out a plastic tackle box full of beads and colored thread and embroiders a colorful oval, while I laugh at the absurdity of doing crafts in an emergency room. *I love that bitch.*

An ultrasound tech peeks her head behind the green curtain to my room and announces she's here to check my legs for deep vein thrombosis. I wriggle out of my pants while apologizing for my still-shaking legs. "I just can't get warm."

The woman is blond and probably in her early sixties. She tells us about her grandkids and is starting to apply cool jelly to my groin when she looks up with concern. "Did *you* get the vaccine?"

Mish and I glance at each other with eyebrows raised. *Covid landed me in cardiac rehab, so yeah, I don't take it lightly.* The ultrasound tech tells us all about how she just *wouldn't* take the vaccine and drove down to the border herself to pick up a large supply of Ivermectin. I can't lasso my eyebrows from the peak of my forehead. My eyes dart from the lady to Mish, back and forth, and now I'm shaking not just from the cold but from trying to hide my horrified laughter inside. *Is a medical provider at a hospital really telling me she is a science disbeliever right now?! I mean, she's entitled to her own opinions, but surely this isn't the time or place to share them!*

The tech traces my veins hard with her transducer as she prattles on about Jesus and having faith over fear, and Mish sits at the left end of my bed, looking up from her embroidery to me every few seconds with her eyes round as golf balls. I know she knows I'm pissed, as well as amused. We've been friends since I was seventeen and she was eighteen. We can read each other's body language like a book. *Welp,* we both are thinking, *we're definitely in a hospital in the Springs, not Denver.*

As soon as the lady leaves, we laugh so hard I'm afraid I'll dislodge the tubing snaking out from the port in my chest.

TOO MUCH

THE ULTRASOUND WAS clear. With the threat of a blood clot behind us, I tell Mish it's okay if she needs to go home to let out Hemi, her heart-melt of a pit bull. This was clearly longer than the hangout we had planned. I text Alex and his wife Nicole, since they live about five minutes from the hospital. Alex says he can get here quickly, and he and Mish change shifts at my bedside.

Alex is my friend, but since he's also my agent, I'm sheepish to let him see me so sick again. It's hard to let anyone see me like this, but especially someone I work closely with professionally. I'm pretty sure neither of us can unsee the memory of me projectile vomiting out the door of his rental car on the side of a Nashville highway nor how I almost passed out before that steroid shot stabilized me.

I tilt my head toward Alex, sitting in the folding chair to my right. "Remember when we first met? At that coffee shop in Castle Rock?"

He nods. "Of course I do."

"Remember how I warned you about working with me—that weird shit seems to happen to me more than most people?"

We both laugh. "I know you thought I was exaggerating, but I bet you don't now!"

Alex chuckles. "You definitely weren't exaggerating!"

I'm wearing my favorite T-shirt, a faded red one with logos for all the national parks. The collar is pulled down on my chest so the nurses can access Simone. Yesterday's mascara is blurred black beneath my glassy eyes. I'm still pants-less under my hospital blankets, and I smooth over the rough fibers with my hands to make sure my underwear isn't showing. My long brown hair is matted with sweat. The tangled lines of a heart monitor and IV tubing stretch out from under the collar of my shirt like weedy vines.

I look over to Alex. "Thank you for being here."

He sits there in a black hoodie and ball cap, shrugging his broad shoulders, and smiles back. "Of course."

I said thank you, but I'm also saying so much more inside. *Thank you for not treating me like I'm too much. Thank you for seeing me as more than sick. Thank you for believing I am more than my messiest moments.*

A doctor comes in and tells us they think I had a bad reaction to yesterday's IVIG treatment and crashed after my IV steroid pre-medication wore off. They're sending in a refill of Solu-Cortef to my pharmacy and sending me home.

I see Nicole by the nurse's station outside and call her in. Alex steps outside, and Nicole gently helps me out of the bed and into my pants.

Alex leaves to get my prescription and a big green smoothie with extra protein powder, since it's been twenty-four hours since I've eaten anything, and Nicole drives me home. She wraps my arm over her shoulder to help me up the stairs and tucks me into bed. We turn on a Nora Ephron movie I've never seen before and definitely won't remember. I'm hot and exhausted and then cold and groggy. I pull on a sweatshirt. Ryan's racing home from Mesa Verde, and Nicole stays by my side until he arrives.

TOO FAST

I WAKE UP hot as morning coffee and assume I must have slept too hard. I peel off my black hooded sweatshirt and barely glance at myself in the bathroom mirror while splashing cool water on my hot face. In the lower left corner of the mirror is a decal that reads *This is a good body,* and I reflexively bring my right hand to my port in recognition of its truth. *Still good.* I dry my face and head downstairs where Ryan sits, ready with a cup of black coffee for me, like every other morning of our thirteen years of marriage. I barely remember him arriving and Nicole leaving, but I'm glad we both are home.

I sit in the corner of the leather couch, legs up on the chaise longue, coffee mug in hand. I'm still burning up. After a few sips, I open the camera on my phone and point it toward myself as a makeshift mirror.

Whoa. My face is a fire hydrant. I pull down the collar of my black shirt to check my port incision and notice that the blotches of red all over my face extend down my chest. Rouge peeks out from the edges of the joggers at my ankles. Angry red splotches cover me from head to toe.

"Um, Ryan, is this what hives look like?"

He frowns in concern. "I don't know, but maybe?" He pauses, clearly shocked. "Probably . . . That looks weird. Call my mom."

I FaceTime Ryan's mom. I've never been more grateful that marrying Ryan gave me a bonus mom who is a retired nurse. I swallow back a couple of pink Benadryl pills. As I show Mom my splotches, it becomes hard to talk.

"Mom." I struggle. "It . . . feels . . . like my throat . . . is starting . . . to close."

"Get help wherever is closest."

I hang up, and we jump in the Jeep and head back to the urgent care that turned me away just the day before, because it's the help that's closest. Before I know it, I'm on an exam table, struggling to swallow. My skin is a flame and my body is the fire. A doctor examines my skin, shines a light in my throat, and says they have to call an ambulance. I can barely speak. Someone tells me to pull down my pants so they can give me a shot of epinephrine. *I was just waking up. I was just in the hospital yesterday. They said I was fine. How is this happening?* ***What*** *is happening?*

Paramedics stand over my body while Ryan explains what happened yesterday and what has happened before. One paramedic pokes me four times trying to start an IV, and I roll inside like the earth is a sphere flying down a hill and my body is a bullet racing from a gun. I am speed and fire and sound. My heart beats faster than any voice could match. *Lub dub lub dub lub dub lub dub lub dub lub dub.* A drum so loud it whooshes in my ears.

The ambulance ride is only about six minutes, but within that time, my blood pressure plummets. *Breathe,* I plead with myself. *Keep breathing.*

I am alone except for the paramedic tending my IV. He pushes more epi, and through the snare drum of my heart, I barely hear his voice.

"Just hold on. You're going to be okay. We're almost there. Just hold on."

TOO SOON

THEY WHEEL ME into a room larger than I've ever seen in an ER. The walls are distant and lined with drawers. Bright lights glare above my head. I'm shaking uncontrollably on a bare bed. My whole body pulses like my drumbeat heart. I am pure percussion now.

My teeth chatter so hard it hurts, and I glance at my arms. *Still red.* Bodies rush around me like waves that crest and fall. Someone explains that I'm shaking so much because of how much epinephrine I've been given.

I must be stable now, because the waves of doctors and nurses have slowed. Through rapid blinks, I see Ryan. They've let him sit by my side, the two of us an island in a strange and sterile sea.

After a long stretch of quiet, someone tells us that they're transferring me upstairs.

I was just here yesterday.

A doctor explains that I was in severe anaphylactic shock, and they'll be observing me overnight to make sure I'm okay. They'll be giving me an infusion of high-dose steroids to help the swelling in my face and throat go down.

Once I'm admitted in a room and the doctors are gone, I grab my phone to take another selfie. After all that epi, I'm so curious to see if I still look like an angry lobster fighting the pot.

The swollen, splotchy face staring back at me is shocking. And then, inexplicably, I smirk into the camera and snap a photo. Somehow, even though this all has been too much, too fast, too soon, I'm still amused. I'm still *alive.*

THE GIRL WHO LIVED

BY EARLY EVENING, I am contentedly almost back to looking like any other white lady. I didn't know a face could change that much in one day.

I've changed into the comfy pajamas I had Ryan bring me from home—no scratchy gowns for me, thanks. I end the scariest day of my life by streaming the first *Harry Potter* movie on my iPad from my hospital bed, in honor of my younger sister.[15] Nine years ago, Kenzie was diagnosed with lupus, and just weeks later, it caused a rare and massive heart attack. At twenty years old. We almost lost her just days before Christmas. Kenzie was life-flighted from Montana to a much larger hospital in Salt Lake City, and once she was finally awake in the cardiovascular ICU, the *Harry Potter* movies were the only thing that sounded remotely comforting to her.

I drove all over Salt Lake, desperately looking for the DVD set like it could save her life, and I finally found it after trying about ten stores. The only way I could bring my sister comfort during the worst days of her life was bringing *Harry Potter* to her bedside, and now I'm drawing from the same comfort. The memory of seeing my sister survive is making this less scary.

I am no stranger to hospitals, but I've never been on this side of the bed. Somehow, in fourteen years of autoimmune disease, I have eluded hospitalization. I sleepily watch "the boy who lived" and I get the sense that I just did, too. It's strange, to sit here in peace, with only the beeping of IV pumps and a pulse oximeter, when I know that just hours ago, I was begging my body to keep breathing.

15 While I still love the *Harry Potter* series, I do not condone or support J.K. Rowling's transphobia.

There's no way I can swallow solid food yet, since my throat is still a painful, loose knot. So Ryan gets me another green protein smoothie before leaving for the night. A few minutes after my first sips, my skin itches—at first on my arms, and then everywhere. The knot of my throat tightens. I push my call button.

I scratch like fire ants have covered every inch of my skin while IV Benadryl whooshes through my heart and the room tilts left and right. And it is not enough. I cannot swallow the knot in my throat, and I sense a silent choice.

I could let it close. I could let my story end.

But I am not done. I do not want to die.

Breathe. I beg my body again. *Breathe.*

A nurse rushes in with more epi, and I pull the fabric of my PJs up, exposing my left thigh for the shot.

IT WAS JUST A SNACK PACK

MY DOCTORS, RYAN, and I have all assumed something in that green smoothie must have caused anaphylaxis, since it happened directly after drinking it two days in a row. We made a list of ingredients I might be deathly allergic to: pineapple, collagen, coconut water, dates, kale. *No more smoothies,* we said—as though hell were that simple to escape.

Ryan drove to the airport to pick up my mom, racing down from Montana. We both figured I'd be fine for an hour alone.

Minutes after he left, a speech therapist arrived, saying that since my throat swelled so much yesterday, she needed to assess my swallow functioning. She handed me a small piece of cheddar cheese and a cup of chocolate pudding for the test. I laughed and told her I haven't had a snack pack since I traded my sandwiches for them in elementary school. *Cheers!* I took one bite of cheese and swallowed one spoonful of pudding under her watchful eye.

Fifteen minutes later, I was red, itching my hot skin with one hand and holding the other to my throat, trying to coax my airway to stay open. Minutes later, another shot of epi gave me air again.

The doctors are putting me on a liquid diet and moving me to the intermediate care unit, right next to the ICU, where they can monitor me more closely. I thought I'd just be here for a day, but I'm relieved help will be closer if my throat starts to close again.

It was awful, being alone in a hospital bed, save for a nurse, trying to beg my body to stay alive without Ryan by my side. But I realized something essential in those long, terrifying moments: when it comes down to it, *I* am the only one who can choose to stay alive.

THE PHOENIX IN ROOM 5516

MY NEW ROOM faces Pikes Peak. Even when I cannot leave bed, beauty finds me. Distant clouds above the mountain contrast against an aquamarine sky like ships in a sea. I feel safer here, with nurses hovering. The machines connected to me beep and beep, but I know the nurses hear them. They rush to my bed when my heart sprints or my blood pressure drops.

I'm NPO—*nil per os* in Latin—which means I'm no longer allowed anything by mouth, including liquids as well as food, after even a bite of food that's never caused as much as an upset stomach before made my entire body rebel in anaphylactic mutiny yet again.

My mom is here now. And Ryan is, too. We were just watching more Harry Potter when it happened again. Out of nowhere, I burst like a dying phoenix into flame. My cheeks burned red hot, and I tried but failed to stop scratching the itch inflaming every inch of my skin. Within ten minutes, my throat began to close. I'm losing count of how many times a nurse or doctor has pierced my skin with epi. Every time is a brutal relief. My symptoms only stop with those shots. I shudder to think of what would happen if they didn't work.

While I fought to breathe, my mom climbed into my hospital bed and stroked my hair. I could breathe so much better with her by my side. I'm not sure I could have let her comfort me like this not too long ago, but we have come so far. I can endure so much more when I am held.

We're back to watching *Harry Potter and the Chamber of Secrets.* My tan steel water bottle sits beside my iPad, since the very generous doctors have decided to let me take small sips of water to moisten my mouth. Underneath a new decal depicting the bright blue waters of Crater Lake, I've placed a red sunflower sticker Kenzie sent down with Mom. It reads, in pretty cursive script, *Shit happens.*

IN WHICH I BECOME A TV CHARACTER CARICATURE OF MYSELF

I KEEP HAVING attacks of anaphylaxis every four to six hours. My nurses are letting Ryan or my mom stay here tonight, because anaphylaxis is so much less scary when I'm not alone.

The doctors here have no clue what is happening, though. I'm really hoping the attending doc can get ahold of my immunologist in the morning.

Nicole just checked in, so I text her back. "They're basically trying to stabilize me enough to stop having anaphylaxis so I can get home and go to my immunologist. There's been a little bit of discussion about transferring me to a more specialized hospital, but no one's brought it up in a few hours."

A doctor just prescribed me Ativan in hopes that I'll sleep tonight. All of the epi shots and high-dose steroids flowing through the IV have me *up*. It's like I'm exhausted but . . . excited? My body feels like how I imagine a cat who got *way* too much catnip would feel—except also, the cat has been hit by a car and the cat periodically almost stops breathing but the cat also really wants to be stroked by warm, soft hands and told she is a very pretty girl.

I copy and paste my text to Nicole to Mish.

She replies minutes later. "This feels like an episode of *House*."

HUMMINGBIRD HEART

THIS MORNING, I tried the tiniest bit of applesauce and went straight into anaphylaxis yet again. I've counted it up: so far I've had eight shots of epi, and there doesn't seem to be an end in sight. I'm back on a steady stream of dextrose and saline dripping straight into my heart via Simone. This is day three of being sustained by sugar in saline and nothing else.

When I was maybe ten, my family visited Colorado's national parks for our annual summer trip. What I remember most from those days, beyond my dad bringing far too little water on a hike in Colorado National Monument on a 110-degree day, are the hummingbirds. Their tiny green-and-orange bodies, flitting fast past my eyes, always mesmerized me. Mom brought a hummingbird feeder home and has kept it full of sugar water for them ever since. It might be the high-dose steroids talking, but just now, when my nurse restarted my dextrose drip, I thought of those hummingbirds and smiled at my need for nectar. There are worse things than imagining I have a hummingbird heart.

I cannot leave this bed and can't even get to the bathroom without someone holding me up, but a hummingbird can fly over five hundred miles without stopping. Flowers are their food. I envision my bed as a bird. I am traveling many miles with every breath. I am one tiny life in one small hospital, and I imagine my pain as pollination. As doctors and nurses and friends and family flit to and from my bed, I daydream that these terrifying days are but a flight to flowers. Maybe my medical mystery will pollinate plants that might have otherwise died.

IT DOESN'T HAVE TO MAKE SENSE

I FEEL AN urge to write and pull out my yellow notebook and open to the empty pages I intended to fill with adventures and awe. I will fill them instead with my fight to stay alive.

Because the severe anaphylactic episodes have not stopped, my doctors are discussing giving me a feeding tube. Jargon buzzes around my room like flies. Maybe I have Mast Cell Activation Syndrome. Or Mastocytosis. Maybe I'm severely allergic to Bactrim, the antibiotic that interventional radiology prescribed for the possible port infection. Maybe that activated everything. Maybe this is a massive autoimmune flare. Maybe someday I will not be a mystery. Even though I've essentially been living off sugar water and nothing else, I'm still going into anaphylaxis daily, and they won't discharge me until it stops.

Every time, I beg my body to keep breathing.

Every time, I'm not sure if she can.

Every time, we somehow do.

Each time I've entered the storm of severe anaphylaxis, inexplicable peace meets me. Peace about my life and self floods me more than histamine.

My knee is swelling, fingers tingling, foot itching—all on my left side. And I'm thanking my body for speaking up, for alerting me to her needs. I breathe into the pain. I exhale the panic. I call my nurse. We intervene. And then I go back to laughing at Moira's antics on *Schitt's Creek* with my redheaded love by my side. None of this makes sense, but I am supported. I am alive.

TORPOR

MY HEART HAS been crawling for days at forty beats per minute. I've never heard this much space between beats. Eighty. Ninety. I knew that *lub dub* pace as predictably as a hymn. But now I'm too tired to even hum. Nurses outside my door listen all day and night to my heart's faint song.

Sugar water via my central line is still all I can tolerate without triggering anaphylaxis. My new hospitalist is Dr. Knope, a tiny but fierce-looking Asian American woman. Today she grasped my hand while asking me to try to eat again, this time asking me to endure the allergic symptoms as long as I can without intervening with epi.

Every tiny attempt at eating—like the half cup of plain white rice I diligently spooned into my mouth earlier—becomes fury. I scratch and moan and sweat and swell until the shot finally pierces my skin again.

My heart has slowed because I am starving.

I have never seen a hummingbird halt. I've watched them in wonder, wings all color in blur as they flash from flower to flower. I've never seen them slow or stop. But they do.

When food cannot be found or the air becomes bitterly cold, the hummingbird's heart slows from 1,200 beats per minute to 50. Unless the cold heart warms, the bird will not survive longer than a night.

The average hummingbird weighs less than the pen in my hand, and it is taking all my strength to hold it. I have not been intubated, but if we cannot get my body to believe food won't kill me, my doctors are going to place a feeding tube tomorrow or the next day. A hummingbird can survive short spells of torpor, but the human body was not made to hold on like this.

HOSPITAL SURVIVAL TIPS

1. If you can get around being in a horrible hospital gown, get yourself into something else. Having your ass hang out when you have to leave your room for a scan isn't gonna help you heal.

2. Get yourself the softest PJs your central line and various beeping shit monitors can go around. Get what you need via family or delivery orders to make yourself even just 10 percent more comfortable in your skin. This is not silly; this is survival. Your comfort is like a reservoir of strength to endure the symptoms that feel too cruel.

3. Have someone bring you a sleeping mask. All the lights and monitors are DEATH TO SLEEP. Every hourly vitals check means you not only get poked and prodded but get fluorescent light–boarded just after you've convinced yourself to not have a panic attack. BLOCK THAT SHIT OUT.

4. On that, one word: EARBUDS. The type doesn't matter, just get them in your ears and get the beeps out. Listen to calming music or an audiobook. I'm making my way through *The Chronicles of Narnia* while I wander through this hellscape. It's probably better for my mental health to hear Lucy's and Aslan's voices than my scary low heart rate alerts. Sometimes the mind needs a wardrobe to walk through. Amen?

5. Do not let any nurse or family member shame you for needing anti-anxiety meds to sleep. Anyone who shames you for your need for comfort can fuck all the way off.

6. On that point: Don't cuss out anyone. But do feel free to let the f-bombs fly when you are alone. Studies have shown that cussing lowers pain and improves health outcomes.[16] Fuck yes they do! Now is not the time to impress your religious aunt. It's the time to survive, babyyyyyyy.

NIGHT

MY HOSPITAL ROOM is empty and silent, except for the beeps alarming every time my heart rate drops into the thirties. I've decided to send my family home. Dad's here now, too, and he, Mom, and Ryan all need a good night's sleep just as much as I do. And I want to be able to endure the long nights on my own.

One Ativan and several chapters of *The Lion, the Witch and the Wardrobe* got me to sleep, but not far into the night, a string of beeps rouses me straight into a waking nightmare. Suddenly, my throat feels like it's closing again. I push my call button in what is now a reflex.

My night nurse, Brittany, rushes in. After checking my vi-

16 Richard Stephens and Olly Robertson, "Swearing as a Response to Pain: Assessing Hypoalgesic Effects of Novel 'Swear' Words," *Frontiers in Psychology* 11 (April 30, 2020): 723, https://www.ncbi.nlm.nih.gov/pmc/articles/PMC7204505/#:~:text=It%20is%20established%20within%20the,perceived%20as%20humorous%20or%20novel; Nicholas B. Washmuth and Richard Stephens, "Frankly, We Do Give a Damn: Improving Patient Outcomes with Swearing," *Archives of Physiotherapy* 12, no. 1 (March 17, 2022): 6, https://www.ncbi.nlm.nih.gov/pmc/articles/PMC8928588/; and Katie Brown, "Profanity Can Sometimes Be the Best Medicine, Increasing Pain Tolerance by ~33%," Psychiatrist.com, July 11, 2023, https://www.psychiatrist.com/news/profanity-can-sometimes-be-the-best-medicine-increasing-pain-tolerance-33-percent/#:~:text=Swearing%20can%20actually%20lessen%20pain,to%20a%20soothing%2C%20analgesic%20effect.

tals and port, she assures me that even though my heart rate is very low, I'm safe.

I look into her warm brown eyes; she's like a candle in the dark. My fear moves toward her like a moth to a flame, and I whisper how over and over I've had to consciously choose to keep breathing.

"I'm afraid," I confess. "I'm afraid I'm going to die."

Brittany kneels beside my bed and squeezes my shoulder, looking me straight in the eyes.

"You are not going to die tonight."

She describes how closely they're monitoring me. She explains every step standing between me and dying. She tells me how many interventions are ready, waiting to sustain me should we need them. Hot tears of relief stream down my face, and Brittany wraps me in a hug, holding me as I weep. "You are going to be okay." She repeats it again and again, until my eyes grow heavy with sleep.

DONUTS?

A DIETICIAN JUST called my room from the hospital cafeteria and accused me of starving myself.

Heard of a chart, lady? It's well documented by my doctors that I've lived like a hummingbird for almost an entire week due to severe anaphylaxis, and you think I'm starving myself to death on purpose?

Dr. Knope came in minutes later, so I shared the asinine interaction with her, in hopes that no other patient fighting to stay alive will be met with that sort of unnecessary food shaming bullshit again.

Dr. Knope was horrified and said she'll be reporting the dietician right away. But she also asked me to attempt eating a few bites of something small again. So, as a nice little *fuck you* to that dietician, I chose the least healthy food I could think of that sounded great: a gluten-free mochi donut.[17]

It was the first food I'd eaten that didn't cause full-blown anaphylaxis. *Maybe the anger helped?* A dear friend was visiting, and she held my hand through the tyrannical itching that started after I took just a few bites. After one woman shamed me, another held my hand.

One of my editors happened to text some encouragement right afterward, so I relayed the ridiculousness of what had just happened.

"Don't fuck with an author," my editor texted back. "That lady doesn't know she just made it into a book."

WITH

EVEN THOUGH I still had severe itching and a migraine after eating it, that donut got my heart rate back up into the seventies. Don't ever try to tell me that donuts don't have healing powers.

But so does presence. The friend who held my hand when I tried eating again—she lost her dad to brain cancer when she was just a kid. Alex and Nicole visited today, too, and brought me a stack of books, including one on fungi and a collection of Wendell Berry poems. Nicole has shared with me about the

17 Because GF folks know how hard it is to find a decent donut: shoutout to Mochi Thai'm Donuts in Colorado Springs. Your donuts are divine.

days her own life hovered near death, after delivering their youngest son. Now that I think of it, every person who has sat by my hospital bed has come carrying the silent wisdom of surviving horrible things.

We don't have to be as afraid of the dark when we sit with people who have been there before.

ALONE, BUT NOT

I'M IN A new room now, in isolation. Dad came down with Covid right as they were planning on flying back to Montana, since I've been trending toward being able to eat enough to be discharged. But now my white blood cell counts have jumped, as well as infection symptoms, and my doctors are presuming I'm positive, too, since my special immune system has historically not been able to pop a positive on a Covid test even when antibody levels later show I've definitely had it. They're talking about starting me on Remdesivir. Ryan is home in bed, fighting symptoms himself.

I've been moved to a lower level of care, which is encouraging, but being in isolation after having family and friends by my side every day is more than a bummer.

Outside my window, the wide blue sky over Pikes Peak reminds me there is still so much space to thrive. I let my gaze rest on every flower arrangement friends have sent. Earlier, when a speech therapist came to assess my swallowing again, she said that in eighteen years of working in hospitals, she's never seen so many flowers in one patient's room. Everywhere I look are flowers. Chrysanthemums, roses, and lilies from the

Stabiles. Tulips from Chase. Hydrangeas from Pat and Sarah. Echinacea from Liz. Orchids from Katie. Gerbera daisies from Johnna. Plants and arrangements fill every open surface in the room.

People may not be allowed to visit me right now, but their presence remains. I'm not really alone. That's what I'm telling myself.

HUNGER GAMES

I SPREAD BUTTER across gluten-free bread and sprinkle the entire piece with salt. You'd think that after a week of near starvation, I'd be gobbling this down. But eating spreads me thin. I'm working hard to get more calories in, especially because if I can't, they plan to put me on TPN. Total parenteral nutrition—feeding me straight through Simone the starving mystic's silicone mouth. That doesn't sound ideal.

They're starting me on Remdesivir tonight, a strong antiviral to fight Covid. I swallow lukewarm chicken broth and tiny bites of mashed potatoes, knowing that each ounce moves me one ounce further from TPN. Chewing food feels like running two miles. Swallowing each bite is like forcing whole wadded socks down my still-raw throat. The effort exhausts me, even with the raised hospital bed doing most of the work of holding my body up.

So, I'm making eating into a game. For every two bites I get down, I get to watch five minutes of a movie. Then I pause and start again. So far, I've watched thirty minutes of *The Secret Life of Walter Mitty*. You do the math.

I need this nourishment to not just be my fight, but my play, the hand of cards I deal myself.

TENDING

I PEER OUT the window, wrapped in my fuzzy pink blanket, watching the morning sun stretch her arms across the blue sky to the sleepy mountains in the west. My white blood cell count fell overnight after receiving the first dose of Remdesivir. I slept harder last night than every night in the hospital so far combined. It almost feels luxurious.

Last night, my new night nurse was a woman named Fae. She's a charge nurse on this unit, and when she entered my room, it was obvious that she had already familiarized herself with my chart. I was nervous to be moved to this unit, worried that something bad might happen while I'm less closely monitored. But Fae clearly saw my complex medical history with respect.

We got to talking about our occupations, of the shared calling of taking care of others. Fae asked how I recharge, since I also work in a job heavy with secondary-trauma exposure. I told her I prioritize listening to my body and giving myself room to release the weight of the stories I hold in the therapy room—through walking, tapping, and other gentle movement. It was the first time in this hospital that I've felt like a person beyond being a patient.

Fae loved my response and said she struggles to answer this question for herself. She crossed her arms and sheepishly looked away. "I'm a Gen Xer, a born and raised mid-wave feminist," she confessed. "So, I'm embarrassed to say, I love making my house a home."

She reached for the purple orchid on my hospital table and submerged the base in water. "I love keeping plants alive and flowers fresh," she said. "I love making beer and gardening, beekeeping—anything that returns me to my roots."

Fae moved to the computer to chart my night meds and started sharing about her young adult daughter, who is trans and probably autistic. I noticed pain yoked across her shoulders, a heaviness, but also a pride shining from her eyes as she talked about her kid.

We talked about how living here in the Springs—a place marked by violence against LBGTQ+ persons—can add to the pain of being different. I sensed that Fae carried respect into my hospital room because she knows how to love in the societal absence of it. The complexity of illness in my body leads many providers and people to treat me with subtle suspicion or even disdain, but Fae entered my room with deference for what I've already endured, respecting the complexity within me rather than dismissing what is hard to understand.

STRIKE POINT

I'VE BEEN WRITHING in bed for hours. Ever since my first days in the hospital, my left side has raged with storms of pain. Electricity surges down my skull, into my left arm, turning my fingertips numb, my hand so weak I can barely grasp anything. My left leg sizzles in bolts. My foot feels like fire. No one knows why.

I'm coming down from some of the worst pain of my life, a fire dulled to embers by Ativan and opioids. I'm trying to tell myself the truest story I can from the ash.

I believe that the borders I crossed before this descent brought me into awareness of the alignment my body needed to make it through this trauma without losing touch with my spirit.

The work of witnessing my wounded younger self welcomed me into a fierce wholeness that is hard to explain. Not yet in this awful situation have I entirely lost my shit.

My body has never been weaker than in these weeks, and yet my mind is still sharp, and my heart is still willing to hold every part of me that hurts.

I believe that rather than a tragic setback, this has been an inexplicable setup into a strength no scale, white blood cell count, nor need for medicine can measure.

Every step that brought me to today has been hallowed, hard, and more effective than I could have imagined. This hospital stay is not a regression of epic proportions. It is proof of the peace that resides within my marrow, the peace that no anaphylaxis nor medical mystery can kill. I watch my weakness like lightning splintering across a pitch-black sky.

We do not merely heal from trauma to prevent future pain; we heal so that we can be present in the midst of any pain that comes.

STETHOSCOPE

INSURANCE MADE ME get a spine x-ray instead of the MRI Dr. Knope wanted, even though we both know it's not going to give us an adequate picture of what's happening on my left side.

I do not trust the system to not silence me.

My nurses and attending doc are so compassionate, but the American medical system drops hurdles in front of every need for help.

If you were to play hide-and-seek with my symptoms, you would lose. My body is sneaky stealthy. She can slip past the detection of blood work. She can camouflage damage like it's an Olympic sport. I wish she wouldn't, but I can't deny that she deserves a medal.

A person's left side should not feel like this. I am listening. Just like a doctor holds a stethoscope to a patient's chest, I am tuning to the sounds you can't detect on the surface. And I know from my sensations that something is wrong.

Before the radiology tech came to wheel me downstairs, Sister Lizzie, my daytime CNA, helped me shower. She's the only provider I've had who is a nun, and I'm grateful for her sensitivity to the spiritual aspect of this fight. Bewildered by pain, I asked Lizzie to pray over me. She wrapped my tears with words: first in English, then in Hindi. We can do the hardest things when we feel heard.

HYSTERIA

I'M GETTING A brain and spine MRI after all, because Dr. Knope advocated for me. Who knows if it will show what's wrong. But her advocacy is showing me what's right.

Dr. Knope has fielded my and Ryan's questions daily without ever rushing us. On her second day as my hospitalist, she jotted down *her cell phone number* and slipped it into my hand. "Just in case you need to get ahold of me fast," she said. "I know your case is complex." She's made me feel safe enough to actually tell her when I reached the limits of my self-advocacy in this system. I know not every doctor can do this for every patient, but I thank God I have a female doctor who is taking my struggling female body, pain, and special immune system *seriously.*

I value my doctor's advocacy because much of my adult life has swelled with its absence. My experience has often been consistent with Dr. Grace Kao's summary of how women in pain get treated by medical providers: "Simply put, women are less likely to be believed about their pain, more likely to be undertreated for pain, and left in pain for longer periods of time."[18]

I am *done* with women being left alone with their pain.

What would this world look like if we took women's pain seriously? The world is missing out on so much goodness simply because many doctors aren't willing to treat women as reliable observers of our own bodies.

18 Grace Kao, "'But You Look Fine . . .': Gender Bias and Pain Care," Meg Foundation, accessed August 8, 2024, https://www.megfoundationforpain.org/articles/but-you-look-fine-gender-bias-and-pain-care/#:~:text=Simply%20put%2C%20women%20are%20less,for%20longer%20periods%20of%20time.

BUTT STUFF

THE MAIN THING standing between me and going home is poop.

Turns out, when your body has been near starvation for weeks, it takes a while for your bowels to believe it's safe to work again. It's been fifteen days since I've had a bowel movement; I know this, because my nurses won't stop asking about it. For days now, my nurses have been giving me laxatives and making me drink curiously weird concoctions called *brown cows*—hot prune juice, MiraLAX, and God knows what else—all to convince my gut to get going. But no matter how many brown cows I've sipped, nothing has mooed. Today my doctor informed me that if I don't defecate tonight, they'll be sticking things up my butt tomorrow to make it happen, whether I like it or not.

Ryan is finally feeling better and testing negative, so he was allowed to visit again.[19] Someone on social media suggested I should have him massage my stomach to coax my colon to move, so I just got a nice Swedish Shit Massage. I also had him bring me frozen custard to the hospital, because I figured, if anything is going to give me the runs, that'll do it. And, damn, I want to go home.

I'll spare you the straining, but I need you to know: this is part of being human. Most of us don't even think to give thanks for our guts. It's often not until you lose a function that you learn to give thanks for it.

By the time Ryan was almost ready to head home for the night, the custard had christened my insides. Never has a toilet felt so holy. I didn't know you could feel so much joy dropping a deuce.

19 Not for that, you rascals.

I WILL.

PLEASE EXCUSE THE twelve-year-old boy who likes to take over my pen. To pass . . . the time I had to spend in the bathroom all night long, I got on Instagram and took a tour through much more pleasant images than the one I just gave you. I pulled up the favorites photo album on my phone and started posting stories of moments of joy from the last year along with resolutions for the future. What started as a way to get through a painful, lonely night turned into a manifesto of hope.

In one of the first photos, I'm soaking in a hot spring with a contented smile on my face. *I will adventure again.*

Next, I'm standing in a forest, surrounded by yellow aspens, the ground gilded with fallen leaves. *I will walk through a golden cathedral of ancient towering saints again.*

Then there's an image of my hands holding open the pages of my last book. *I will hold new books that I WROTE with my own mind and hands AGAIN.*

The images go on and on. Me in forests. Me with Ryan. Me with friends. Mushrooms. Wildflowers. Lakes. Sunsets. Stunning skies. I state audacious and simply human hopes. I set intentions for how I want to spend the days I now intimately know easily could have been lost.

- I will love Ryan with my whole body and soul.
- I will forage again. I will be the nerdiest mushroom lover and make all my friends feel awkward about my excitement.
- I will honor the land I walk on as sacred to people long before it became sacred to me. I will steward my place on this earth. I will keep visiting the national parks and be astounded at the space they hold for human kindness. I will

advocate for a return to Native stewardship of these sacred lands.

- I will stand by my sisterhood of fierce women, and we will howl with laughter and let our tears become tapestries of wholeness. I will celebrate every courageous woman in my life who makes a way into a wholeness no one else gave them permission to pursue.
- I will hold space for the little girl who grew up with an amazing family that also had to hold too much pain.
- I will love my frustrating, adorable, quirky-as-hell dad and soak up every minute we're able to be together.
- I will love my mama like hell. I will value her heart and honor her help. I will laugh by her side as often as I'm able.
- I will go to Disney World with my family again and let myself be a total child.
- I will let my friends carry some of the load of how hard having so much treatment is. I will listen when they cry. I will let them comfort me. I will keep inviting my friends on imaginative adventures, even if they mostly start at my bedside for a long while.
- I will, hopefully, someday, hike alone again. But if not, I will learn how to accept company and help when I want solitude.
- I will keep texting my friends inordinate amounts of pictures of beautiful things.
- I will do whatever it takes to stay alive in my body—EpiPens and steroid shots at the ready.
- I won't be a victim of my vulnerabilities. I will welcome every version of myself. I won't turn away from my own face, no matter how much steroids or suffering change her.
- I will stay attuned to my heart. Diastole and systole. Drama and delight. I won't silence my sensations.
- I will find my strength again.

- I will delight in the land of the living, every day of my life.
- I will never treat my life as a curse. It's a basket that sometimes overflows with burdens, but also with beauty. I will tend to my basket well.
- I will rise.

THOSE WHO BEAR WITNESS TO DEATH

MY FINAL NURSE just poked his head into the room—at least I hope he's my last nurse. I hope I'm going home. Chase looks around my age. He's slight but strong and carries what I can already tell is a generous sense of humor twinged by some sense of grief. Somehow, we go from "Wow, a lot has happened to you" to swapping stories in the time it takes for him to scan in my morning meds.

I tell Chase how last night I had a CNA named Beth who shared that this floor was a Covid unit during the height of the pandemic. Beth had told me through tears about helping a dying man call his family before he took his final breaths.

Chase hands me a small paper cup of pills. He starts checking Simone's dressings. "I had a Covid patient like that here, too." He steps back. Tears pool under his clear-rimmed glasses. "He was only twenty-two."

Chase crosses his arms and looks away for a moment. "His mom never got to say goodbye to her son. She missed him by a mere two hours. I sat with him until the very end."

Chase wipes back tears. "I'm sorry. I never do this. I never get emotional with patients."

"It's okay. *I asked.*"

Chase gathers himself, replacing the bag of saline on the IV pole to my right.

I tell him that since talking with Beth, I've been forming a theory. "All right . . ." Chase holds his hand to his chin, "let me hear it."

"Well, in my entire time in this hospital—except for one exceptional night nurse when things were really life-threatening—I haven't experienced such constant compassion anywhere else than I have on this unit. The nurses and CNAs here are different."

Chase folds his arms over his navy-blue scrubs and tilts his head.

"It's clear to me that so many of the staff on this unit are uniquely charged with compassion, and I think it's because you each have cared for so many crushed by death. That's my theory: I think what you all witnessed during the pandemic changed you." I pause, trying to gather my thoughts. "Those who bear witness to death become conduits of compassion."

Chase brushes away a tear before meeting my eyes.

"Thank you. I've been terrified, but the compassion of the staff on this floor has given me strength to face my fear and pain."

Chase guffaws. "Everyone warned me before I came in your room this morning. They said, 'You have the patient in sixty-five twenty-six? Oh, she's a therapist. Watch out. She'll make you cry!' "

We burst out laughing, laughter that bends our bodies and fills the room, more than any beeps or alarms have.

PINK

I LIE IN the hospital bed, rubbing my hands back and forth over my pink blanket. I don't know that the doctors here are going to figure out why I almost died. Instead of analyzing that awful mystery, I'm pondering a more pleasant one.

I have hated pink for as long as I can remember. When I filled out my publisher's forms on my preferences for my first book cover, I'm pretty sure I added extra lines to articulate that no amount of pink would be acceptable. I've quietly judged women who love pink as superficial, as though pink makes us look silly, not strong. I'm not proud of this particular preference; I'm just painting you a pink-less picture.

This season has been about welcoming home the little girl in me who didn't fully get to be safe as herself.

I was a tomboy as a kid. At five, I decided—temporarily—to set down my figure skates to join the boys' hockey team instead and had my mom take me to get my perfect long brown ringlets cut as short as my brother's. I wished I were a boy.

On my national parks trip, I met a self I had only previously seen in pictures and sensed like a ghost. She was no longer two-dimensional, but present; no longer wishing to be someone else to belong; ready to seek what her soft body loved.

When we moved into our house, I picked out a massive rug for our living room, covered in shapes shaded in tones of pink. I was surprised I wanted it. Then I picked framed pink desert scenes for the large wall above our stairs. I recall asking friends, baffled, *Am I becoming a pink person?!*

Then Amy sent me this pink blanket for my port surgery recovery, the one that's covered me every day and night in this hospital. And now I'm a thirty-four-year-old woman who has a pink blankie. *And I love it.*

Today I ordered a pink cashmere cardigan that I plan to wear home, wrapping myself in feminine comfort my child self couldn't. And it's becoming clear.

In the past, wearing pink felt like making myself prey. My wish to be a boy was about wishing to be safe.

But now, I'm fully safe to be who I am in body and soul. My feminine self no longer has to fight or flee. Pink means I am free.

DAMAGE

I'M NOT GOING home today. They haven't been able to get me downstairs for a brain MRI yet, and without that, it's not safe for me to leave. It's dawning on me: going home doesn't mean things are going to get easier.

This morning on her rounds, Dr. Knope crouched down at my bedside so she could listen from my eye level. That subtle shift in posture communicated so much about how she sees her own power.

Dr. Knope grasped her chin while listening carefully to my perplexed descriptions of pain: how I can barely hold my phone with my left hand, how when I walk to the bathroom, my left leg drags behind me like a decaying log. She carefully checked my hand, arm, and leg, assessing how much dexterity, feeling, and function I've lost in my left limbs. (Thank God I'm right-handed, or I wouldn't even be able to journal.)

Dr. Knope prepared me for a puzzle, explaining that if all those shots of epi damaged my nerves, the MRI likely won't reveal it, because those scans typically miss more subtle damage. She's referring me to long-term physical therapy to learn how to walk and use my left hand again.

It's so hard to acknowledge that.

I have to learn how to walk well again. I have to learn how to use my left hand fully again. I can walk—but barely. I can grasp—but hardly. *How do you forget how to do something you've done your whole life?*

Today it finally hit me: I probably have a many-months-long recovery ahead of me, not a "rest for two weeks and get back to life as usual" one. Whatever happened to me, harmed me. And though the damage is still nameless, it is no less real.

UNFURL

I'VE BEEN BAWLING, and a pile of tissues sits crumpled beside me on the bed. *Knock, knock.*

I'm not surprised to hear a knock at the door. Somehow, in almost every moment I've wept in this hospital, *someone* has interrupted my tears with presence. It's usually been a nurse or CNA; this time, my friend Tara peeks her head into the room.[20]

"Can I come in?"

I'm stunned it's her. "Yes. Yes! Of course!"

Tara folds me in a huge hug, completely unfazed by my

20 Tara's name, by the way, is pronounced *Tar-uh*. If I were her, I'd want you to know that.

tears. She grabs a chair from the corner and sits as close as she can to the bed.

"I'm not—" I choke back tears. I can barely get words out. "I'm not being discharged today." I burst into tears again.

"I know."

Tara sets down a book and small potted prayer plant on the hospital table that stretches across the bed. *Why am I not surprised Tara already knew I wouldn't be going home yet?* Tara's the type of person who senses realities we can't always see. She's a writer and spiritual director who lives with a life-threatening disease, too, and after having a heart attack quite young, she fought to regain her health doing cardiac rehab in this very hospital.

I tell Tara about the disappointment of not being discharged, but also, the even larger disappointment of realizing that it's probably going to take months to regain my health and mobility. There's a part of my heart I only show others whose hearts have been broken. I'm undone. But Tara doesn't interject. She just meets my stormy eyes with her own tears. This is a language I can only speak with those who honor the limits of words. There is so much said in that silence.

Finally, I have to ask. "How did you know I wasn't going home today?"

Tara reaches for the book she brought me, a soft, small leatherlike book with a brown ribbon bookmark. "It's called *Seeking God's Face,*" she says, "and it contains daily readings from the lectionary along with brief prayers."

Normally, if someone gifted me a "devotional," I'd smile outwardly while inwardly planning to dump it at the nearest Goodwill. But Tara's different. Tara wouldn't give me something saccharine; she would only offer substance.

She opens it to today's reading. "*This* is how I knew you weren't going home today." She points to the page, handing me the open book.

It's Psalm 22—the words of a despondent King David that Jesus himself prayed while pinned to the cross, about to die. "My God, my God, why have you forsaken me?"[21]

Tara says that as soon as she saw that, she knew that tomorrow, Friday the twenty-eighth, would be the day I would go home. *Pretty bold of her, but probable.*

I turn the thin page. Tomorrow's reading is Psalm 23—words that have become friends to me over the past few years. Words I still want to carry home, regardless of how much new damage I am bringing with me. *Surely*—the words rise like a reflex—*Surely your goodness and love will follow me all the days of my life, and I will dwell in the house of the Lord forever.*[22]

Surely, grief does not preclude goodness. Surely, lament does not cancel out love.

Tara pierces my reverie. "In Psalm twenty-two, *forsaken* actually means 'loosened.' "

"*What?*" My jaw hangs open. "Tell me more."

Tara regularly studies scripture with Jewish rabbis. She steeps herself in ancient wisdom like tea. To explain the nuance of *forsaken,* she paints me a picture of swaddling; a baby wrapped tight in a blanket by their parent to sleep or be soothed must be unwrapped if they are ever to crawl or walk.

Forsaken means loosened, for the sake of expansion.

Tara doesn't drop a sermon. She doesn't dangle a pretty pur-

21 Psalm 22:1, New International Version.

22 For the sake of transparency, I would like to note that while in the hospital, words from the bible welled up inside me in a way they had not in years. At times, I was mystified by what met me as true and real in my fear. In other moments, I felt a little like a spiritual mascot. It is a mystery, but what I felt and said in those days was just as true as what came after.

pose for my pain. She just lets the words sit beside my own unraveling.

There are hundreds of humans in my life from whom I could never hear these words. They might say something that sounds like them, might tell me of God's goodness or kindness or plans, but they would only beep like the alarms on the monitors beside my hospital bed. As a kid, I was taught to not take God's name in vain, but the real vanity is claiming to be a Christian while opposing those Christ sought with love—the poor, the sick, the immigrants. God-talk becomes empty when it is used to gain and hold power rather than give it away. When you've lived around evangelicals as long as I have, sometimes all the faith words become beeps, cloying background sounds you just have to put up with until you can get out of the room.

Too many people speak of spirituality when what is most needed is silence. Too many people claim confidence in God's will and ways when what would be more comforting and honest is to just sit together and feel sad.

Maybe most people of faith never really expand because we rush past feeling forsaken.

I breathe deep, grateful to have a companion who isn't afraid of my dark, comforted that the God who became human has felt as forsaken as I have, surprised that somehow, stripped down by sickness, Jesus—God with fingers, toes, and fears—has risen within me as not less but more real. The deep green leaves of the prayer plant Tara brought me are the size of my palms, veined with burgundy. As a plant lover, I've long known and loved that when it gets dark, the maranta raises her palms instinctively, like hands in prayer. Tara tells me the word for this is *nyctinasty,* the movement a plant makes in the absence of light.

PART III

We were heading toward all that makes life intolerable, feeling the only thing that makes it worthwhile. That was joy.

ZADIE SMITH,
Feel Free

RAINBOW

THE COMPROMISE WE made with my attending doc was that I could be discharged, as long as I went directly to see my immunologist in Denver first. The whole hour drive home, I watched the mountains and sky and green grass as though I had entered a fairy tale. It's a strange thing to realize you haven't seen a tree in two full weeks. My eyes were just as starved for beauty as my stomach was for food. Deprivation is a potent drug. Everything glittered.

As soon as we merged onto the final stretch of highway before home in the Springs, I saw a rainbow on the horizon. "No way." I turned to Ryan. "Doesn't that look like it's around where the hospital is?!"

We had to pass the hospital to get home, and the closer we got, the more I could see. A double rainbow stretched over the building, ending exactly over the room I left. The dark band between the bows sat directly over the rooms where some of my scariest moments happened. I snapped picture after picture. If I hadn't seen it, I wouldn't have believed it. In this, my first time seeing the hospital since leaving its doors, I saw it touched by light. I saw a dark place crowned with color.

All the light we see from the sun contains all the colors of the rainbow. We just can't perceive the whole spectrum of the sun's light without the rain to bend it. Sunlight slows down within millions upon millions of water droplets, bending into beauty through the inconvenient medium that sometimes drenches and distresses us.

It didn't just rain on my wedding day; it poured. We were taking photos in a bright green field with our wedding party after saying our vows when the sky split open. We ran through the rain toward the reception tent, laughing. No one wants rain on their wedding day, but somehow, we didn't feel disappointment, but delight. We danced, slightly soggy, under a tent with our friends and family late into the night. The pouring rain kept us all from leaving the joy sooner than we otherwise would have.

As we passed tonight's rainbow, I clutched Ryan's hand. Light needs the medium of water to refract into a rainbow. Love needs limits to become luminous.

My Sunday-school self was taught that rainbows are bows, weapons turned into welcome, punishments flipped to peace. But a rainbow actually has no end. What looks like an arch or bow is actually a circle. We just can't see the whole disc of color from where we stand. With the sun at our backs and rain on the horizon, we see half of a whole. We're not high enough up to have the full perspective.

When we finally got home, I saw flowers on our doorstep and a message in pink letters a friend had stuck to our front door. "You are home and held!" Ryan helped me hobble inside, and I collapsed onto the couch while Resa, our puppy-hearted German Shorthaired Pointer, wagged her tail and kissed my face, already wet with tears of joy. Merton, our older GSP, seemed afraid to come near me. I was just glad to be home. For a while, I wasn't sure I'd ever see our dogs again.

After Ryan helped me upstairs and into bed, I opened the book from Tara. I had only read the first part of the lectionary this morning, Psalm 23. My jaw dropped as I finished the next passage in the day's reading:

"This is the sign of the covenant I am making between me and you and every living creature with you, a covenant for all generations to come: I have set my rainbow in the clouds, and it will be the sign of the covenant between me and the earth."[1]

No two people see the same rainbow the same way. The way we see the light depends on where we stand. Neither can anyone touch a rainbow, but that doesn't make it less real. From where I lie, I see a gift I don't fully understand. And with hard things in my hands, I'm receiving it as real anyway. It might just be refracted light, but I imagine my own bending can become beautiful.

WOVE, TWUE WOVE

RYAN IS DOWNSTAIRS in the living room relaxing with his parents, who flew from North Carolina to help take care of me. I'm not strong enough to leave bed yet, so Ryan and I are communicating across the chasm between our bedroom and the main floor downstairs via walkie-talkie on our Apple Watches. I just requested a cup of crushed iced and gluten-free red licorice, followed by *over and out*.

I grin. All those childhood summers, our family used walkie-talkies in the woods, on hikes, across campgrounds.

The watch on my left wrist buzzes.

"You don't need to say 'over and out' every time, KJ."

1 Genesis 9:12–13, New International Version.

"Ten-four."

Two minutes elapse. I tap my watch walkie-talkie again.

"Also, I need my knee ice pack in the freezer so I can use it in bed. Over . . ."

Ryan beeps back before I can finish. "That'll be five extra dollars."

"I can do five extra kisses, but no more."

I giggle until he arrives.

Later, I request the squatty potty I ordered online yesterday, since my sleepy post-hospital bowels still need some help waking up. Ryan arrives ten minutes later carrying the folded squatty potty on a wooden tray, with a bouquet of white hydrangeas on top.

"Shitter is served!"

BLOCKED

"FOR HEREDITARY ANGIOEDEMA, press two . . ."

A specialty pharmacy tech answers and asks for my birthdate and address. "Have you had any hospitalizations in the last month?"

"Yes . . . um . . . a long one." I stammer, twisting the comforter on my lap, trying hard to explain why I was hospitalized without saying too much, but it's too strange of a story to be succinct. I wish something simpler had happened to me so I could just say, *I had a pulmonary embolism* or *I had pneumonia*. How am I supposed to explain something I still barely comprehend?

"Okay . . ." The tech moves on. "Have you had any HAE attacks in the last month?"

"Um . . . maybe?" I'm struggling to answer. I have Type 3 HAE, and that can make "attack" harder to define. Most of my swells are internal.

My throat tightens. I can't hold the phone up anymore. I can't speak. Can't think.

"Mom." I mumble the word, too weak to cry out.

Suzanne shuffles around the bedroom, putting away laundry. I hold out the phone. "I'm so confused. I . . . I can't talk to them . . . but someone has to. It's the specialty pharmacy."

Mom takes the phone and turns it on speaker. Her nursing skills and sweet Southern accent make the rest of the call smooth as butter.

But I'm shook up and ashamed. A specialty pharmacy call—something that used to be a simple, though annoying, part of my life—just about spiraled me into a panic attack. It's like my brain is bruised, and the functions I need to communicate are blocked behind the bruises.

GIRL OR GHOST

WHAT HAPPENS TO a person when they almost die is not the same as what happens to those who love them. My family focuses on how far I was from death, but I still feel closer to it than life.

No matter how many interventions were ready to revive me, I can't unsee myself begging my body to breathe. Like a hawk, my spirit hovered overhead, watching breaths become vapor, pink lips fading to slate. I brooded over my own body.

Breathe. Breathe. Breathe.

The average adult breathes twelve to twenty times a minute, without ever having to beg. Within seconds, without thinking, air travels across alveoli and capillaries over the roughly 1,500 miles of airways in our lungs—around the same distance between my home and the Redwoods. Each time my airway swelled and my breath sputtered to stretch through my lungs' highways, I traveled to a shadowed, distant place. Part of me still hovers there.

My family focuses on the fact that I survived. But they don't understand that I can't unsee the shadow of death. Even now, I feel so weak, as though I am spectral, slipping away in slow motion.

ROARRRRR

AUGUST

IN A LITTLE bit, I'll go downstairs for the first time since I was discharged from the hospital. It will be my first time leaving the house. And even though I'm only leaving to get some IV support at my immunologist's office, it feels monumental to leave bed.

I decide I need some extra adornments to face the world. I drag myself to the bathroom, grab my leather makeup bag, and collapse back in bed, opening a mirror to my face. I blend blush onto my pale cheeks and press powder to the dark circles under my tired eyes. I fan mascara over my lashes, paint my lips with red lipstick, and place a pair of dangling chartreuse cacti earrings on my earlobes. I'm adding color not because I'm afraid to be seen as sick, but because I need an outward expression of care.

Makeup can be a ritual of rising we offer to ourselves, not to conceal but to reveal. When I wake up weary and my face is already downcast, taking time to tend to my face can reconnect me to a story of strength. I've used red lipstick and waterproof mascara like potions and prayers for at least a decade. They are the witchcraft of women who are determined to show up believing we are stronger than we yet sense or seem.

This is my first time putting on makeup in a month. And it's a choice. A choice to be courageous.

When I finish, Ryan wraps me in a hug and helps me out of bed. We take the stairs as a team, his shoulder holding half my weight, my other hand gripping the handrail tight. Ryan's dad stands at the bottom.

"Wait!" I call down. "Dad, take a picture of us!"

I don't *want* to remember every moment. I'm not a masochist. But I won't stop looking for what is good, even when I'm groaning. I want to remember getting up and getting out.

I'm documenting this journey for dignity. There is power in paying attention and power in pausing to register the existence and worth of my body, not only when she stands on the crests of mountains, but when she needs help to climb down a set of stairs.

I once believed pride was a lion to poach. Now, I'm glad to have grown into a person who is capable of being proud of herself. I wish I had learned sooner that real pride is pretending we are needless, not pausing to acknowledge the tenderness and tenacity it takes to keep going.

PERSPECTIVE

EVERYTHING LOOKS ENCHANTING when you've only seen the inside of either a hospital or your bedroom for a month straight. I stare out the window the whole way to Denver, thinking *Are people aware that grass glows?* The sky is like a painting—Berlin blue with whipped cream puffs of clouds over buttes and craggy hills.

Ryan gets a wheelchair from the doctor's office and rolls me in while I clutch a pillow to keep my weakened body propped up. The receptionist's face looks confused, clearly disturbed at how much my appearance has changed since the last time she saw me here. I fumble over my words while trying to check in, suddenly agitated and confused at something that used to be so simple.

I notice a doctor—not mine—staring at me as I struggle to speak. His face is a scorecard of concern. I sink into the arm of the wheelchair, stinging with shame. *He has no idea I write books for a living. He has no idea I'm a licensed professional counselor.* Everything looks different when you notice how others are looking differently at *you*.

We turn the corner to the infusion center, where my old and beloved nurses greet me with warmth. But I can tell by their faces that seeing me this sick is a shock. They give me the one room in the infusion center that has a bed, a spacious room that on multiple occasions I've been jealous of others for getting to have. It isn't until I'm curled up in the bed that I realize it's the room where they usually place the sickest patient of the day.

DETECTIVE

I SAY GOODBYE to Ryan and his mom, thinking this little IV treatment is a good chance for them to take a break from constant caregiving. The nurse accesses Simone, hooking up my port to an IV pump, and after some pre-medications, she starts a yellow bag of a vitamin cocktail to help my immune system recover better from Covid.

I only make it fifteen minutes into the infusion before my body feels strange. My tongue tingles, and I cry out for the nurse. These sensations are too familiar to not be scared by them. The nurse stops the infusion, and Heather, the physician's assistant, races into the room.

Everything speeds yet slows, as though I have entered an alternate reality, like I'm watching my life happen to someone who looks like me but isn't me.

Heather pushes IV Benadryl, and I labor to breathe. She listens to my lungs, and her face scrunches in worry. "I still hear 'stridor.'" Later, I learn that stridor is the high-pitched sound of an airway closing. Though the anaphylactic reaction has slowed, it hasn't stopped.

The clinic's allergist now stands in the doorway, assessing what Heather has seen. He leaves and returns a few minutes later. The team decides to give me another 100mg of Solu-Medrol, even though I've already had 100mg of steroids today.

The allergist shakes his head. "This is so much steroids to give a person," he says to my nurse. "I don't like it."

She pushes the steroids and even more antihistamines, and eventually—I don't even know how long—the anaphylaxis slows just short of them stabbing me with one of the expensive EpiPens that are now always stashed in my purse.

I'm still straining when my immunologist enters the room. I've started referring to him as Dr. Detective. The nickname makes me laugh at the absurd mystery story I seem to be trapped inside. *God knows, my special immune system needs a Sherlock.*

Suddenly, the spacious room shrinks. Providers hover around me and a couple stand in the doorway while I cough and gasp. I gather my strength to speak up.

"How am I supposed to feel safe to recover at home when this keeps happening?" I grip the bed, trying to assert my agency, even though the room is spinning. "What even *is* happening?!"

Dr. Detective sits in a chair a few feet away. His arms are crossed, and under his glasses, his face is creased in concentration. He doesn't answer me, but I know from experience that he's in Mad Scientist mode, weighing possibilities. Benadryl buzzes through my body, making me loopy and covering everything in a humorous haze. I laugh even though I know what's happening is far from funny.

The providers toss theories around like a football. I hear Dr. Detective say something about "possible Stevens-Johnson syndrome" and that this could be a "rejection syndrome." I strain to focus, thumbing the words into Google on my phone. I don't know what's happening to me, but my body sure as hell doesn't look like the images that are popping up. *My skin's not falling off in clumps, but what do I know?*

Heather leans against the doorway, scratching her head with a pen.

"I don't know what this is, but I *know* that it has to have something to do with her port."

Her tone is ominous. My heart drops. "I need my port," I protest. "I *need* to be able to keep getting IVIG!"

Heather nods—she's heard me—but the rest of the providers keep talking among themselves as though I'm not here. They mention some biologic medication they've given to another patient whose body tried to reject his hip replacement. "Maybe that would work for her port."

They're talking *about* me, but not *to* me.

I will myself to make my wishes clear, to come back to my body and into this room, despite the floating sensation of being pumped full of IV Benadryl, despite feeling flattened into a character in a medical made-for-TV drama instead of an actual person with a job and a family and a home and hopes.

Just this morning, I gathered myself to show up in this day, to feel like *me* in a life I don't recognize as mine. And now I'm losing myself again. Even in a room full of providers who I know care about me, it's like I am not here.

Nothing is decided, except that I need to come back to the clinic tomorrow—another two-hour round trip—for more IV antihistamines and fluids to try to keep me out of the hospital. They send me home with orders to eat and drink nothing but water to prevent another anaphylactic attack and urge me to keep my EpiPen within reach.

THE THINNEST PLACE

THE FOLLOWING DAY I return, only for anaphylaxis to strike again. My lips tingle like hail against pavement. My throat clogs like sludge in a drain. My blood pressure plummets like a rock in a pond. It is miserable, and yet, while doom descends over my mind, peace meets me in the middle.

It makes no sense. I am panicked. Every single time. And yet, there is a presence surrounding my panic. It is like making contact with the source of life itself. In that wordless place, I beg but bow. Each time I cannot breathe, I encounter energy beyond my own. I sense my connection to a life that will endure beyond my breath.

"Heaven and earth," the Northern Irish author Kerri ní Dochartaigh writes, "are only three feet apart, but in thin places that distance is even shorter." Perhaps that distance is also slim between peace and our pain. Thin places, the author writes, "are places that make us feel something larger than ourselves, as though we are held in a place between worlds, beyond experience."[2] When I started writing this book, I thought I would travel to the thinnest places I had ever been, to encounter and study the beauty that begets joy. Instead, I have traveled to a threshold within my own skin.

We're on our way home from the clinic again, just barely escaping a trip to the ER, and my phone rings. It's a FaceTime call from Lisa Sharon Harper, an author I've only known of from afar until recently. I totally forgot we had planned on talking.

Many years ago, Lisa had a whole year of unexplainable anaphylactic episodes. When she heard online about what's been happening to me, she reached out in solidarity. From our DMs, I know she, too, has been met in terror by a peace she can't explain. I haven't known anyone else who has waited again and again at this particular intersection of breathlessness and beauty. And the juxtaposition is so baffling that I'm beginning to fear I'm losing my mind. *How can something so brutal be so beautiful?* But if Lisa experienced this, too, maybe I'm not crazy.

2 Kerri ní Dochartaigh, *Thin Places: A Natural History of Healing and Home* (Minneapolis, MN: Milkweed Editions, 2022), 23.

I pick up the call, even though I'm woozy.

I describe to Lisa the peace that just met me, exactly like it did in the hospital. She nods knowingly and then describes almost the precise sensations I've had, and the strange sense that in the threshold of anaphylaxis, she, too, was held.

"It's like a thin place," I tell Lisa. "But rather than being in the midst of great beauty, like at the top of a mountain, it's thinnest where I'm weakest."

Lisa's gaze is piercing. "I know," she says. "The thinnest places are always at the bottom."

I THOUGHT THEY DIED

A MONTH BEFORE I drove west, I planted wildflower seeds. I shoveled old woodchips into a bin, pulled back layers of worn weed barrier, and tilled the soil, wiping back sweat as I went. Words danced down my arms while I worked. Fragments of poems found me in the soil where I scattered seeds to grow the flowers I'd dreamed of having for thirteen years, in this, our first-ever yard.

I till soil for the first time and suddenly it's like Wendell Berry's being born in my body, I thought to myself, laughing, ludicrously happy.

By the time I returned home from my road trip, the tiniest sprouts were peeking their heads out of the dirt. But they were barely growing by the day I went to get Simone implanted in my chest. *Maybe they won't grow this year. Maybe I planted them wrong.* When I landed in the hospital, and the days turned into weeks, I figured they all had died. It's not like anyone in my family was watering them while they were busy sitting at my bedside, hoping I'd be okay.

I just got home from the clinic and paused to rest outside on a rocker on our back deck beside my father-in-law. The sun felt like a smile, mirroring my gratitude to be outside my home instead of inside an ER. I still might end up there, but for now, I'm so relieved to be home.

"KJ, what are the dogs into over there?" Dad pointed over to the far fence.

I squinted. "Oh my goodness. Those . . ." I paused in disbelief. "Those are my wildflowers!"

Mom heard the commotion and came outside. She held my hand and arm, helping me to the flowerbed, where I plopped in the grass, too tired to stand. Pink petals and purple buds dotted the patch of dirt like glitter. Golden clusters and the start of orange poppies sat tucked in their buds.

The flowers didn't die.

WHAT TO SAY IN THE EMERGENCY ROOM

THE NEXT DAY, I see the allergist again, in a video appointment. He helps me form a list of what to say if I have to go to the ER during another anaphylactic attack.

"What's happening to you is too complicated for most ER docs," he says. "If you go in and try to explain what all has happened to you in the last month, they'll be at best confused and at worst suspicious. So, I need you to tell them exactly this instead."

I listen carefully, scrawling out a list in my journal. I swipe yellow highlighter over "WHAT TO SAY IN THE ER" and mark the page with a ribbon, deciding to jot down my phone passcode too in case I ever lose consciousness:

- [Note to self: *Keep. It. Simple.*]
- I am experiencing idiopathic anaphylaxis.
- I have Type 3 Hereditary Angioedema.
- I have adrenal insufficiency and am currently on high-dose steroids.
- I need these meds emergently: IV Benadryl, lots of it. IV Steroids. IV Zofran. Epi.
- You must draw these labs: C1 Esterase. Tryptase. Serum histamine level. Prostaglandin D2.
- I need to be seen by an immunologist, an allergist, and a rheumatologist.

WHAT *NOT* TO SAY IN THE EMERGENCY ROOM

EMERGENCY ROOMS AREN'T exactly enjoyable places for anyone, but they're particularly painful for chronic illness patients. After being judged by ER docs as a drug-seeker or hypochondriac a handful of times, I avoid the ER with all I've got. So, later that night, I imagine a different kind of list, giggling to myself in bed over all the unhinged shit I wish I could say in the ER but ***definitely* will not:**

- Hey doctor, nice to meet you! I know that statistically there's a good chance you're biased against believing women in

pain, but I'm telling you that what is happening is real, and if you are an asshole to me, you better bet I will write about you in a book that many thousands of people will read. I hope your girlfriend finds a copy at Barnes & Noble on the "hot new releases" table and breaks up with you for being a little bitch.
- I almost had a panic attack today while in a video appointment with my allergist. Sometimes I daydream about jumping off a cliff, but don't worry about it. I'm too tired to even reach a cliff right now.
- My sister had a heart attack at age twenty from lupus. My paternal aunt died from complications of lupus around forty-two. My maternal uncle has discoid lupus. Three out of four of us siblings have autoimmune diseases. No fewer than seven members of my extended family have autoimmune diseases. Do you think there's something wrong with our genes? Like maybe there was incest a ways back on both sides of my family? Or is it more likely that we all ate too much genetically modified corn growing up?

JOY, SALTED

I MAY HAVE just reached a new sickness low. It's been about four days since my last anaphylactic attack, and I haven't had a real meal in a week. Not eating is the strongest weapon my doctors and I have to prevent anaphylaxis right now, so I've been living off hypoallergenic protein drinks, forcing them down sip after sip.

I just ate a chewable stool softener as though it were the finest piece of chocolate I've ever tasted and the only piece left in the world. I took tiny bites, savoring every ounce. Eating a stool softener just felt indulgent. *Yikes.*

I'm feeding myself by finding delight wherever I can. Right now, I'm sipping on watermelon salt LMNT electrolyte water to try to get my heart rate down, and *wow,* simple flavored salt water tastes like a literal dream when you can't have anything else. My tongue is being trained by deprivation to taste new delight. My eyes are sharpening to sense wonder at my windowsills. I'm too sick to get to another room right now, but I see light bedecking the trees out our windows. I see my monstera's leaves glow when the sun rises. I'm so limited, but I have become enamored with the light.

Limits have such a nagging way of wearing us down to choose to greet the little we have with acceptance and love. Even electrolyte water can well up joy in me if I let it.

Let it.

WITH-NESS

"YOU'VE USED UP all of your reserve," my mother-in-law explains, tucking me back in bed. "You *need* to lie here and do nothing until you gain a little more strength, or you really will end up back in the hospital."

I'm not exactly happy about being sent to bed like a toddler, but I don't resist, because I'm afraid. My legs feel like they weigh two hundred pounds and my torso four hundred. It's the heaviest fatigue of my life.

All day, Mom and Ryan take turns carrying me the few steps

from our bed to the bathroom, because it's too much of a fall risk to try to get there on my own.

I resent losing my independence, and I'm sure I've been more than bristly. But when I stop focusing on all I can't do, I start noticing what is here.

Before today, every time I've gotten up, Resa has followed me, tail up, pressing her spotted body to my legs like a crutch to keep me from falling. When my heart rate spikes, she somehow senses it. She curls herself against my legs or drapes her head heavy over my lap until my heart can rest. Resa watches me like it's her job, a job for which she was never trained. When she runs downstairs or outside, she sprints back to the bed every few minutes to make sure I'm okay. I've always thought of Resa as an empath, but now I see her as pure gift. Maybe even—I'm not ashamed to say—a furry glimpse of the face of God.[3]

Ryan's mom ferries trays of water and ice chips and bone broth and protein drinks into the bedroom all day long. She sits outside the open bathroom door, ready to rush toward me with help while I shower seated, never once giving me a strange look or saying anything shaming about seeing me naked. She holds me when I break down in frustration on endless phone calls from pharmacists and physicians and then fields the calls for me instead. She hears out my fears, even when I've already repeated myself fifteen times and forgot. I'm beginning to think of my mother-in-law as my friend.

Mom and I spent the majority of the last two days making our way through the phone tree hell that is US Healthcare. *The Four*

3 Resa's presence is a living reminder of something her namesake, Saint Teresa of Ávila, once wrote: "Believe the incredible truth that the Beloved has chosen for his dwelling place the core of your own being because that is the single most beautiful place in all of creation." Saint Teresa of Ávila, *The Interior Castle: New Translation and Introduction by Mirabai Starr* (New York: Riverhead Books, 2003), 3.

Seasons played while we waited on hold, and I'm sure Vivaldi rolled over in his grave. Many phone robots were cursed. *Can we just talk to a human, please? Press 69 if you think this sucks.*

Yesterday we spent most of the day begging old doctors to fill a blood thinner prescription that ran out, one of many details that got lost after I was discharged from the hospital. I have a genetic blood clotting disorder, and the other day at the clinic while getting labs drawn, my blood came out clotted and frothy in a way neither I nor my nurse have ever seen before. I'm clearly clotting more than I should be. In between frantic calls, I remembered that I have a ziplock bag full of pills stashed away on a shelf on the top of our closet. I had Mom grab it, and we found eight days' worth of blood thinners inside. No joke; we hugged each other and cried.

WHAT IS *HEALING*?

I COULD EASILY find a hundred "trauma-informed" influencer therapists and coaches on Instagram who, if pressed in the privacy of their own heads, would probably say that my medical crisis is proof of unresolved trauma and, therefore, a lack of resolution on my part to release it. It would be easy to say that I—a licensed professional counselor who mostly treats clients with trauma—have failed at what I am paid to help heal. The body keeps the score, and I appear to be losing. If I really am healing from childhood trauma, wouldn't I be reversing diseases instead of almost dying from new ones with no names?

The wellness industry in the United States wears a costume of kindness, presenting itself like the crunchy, compassionate aunt who will tell you the truth about healing that no one else is willing to forsake capitalism to share. The gospel of green juice cleanses, essential oils, hip-opening trauma release courses, and coffee enemas preaches the pretty possibility that healing can happen if you work hard enough to receive it. But when the diet doesn't heal you and positive thinking doesn't remove your pain, what's left is shame. And an empty wallet.

It's telling that while the wellness industry markets itself as an alternative to Big Pharma's exploitation, it is nearly four times larger than the global pharmaceutical industry.[4] Every detox comes with a disclaimer, but every product is shared with a discount code. Wellness influencers say they're sharing *hope,* but much of it is just monetized misinformation.[5]

I wanted to believe that my bag of tools for treating trauma could protect me from experiencing more. When I got my port, I was the healthiest I've been in my adult life. A combination of effective medical care and intentional self-compassion toward my nervous system had brought me to a new place of freedom and even ease. We all want to believe that if we work hard enough to heal, more hard things won't happen. Or, we hope we at least won't find hard things to be *as* hard. But what I'm noticing—as a trauma therapist experiencing more trauma—is that we cannot heal our way out of being human.

Dis-ease exists wherever we perpetuate a dichotomy be-

4 Global Wellness Institute, "The Global Wellness Economy Reaches a New Peak of $6.3 Trillion—and Is Forecast to Hit $9 Trillion by 2028," PRWeb, November 5, 2024, https://www.prweb.com/releases/the-global-wellness-economy-reaches-a-new-peak-of-6-3-trillionand-is-forecast-to-hit-9-trillion-by-2028--302295427.html.

5 Quan Xie et al., "Brand Endorsement by Influencers Fueling the Anti-vaccine Movement: The Roles of Misinformation Interventions and Pre-existing Schema in Endorsement Effectiveness," in American Academy of Advertising, Conference, Proceedings (Online), 40. American Academy of Advertising, 2024, https://www.proquest.com/openview/542277d938f12d1d218b0507a8956e63/1?cbl=40231&pq-origsite=gscholar; @this.is.mallory on Instagram has said similar things and is an excellent follow for exposing the shadow side of the wellness industry.

tween hurting and healing. We live in a loud world that shouts that persistent pain is proof of either a failure of faith and personal freedom or a fault in one's commitment to release trauma. But my body speaks a stranger story: pain has a voice, and binaries only box us into believing we must silence it. But healing is hearing the ache that resounds. Healing is heeding the alarms in body and soul that alert us all to recognize that our flourishing is stitched to systems larger than ourselves, that we are made stronger by solidarity and sicker in its absence, that ache can never be fully answered alone.

I couldn't prevent this pain from happening. But I have been able to remain present in the middle of it. I have not been able to transcend trauma, but I have been able to receive love in its midst. I think we've mis-traced the trajectory of trauma recovery. Maybe the hope of healing has never been about the removal of pain but the recovery of full humanness, including our innate interdependence.

DEAR CLIENTS

THIS IS THE hardest letter I've ever written. I'm in bed, drafting an email to all of my therapy clients—many of whom I've worked with for *years*—telling them I need to take at least three months away from work, likely more. Most of my clients have complex trauma histories involving some level of abandonment, and here I am, leaving them suddenly because of my own trauma. It's beyond unfair. And it's beyond necessary.

I last wrote to my clients from the hospital, hanging on between anaphylactic attacks. Now it's becoming clear that I can't hope my way out of how long and hard my recovery will be. All the energy inside me has to go toward my own healing before anyone else's.

I write so much more than this—sharing updates, instructions, referrals, and resources. But when I write the final paragraphs, I see the words through tears.

> *I am more committed to our collective wholeness than I am to my capacity to work. I am more committed to holding out a picture of accepting our humanness than I am to being the most consistent and ableism-acceptable licensed professional counselor in the world. I am more committed to your wholeness than my income.*
>
> *I have decided, along with my spouse and medical providers, that on the low end of reasonable and probable, I need to take at least a three-month medical leave from my therapeutic practice . . . As I choose the work of rest, I am coming home. Whether I get to stay in my cozy king bed facing plants and my pups—or I return to a new hospital room—I am always at home when I hear my body's breath.*
>
> *It's funny—I'm always reminding you to come home to your bodies. Well, we just get to all watch ourselves learn the way home. Open that door, even if it feels heavy—there is comfort and connection and astounding courage inside the home of your body, too. Let your grief and your internal goodness show you the way.*
>
> *Warmly,*
> *KJ*

I fold my iPad into its keyboard, and the tears that were trickling become a full-on fountain. Witnessing my clients show up to love themselves more fully has been the holiest work of my life. I know that by sending this letter, I'm opening my hands to let these precious people go wherever they need. I'm also releasing my grip on the work I love. I sense that "three months" could easily turn into three years. I'm that sick. I weep and wrap my hands around myself instead.

HELP

I'M STILL ON a mostly liquid diet for anaphylaxis watch, with one new extravagance. I'm crunching into every bite of this morning's gluten-free sourdough toast, complete with the flaky Maldon Salt I now sprinkle on everything because I swear it stretches a "meal" into my imagination of that meal. For example, when topped with Maldon Salt, a freezer-frozen Kate Farms Chocolate Hypoallergenic Nutrition Shake is only a handful of atoms away from being fries dipped in a Frosty.

Some author friends have asked if they can raise money for my medical expenses. I've wiped back tears watching others receive support like this. It's a beautiful thing to see. But if I'm honest, GoFundMes have also made me green with envy, wishing just once someone would swoop in and set me free from the invisible financial burdens of my fragile body. It takes a real sick person to be jealous of someone with cancer, but I assure you, I am that terrible.

When Anjuli, Jessica, and Jennifer texted to ask if they could spearhead a fundraiser for us, I was surprised I felt resistance right beside relief. I've always needed more support than I have, but even *I* am scared to be standing on the cliff of *more* than chronic illness. This close to the edge, I can see that if this strange sickness doesn't ruin me, it could easily ruin our finances. We only just bought our first house. I don't want to lose that, too.

This morning, I read from Psalm 37 in the lectionary. *Commit your way to the Lord; trust in him and he will do this.*

I don't like to treat scripture like a magic lamp I can rub just right to get what I want. When I read that verse, I'm prompted to take a different posture, one that's terrifying to take when you are holding tight to life. I need to open my hands.

I pull up the group text and type *yes.*

THANKS

AT SIX A.M., I pressed send on the most audacious Instagram post of my life—asking for ten thousand dollars for our medical crisis. And then more. When my friends shared it with their own social media communities, I shivered. *I can't believe I am asking for this much help.*

After a few hours, $25,000 sat in my Venmo account.

Around $27,000—more than my first salaried job fresh out of undergrad in 2010—I stopped looking and took a shower so the water could wash away the shock and leave me with the awe.

I slowly washed my long hair and scrubbed at the sticky heart monitor splotches still dotting my body. There in the water, I started to talk; I started to pray.

I am amazed. There is love.
You are here. I am alive.
Humankindness is present.
It is enough.

Steam curled around me, and I sat up on my shower chair in sudden recognition. *This* is what I wished for years ago when I was jealous of others on the receiving end of fundraisers.

Back then, I'd been ashamed of my wishes, but what I most needed was to feel less alone with my wounds. The absence of the answers I wanted led me to the attunement I needed. I dreamed of this day coming sooner—like the year we were on food stamps, or the year we lost so much by leaving the church that we were nearly unhoused but our friends took us in. But now, I'm glad I learned how to persevere when a bigger rescue didn't come. I'm glad I learned how to let others in, even when they couldn't lift my burden.

Now, all I have left is thanks. Thanks for the help that came when it looked like almost no one cared. Thanks for the help that is coming even now, when more people care than I could have ever imagined.

Thanks.

WOW

ALL DAY, MONEY poured into my Venmo and PayPal accounts.

All day, I realized that the church isn't as dead as abuse, Christian nationalism, racism, and homophobia have made her seem. She lives wherever there are tears.

All day, I fought anaphylactic symptoms, trying hard to breathe without taking another shot of epi. I saw Heather virtually today, and she and Dr. Detective want to readmit me to a hospital with more help. I'm trying hard to hold on. But I need, in a way, to let myself break.

All day, my mother-in-law sat beside me, holding my hand while I tried to stay calm, reading me Ada Limón's poetry, feeding me bone broth and nutrition shakes.

All day, pain and possibility merged as one invisible thread, knotting me to *here,* weaving me to *now.*

COMPLEX

THE NEXT DAY, Ryan and I sit in Dr. Detective's office, since he wanted to assess me himself in person before sending me to a bigger hospital. Worry lines his face as he thumbs through my lab results.

He sighs. "Well, you're officially my most complex case."

It doesn't exactly feel good to currently be the most complex case in a practice whose tagline is "Excellence in complex care."

Since this is a private practice, Dr. Detective doesn't have admitting privileges at local hospitals. But an old friend who has lupus and works at the largest hospital in town reached out, wanting to help. Lana connected with her colleagues and found an immunologist who wants to directly admit me. I show my doctor a text she just sent me:

"Apparently, we have another patient right now who also started having weird anaphylaxis after a port placement."

I shrug. "Maybe I won't be as much of a mystery there."

Dr. Detective leaves the room to coordinate my admission. We wait. I clutch a small olive-wood cross, running my thumb over its smooth edges. Two vials of Ruconest rest on the journal on my lap. Ryan squeezes my other hand tight.

I can hear my doctor in the room next door. It sounds like he's on the phone with another doctor. He pops his head back in the exam room. "I just don't want you leaving here without confirming you have a bed." He ducks out again.

We keep waiting. I open my giant illustrated copy of *Harry Potter and the Sorcerer's Stone,* forcing myself to focus on a story where I know the ending is good. Another hour goes by.

Dr. Detective says the attending physician has confirmed they'd like to admit me, but they still can't tell me an exact plan. He hands me a huge stack of papers—clinical documentation of my diagnoses and history to give to the doctors at the hospital. He doesn't want me waiting any longer while I'm this unstable, so Ryan loads me into the car. I'm hopeful. I can't keep holding out like this at home. It's too scary. I'm too weak.

FEMALE IN PAIN IN AN ER IN THE UNITED STATES OF AMERICA

THE HOSPITAL I was in before could fit into a wing of this one. It's a city in itself, sprawling in gleaming steel. We head upstairs to the floor where Lana said to check in, but after an hour, the receptionist says the admitting doctor wants to admit me through the emergency department.

Okay . . . I think. *As long as I'm admitted.*

Downstairs, I hear sirens and shouts, coughs and confusion. I put on a KN95 mask. The emergency room is the last place an immunodeficient person wants to be, particularly when already this sick.

They get me into a room right away, and minutes later my friend arrives. Ryan walks outside to greet my mom, fresh off a flight from Montana, here to help us again now that his parents have returned home.

Lana's an angel. I'm overcome by her kindness, her advocacy. A CNA enters to help me to the bathroom. I almost fall on my way. My balance is worse than ever. Mom sits by my side, arms crossed, afraid.

A doctor finally arrives, but he seems confused at my adamance that I'm supposed to be directly admitted. I open my notebook to the bookmarked list of "What to Say in the Emergency Room." It's hard to focus on keeping the story simple when I thought someone was here who already respected that it's not.

The doctor folds his arms across his chest. "I'm going to have to speak with the immunologist on call." He brusquely leaves the room.

This isn't going as planned.

He returns thirty minutes later. Apparently, the shift just changed, and now the doctor who agreed to directly admit me is gone. We missed our window for getting help without having to explain all the crazy-sounding things that have happened to me.

I'm scared.

After more hours of waiting, another doctor enters the room. She introduces herself as an immunologist, Dr. Dwyer.

I clutch my stack of medical proof for the pain I'm in. She glances at me, then my friend. Nothing she is saying sticks. All I know is that I can tell she doesn't believe me. It doesn't matter that I have a mountain of proof in my hands. It doesn't matter that I have a port clearly sticking out of my chest. It doesn't matter that my swollen cheeks practically scream *high-dose steroids on board!* It doesn't matter that a CNA saw me almost fall walking to the bathroom.

"I'm not sure you even need to be on IVIG," Dr. Dwyer says, "but I'd be happy to take on your case in my outpatient practice."

I look at Ryan and Mom in disbelief, then rage.

She doesn't even think I need to be on the treatment that gave me back my life last year.

I try to hand the doctor my medical records. She shrugs and takes them, but I can tell it's just a courtesy. That woman's not going to look at a thing.

Lana leaves the room after getting a text and comes back a long while later. The ER charge nurse lodged a complaint about her, saying she misused her credentials in coordinating my direct admission. Lana is crestfallen. I apologize profusely, knowing her job might be on the line because of *me*. She says that even if she gets officially reprimanded tomorrow, standing up for me was worth it.

At 1:23 A.M., I'm told I'm not being admitted. I can wait a

little longer for a psych consult and to be evaluated by the neurologist on call, but that's all they can offer me.

I'm aghast. They're sending me right back home hours after being told by my own immunologist that he doesn't believe it's safe for me to be at home.

This is healthcare in the United States of America.

Many physicians would rather give a psych consult to a woman in horrific pain than confront the reality that her body may be experiencing disease processes beyond the scope of their intelligence.

LIVING HELL

THE NEXT DAY, I end up back at Dr. Detective's office for yet another infusion of antihistamines and fluids. They try to give me some of the support the hospital didn't. But my body's too fragile, and anaphylaxis hunts me down *again*. Carly, the physician's assistant on call, is too disturbed by what she sees to not take more drastic action.

"If this doesn't improve quickly, we'll have to use your EpiPen," Carly warns. "And if I do that, I *have* to call an ambulance."

After a tense fifteen-minute wait, watching my throat swell and oxygen saturation drop, a nurse administers my tenth shot of epi in far fewer than that many weeks. It doesn't help enough. She shines a light down my throat and says it's closing. Another shot of epi pierces my skin right before the ambulance arrives.

I'm rushed right back to the hospital that turned me away

less than twenty-four hours ago, the hospital that could have prevented this hell.

Only to sit there for hours and get pushed right back out the door.

SAFE HARBOR

I WAKE UP the next morning to pale lilac and lemon light, my eyes catching the comfort quick and kind like a mercy against the memory of the last two infuriating nights in the ER.

Nothing in me wants to recount the disrespect doused on me while my doctors tried to get me a higher level of care in the hospital. The dismissal I experienced in the ER has cast a shadow over my hope. I hate that *this* wrong is now part of my story, when I've already experienced more wrong than I can bear.

I'm thinking about something I wrote in my last book: "Trauma happens and harms us. But I often wonder if the worst trauma is the second wave—when your story is misbelieved, mistrusted, and maligned. May your story find safe harbor in the presence of people who will honor both your vulnerability and resilience."[6]

I want to focus on the humankindness holding up the edges of the enigma I am living. Lana's advocacy. My mother-in-law's voice. My mom's presence. Ryan's constant care. I want the relief of resting in a safe harbor, but I have so little energy left to keep bailing out water from my boat while I do.

6 K.J. Ramsey, *The Book of Common Courage: Poems and Prayers to Find Strength in Small Moments* (Grand Rapids, MI: Zondervan, 2023), 126.

Yesterday as I waited and waited in the emergency room, I could tell the doctors there were strangely suspicious of my immunologist. A year ago, a doctor friend told me how fraught a field immunology is. Many doctors, both within the field and beyond it, disagree about the use of new tests and measures to diagnose and treat complex diseases in novel ways. And my immunologist is a researcher; he's always running clinical trials and studies to bring new and better treatment to patients who have often been overlooked and misdiagnosed elsewhere. Being a complex case already makes coming to a hospital a crapshoot, but I think I stumbled into some strange professional feud and got caught in the crossfire.

I can hear Mom and Ryan talking downstairs about how horrible last night was. Ryan is exasperated.

"You *can't* do that to a person! You can't call into question a person's whole care plan and experience of progress right when meeting them!"

His anger is like a lighthouse, radiating rage to protect what he loves.

I sit alone upstairs in our room, rocking back and forth.

DON'T TOUCH MY BARBIES!

IT'S BEEN TWO days since my ER nightmare, and I'm reeling after yet another sleepless night. It turns out sleep is nearly impossible when you're on 100mg of Prednisone. Forty milligrams of Prednisone is considered "high dose," and I've been on far more than that for weeks now. I am a live wire, a buzzing brain in a bed, a high and a low, a floating fury of survival.

Mom enters the room with bone broth and toast. It's still all I'm eating, along with the nutrition shakes. I reach for the bed table to clear room for my "meal," but I accidentally knock over several tiny trinkets people have brought as gifts.

I freak out. *I'm ruining everything.* I'm not sure if I screamed that out loud or just in my head. I try to reach for what's fallen but almost fall out of bed.

Mom interrupts my anxious tidying. "This reminds me of when you were around three and would line up your Happy Meal Barbies." She chuckles.

As a little girl, I collected every tiny Barbie that McDonald's made and would line them up daily on my bedroom windowsill with painstaking precision. This was during the same years that I washed my hands so frequently and intensely that they often were raw.

"You'd always come down from your room yelling, 'Mom! You moved my Barbies!' "

I don't hear what she says next. My hands are hyper-focused, rearranging trinkets. A glass tube of dried purple flowers from Tara. A palm-sized gilded icon of Mary holding Jesus, the Theotokos, from Felicia. A metallic stone from Nicole. A tiny apothecary vial from Stacey with living sea moss inside that's smaller than my fingertip. I hold the tiny things, wiping microscopic dust away with my sweater sleeve, and it's like no time has passed.

When Mom leaves my room, I think of the way I barked at my mother-in-law last week about all the things piling up on our dresser. And then I think of the way I demand Ryan to remake the bed every few days, because it feels like if my sheets aren't clean, I will cease to exist. The distance between my desire for clean and my ability to do it myself is driving me to rage multiple times a day. And it's not pretty.

But I'm also glimpsing something important through the grimy looking glass of steroid-induced agitation. I coped with chaos as a kid by creating order in the one place I had control. Those Barbies were a line of dreams for a life that was free of anyone else's dirty hands. And I'm coping the same way now.

EVICTION NOTICE

MY IPAD IS propped up on an overbed table. Ryan sits beside me in bed and wraps his arms around me, speaking softly in my ear. "We will do what we need to do. I will make sure you get the help you need."

We open Zoom for yet another virtual appointment with one of the physician's assistants from my immunologist's office. Ryan grips my hand as Carly comes onscreen.

It's been three days since I was taken by ambulance to the ER, and while I haven't had to use another EpiPen, I still can't eat without horrible itchiness and pain. During the night, when I finally fall asleep, I wake up about once an hour, gripping my throat, struggling to swallow. During the day, I've set a goal for myself to walk the length of our upstairs hallway twice, but instead of getting stronger and more stable, my left leg drags, and I can barely feel the floor. When I lie in bed, that foot often feels like it's on fire. And sometimes, the fire spreads to the other side. I keep dropping things—the trinkets beside my bed, my phone. Even my coordination is confused.

Carly listens and makes a note to work on scheduling a peer-to-peer review for the brain MRI that just got denied.

"Carly, I'm miserable." I shift against the pillows, trying to sit up. "Can you give me anything to help me sleep? Maybe more lorazepam?"

Carly tucks her curly hair behind her ear and sighs, holding a hand to her chin. She takes a deep breath. "KJ, our team has been discussing your case. And, well, we've all decided that the best thing we can do right now to keep you out of danger is to remove your port."

I clutch my hands over Simone without thinking. *This can't be real.*

"There's nothing else we can do? We can't consult with other interventional radiology departments? Find other options? How am I supposed to keep getting treatment?"

Carly shakes her head. "At this point, we know that even infusing just saline through your central line causes severe anaphylaxis. The one common denominator we can control is that port. Removing it is the best chance we have at stopping whatever storm is happening in your body."

I glance at Ryan. The corners of his mouth are a low cloud. He nods in defeated agreement.

My shoulders shake, unable to contain my grief. Carly explains backup plans for my treatment—subcutaneous IG, though it's not the best option for me, could work, if my veins don't hold up enough for IVIG. Or, we could try less frequent, higher dose IVIG to give my veins a break between treatments. Both options sound scary to me, but what's scarier is staying this sick.

I hold my hands over my wet face and take a deep breath. "Okay." I wipe back my tears. "If this is what it takes to get better, it's what I have to do."

PILLS I SWALLOWED TODAY

- Prednisone XXXX
- Zyrtec XXX
- Pepcid XXX
- Celebrex XX
- Gabapentin XX
- Montelukast X
- Hydroxyzine XXXXXX
- Xarelto X
- Lorazepam half-X
- Tramadol X

HARDER PILLS TO SWALLOW

- DON'T FUCKIN QUIT.[7]
- BREATHE WHEN YOUR BRAIN IS FEELING BAD.
- REMEMBER TO BE KIND, EVEN WHEN CONFUSED.
- GETTING THROUGH THIS FOR YOURSELF + RYAN IS MORE IMPORTANT THAN GETTING ANY OF IT DOWN ON PAPER OR EVER WRITING A BOOK ABOUT IT.

7 Hat tip to John Blase, who messaged me this phrase in encouragement, which I then wrote on a whiteboard on the wall beside my bed, giving me tough love when I feel like a puddle of self-pity.

SCRIPTS GO OFF SCRIPT

I'M ON THE phone with the specialty pharmacy, updating our insurance info. Because of course, Ryan's employer just split into two and changed us to a new insurer right after I was discharged from the hospital, because the thing we really need to be dealing with right now is a new huge deductible right after meeting the last one from almost dying. *How is this not illegal?!*

Since I'm a super mature woman in her mid-thirties, I'm clutching the weighted stuffed animal someone bought me recently for support—a pink dinosaur I've named Father Richard Roar. I like my comforts priestly, with ready-made reasons to smirk.

Mom stands at my dresser, tucking away laundry. I sit up in bed, trying to swallow my own hard pill by choosing to remain kind instead of pissed at the entire unjust world while reading off my new policy number to a person at a call center who definitely does not deserve to be the object of my wrath.

"It's O—as in 'Overwhelmed!' Two. Eight. One. Nine . . ."

Gosh. I roll my eyes at myself. Leave it to a poet to make reading off a policy number a chance to share her feelings.

Mom overhears me and starts laughing so hard she has to leave the room. The agent accepts my answer but is far less amused than us. I giggle through the rest of the annoying call.

Silliness = success.

I smile. It's more than that.

Silliness = I am still me.

LORELAI

LATER, MOM CURLS up beside me in bed, and we start season one of *Gilmore Girls.* Lorelai and Rory were more than a distant reflection of our mother-daughter relationship when the show aired while I was in high school—down to my obsession with reading and the fact that I'm pretty sure I mostly made friends because they liked hanging out with my mom, who, to be accurate, was way more fun than my study-obsessed, intense self. But also, like Lorelai, Mom has always been good at getting around the grief of her own past with work and fun. Mine, too. But now? It feels different.

In this apocalypse of two months straight of anaphylaxis and angst, I can see that I am being given something precious. My mom is right here, giving me her full attention—ready to help, holding what hurts. Earlier today, she held me in her arms while I wept in bed over having to remove Simone.

Today can heal yesterday.

Perhaps not in replacement—this is not a removal of the emotional void I experienced early in childhood. This is something stronger and stranger. This is love that can reach into the sinew where I still feel scared and alone. The Hardest Thing in your life can become healing ground.

BRING YOUR OWN RAINBOWS

I'M IN THE back seat of Reepijeep. I like sometimes calling the Jeep by her ridiculous name, as though I'm still living in the same universe where I could set off on a cross-country road trip. Ryan's driving, and Mom's in the passenger seat. Ryan and I were supposed to be driving to Montana today to spend the week with his family at our favorite national park, Glacier. Instead, we're traveling just down the road to another surgery.

I'm wearing a hot-pink camisole topped with my pale pink cashmere sweater. Draped over my shoulders is a pink shawl from Mish. Last night, I took one last pre-surgery bath, and Mom helped me curl my hair into gorgeous waves. *Who shows up to surgery with perfect hair?* We hold on to our dignity however we can.

I still can't believe I named my port Simone. I worked so hard to accept her, but Simone the starving mystic almost starved me to death. And though none of my doctors can explain her anaphylactic assassination attempts, we do know that evicting Simone is the only way to make the home of my body safe again.

The thing that was supposed to help me hurt me.

The fact that I named that thing after a woman with a death wish can only be described as absurd. I know. But it would have been absurd, whether I had named it or not.

The last time I left this hospital, I saw a double rainbow stretched over it—the universal symbol of the beauty that comes after a storm, a symbol of the hope that harm will be flipped on its head. I didn't expect that sight to lead me right back to where this story first got scary. I didn't expect the storm to continue quite so fiercely or long. I didn't have much choice in gaining two new scars. But I do have a choice in how I will greet them. So, last night Mom and I gave ourselves manicures with ombré rainbow gel strips. This time, I'm bringing my own rainbows right through the hospital's doors.

OPEN HANDS

I BLINK AND am back in the recovery room. I shiver. My fingers find the edge of the thin blue hospital gown before reaching upward toward my heart. It's gone. *She's* gone.

Surgery was a blur. A nurse steps in to check my vitals. I ask for the port. Surely, if it was inside *my* body, then it should be mine.

I've only ever seen a digital rendering of my port on the card in my wallet that they gave me to carry—like a kid's school ID, but to show doctors—complete with a manufacturer's ID number and tiny purple photo.

I feel naked, emptied not just of a part with a number but a thing with a mind. I mean, I'm here in this hospital bed because this *thing* almost killed me. I could list a dozen people who have ports and haven't come this close to dying. People get them every day and have no problem. I need to see the thing to believe what happened to me is real.

"I'm sorry," the nurse says, shaking her head. "We just aren't allowed to give patients anything removed during surgery. It's hospital protocol."

I beg. I try to explain what I need without sounding crazy. (Obviously, I don't tell the nurse my port had a name and a backstory fit for a Mary Doria Russell novel.)[8] She shrugs, apologizes again, and leaves the room.

Twenty minutes later, a thin woman in scrubs walks in behind the nurse, her brown hair still covered by a blue surgical cap. Suddenly, I remember more than blinking awake. *She* was there, standing over me while I wept on the operating table, shaking in the cold with tears running down my face. She stroked my head and hair until I was ready to go under. I counted backward, looking into her reassuring brown eyes.

The woman pauses for the other nurse to finish checking my vitals and leave. Then she pulls out a small plastic bag from her pocket. The bag has an orange biohazard label. "I could get into so much trouble for this." Her voice is low and hushed.

"I cut two small pieces from the catheter after they removed it. I know it's not the whole thing," she apologizes, "but I hope this helps." She hands me the plastic bag. "Maybe your allergist can use this to do testing. Or maybe it will just help you to have. Just don't tell my coworkers I gave you this."

I clutch the bag to my chest like it holds treasure. I look up at her with tears in my eyes before she leaves the room, and whisper, "*Thank you.*"

The unreality of what has happened to me now has substance. I can hold a piece of this pain in my hands.

Minutes later, the other nurse slips into the room, furtively looking behind her to make sure the door is closed. "Here." She sets a long tube and a rounded triangle on a sterile cloth on the hospital table beside me. "I can't let you keep it, but I thought you might really need to hold it. I'll give you a few minutes."

I'm speechless at their kindness. So many medical provid-

8 Side note though, if you haven't read *The Sparrow*, holy Jesuit, that novel is a masterpiece on the meaning of suffering.

ers have shrugged at my story, but these two women each separately saw that I needed something to hold.

I reach for Simone. The catheter tubing is still stained with my blood. The port itself is just larger than a quarter, a grayish-white rounded triangle with silicone at its center, and I hold it in my left palm. I touch the three raised dots that sat under my skin just two hours ago, the guide marks that I and my nurses used to connect me to more bags and vials of saline and steroids and IVIG than I can count.

The port is almost weightless in my hand, and I hold it with awe instead of hate. Something far smaller than my palm almost stole my whole life. We spend decades building careers that can buy us homes of wood and brick and stone, but something smaller than an eyeball can burn the home of our bodies right down.

GIVE ME A MAP

TODAY I WOKE with the sun and the sting of the incision over the place my port so briefly sat. I traced the place where the catheter collided with my jugular. It always tugged when I would turn my neck, and now that sensation is gone.

I've been reading daily from the lectionary Tara gave me, even though it's been a long time since I've wanted to read scripture daily. Something about the Psalms especially feels solid right now; these old words are honest enough to reach my new wounds. This morning's reading was from Psalm 43, and I was entirely captivated by the third and fourth verses. In *The Message* translation, they go like this:

Give me your lantern and compass,
give me a map,
So I can find my way to the sacred mountain,
to the place of your presence . . .

I feel lost in loss, and I'm sure I'll cry out for a compass if this recovery remains harder than I hope. But I know that the pain I'm feeling reveals a path to the places I still need healing. The port was not for nothing. It pointed me toward a part of myself that still prefers the illusion that a life without pain is the only one worth living. The pain of getting that port triggered me again and again, pinpointing shadowed places inside myself that need confrontation and care.

I'm realizing there is mercy hidden in misery. Every bruise and ache and trigger locates the latitude and longitude of land that still needs tending. And when I travel there, love always meets me. Both the map and the mountain have always been within me.

"YOU ALL JUST THINK I'M AWFUL!"

I SHOUT THAT at Ryan. I can barely walk, but good Lord, I can still stomp if I'm angry enough. I heave myself out of bed and slam the bathroom door.

Ryan stands on the other side. "I was *just* trying to ask why you're spending so many hours on your phone in the bathroom at night. I wasn't upset with you!"

"YOU DON'T UNDERSTAND!" I shout back through the door. I crash onto the blue tiled floor, cross my arms, and glare at the door. His question feels like an accusation, as though this is about some phone or social media addiction, not the fact that I'm on so many steroids that it's almost impossible to sleep *and* I'm literally working my ass off to do something that used to take zero effort and maybe ten minutes of each day. I can't believe we're fighting about shit.

I'm so angry, I growl. A deep throaty *uuuugghhhhhhhh!*

I hold my head in my hands, shaking a silent no. *Man, I'm really not myself. Why can't I control myself? Why can't I stop yelling? I'm losing my mind. Ryan must hate me right now. I need to ask him to forgive me.* I sigh and pull myself up from the floor, brushing off dust from my hands. I crack the door open. Ryan's still standing there, with Resa quivering at his feet. Ryan runs a hand through his red hair and relaxes his shoulders. I force myself to meet his eyes—bright blue like a tropical sea—before I look away, ashamed.

"I'm so sorry. I don't understand why I'm so mad. I don't understand what's happening to me."

He wraps me in a hug. "I know." I weep into his shoulder. Resa taps a paw at my leg—*boop, boop, boop*—checking on me.

"It's the steroids, KJ. You're angry because of the steroids."

We sit on the edge of the bed, and Ryan rocks me while Resa drapes her body over my thigh like a canine weighted blanket. And though I feel loved, I wonder if Ryan doesn't deserve a better spouse than me. I wonder if he's disappointed that I'm not stronger, that I can't control myself, that even though I have all the tools to stay emotionally regulated, I can't. I wonder if his life would be better if I and all my illnesses weren't in it.

SATAN'S LITTLE TIC TACS

EVEN WITHOUT HIGH-DOSE steroids, *I've got range.* I can travel between delight and despair in a day, and often do. Ryan sometimes tells our friends that he's jealous that I feel a fuller continuum of feelings than he's ever been able to access. But much of my adult life has been consumed by learning to ride my own waves.

This ride is too much for us both. Earlier, a friend visited and asked Ryan how he's doing with everything we're going through. Ryan said he feels "a rupture" between us over how differently we're experiencing my sickness. He feels confused by me and hurt at how quickly I swing from smiling to crying to shouting.

I hated hearing it, but I know it's true. Each day, I travel between what feels like heaven and hell. I bounce between reverie and rage while everyone around me stays rooted. I feel like I've been living on some strange, alternate plane of existence that is simultaneously here and not.

Every day, I swallow four small white pills of Prednisone, knowing it will fight both inflammation and me. I'm down from 100mg to 80, but even 80 is double the highest dose I'd ever been on before. Many of us in the chronic illness community affectionately call Prednisone "Satan's Little Tic Tacs."

SIDE EFFECTS INCLUDE:

- Dizziness, rapid heart rate, blurred vision, trouble speaking and thinking, trouble breathing, and numbness in arms or legs. Akghjkhkltgkhje . . . Caught you trying to skim this part, just like I wish I could skim the pamphlets from my pharmacist!

- Side effects also include:
  - Agitation so awful you won't even know why you're annoyed and may find yourself frequently reacting irrationally to small statements or situations while feeling both VERY RATIONAL AND LIKE YOU HAVE BEEN WRONGED NOT ONLY BY THE PERSONS WHO ARE SUPPOSED TO ACCEPT YOU UNCONDITIONALLY BUT BY THE UNIVERSE HERSELF!
  - Fluid retention and insatiable hunger along with rapid weight gain in your arms, face, and stomach so unevenly distributed that you may appear more like Violet Beauregarde than yourself.
  - Sleeplessness unparalleled maybe even by new parents, but the baby is you. The baby is the brutal reality of being a grown-ass adult who cannot stop herself from shouting, just moments after crying with joy at being so grateful to be alive.

The reason we make this deal with the devil is that this shit saves your life. And I've been on a higher dose of it than anyone I've ever known. No wonder I'm living in a different reality than Ryan.

DIVING

LATER THAT EVENING, a warm breeze blows through our bedroom windows, where Ryan sits in an armchair with Resa curled in a dappled chocolate-and-white circle of fur at his feet. The sun has just begun to drop behind the ridge, filling our room with golden light.

"I want you to listen to this new Bombay Bicycle Club song," Ryan says. "It's giving meaning to this season for me."

Two voices join a looping acoustic guitar and building beat. The chorus is pure consolation, like two young lovers echoing promises to see the best in each other, even while holding their breath after diving in the depths of some dark water.

In the aftermath of my recent roid rage moments, I've felt contempt for myself. I have believed in my own reduction. My partner and loved ones don't deserve better than me; they deserve my commitment to tell a better story about myself.

Ryan and I cannot be our best selves right now, but we can choose to believe the best is still inside each other.

We play "Diving" again, and Ryan sits beside me on the foot of the bed. The song softens the calcified sadness between us. I pause it midway.

"Let's choose to see the best in each other." I squeeze Ryan's hand. "Not in perfection, but as a practice. Not with high expectations, but to hold hope."

He squeezes back and nods his head *yes*.

I push play again. The song swells. We let our bodies say everything our minds and mouths are still learning to speak.

COUNTING RINGS

I SPEND YET another night sleepless and finally drift off around five A.M. I wake after only a few hours, disoriented, as though I've fallen into a puddle. I am drenched in my own sweat.

I snap, disgusted at the sensation, yet too fatigued to be able to strip the bed myself. I burn with anger—angry that I can't accomplish a simple task, angry to need to shower again when I don't even have enough energy to sit on a shower chair, angry that even though Simone is gone, I'm not getting stronger. But the anger comes out sideways, slicing like a sword.

"Ugh! Ryan! I sweat through the sheets *again*. You have to remake the bed. *I don't care* if you're running late for work!"

"It's okay." Ryan pulls on a navy collared shirt and glances up at me. "I don't mind changing the sheets. But you *do* have to try to be nice to me."

"I know," I said, shrugging, "I'm trying. I'm so sorry for snapping again."

He stretches clean celadon-green sheets over our bed. I rest in the chair in the corner. I look from the sheets to him. "Ryan." I pause, apologetic. "*Thank you.*"

He hugs me and leaves for work. Ryan's a chaplain, and even though we've moved to the Springs, he still works in Denver. Every day, he drives an hour north to care for others, only to drive another hour home to come back and care for me. He doesn't complain, but I know he's exhausted. If we didn't have our moms or friends taking turns helping care for me, I don't know how we'd make it. Even with help, I don't know how we'll make it.

On my dresser, a vase of fragrant white lilies sits atop a tree slice, one of the centerpieces from our wedding reception. I climb out of the freshly made bed to smell the lilies and then set the vase aside, tracing the tree's rings, fingertip to pith, counting out from her core. Remembering.

Under our wedding tent, while the rain poured outside, my dad raised a toast to the new life of our marriage. Dad told our guests about the grandmother of the tree that graced their tables, a giant white ash—wider than our arms could hug—who lived at the base of our driveway. Dad shared that nothing could take the tree down, not even the biggest storms nor the time his daughter—*this daughter*—accidentally put the family van in neutral, jumped out in panic, and watched as it rolled down the driveway and crashed into the hulking trunk below.

One spring, Dad noticed a gray residue on the tree's diamond-shaped bark. He brushed it off as nothing. Spring turned into summer, and the tree stood tall. But year after year, the canopy that covered our small forest thinned. The tree's bark began to flake and crack. An arborist was called. *Neither storms nor the crash killed the tree,* Dad declared to our guests. *It was a bug no larger than a fingertip.*

The emerald ash borer had infiltrated our forest and slowly eaten away the life in almost every ash tree. In the months before our wedding, Dad had to cut down most of the trees in our woods to save the whole. He sawed some of those trees into slices to serve as storytellers on my wedding day.

The centerpieces on our tables held not only mason jars of green chrysanthemums and fragrant white peonies; they carried an allegory. The biggest storms and hits are not what will slay us. It is the small things—sharp words, biting moments of blame, small resentments building up day after day.

I count fifty-two rings on the tree slice on our dresser, a

hundred and fifty or more years fewer than the tree could have lived without the ash borer's bite.

Pay attention, my dad was saying. *Protect your love.*

MOON FACE

I CLUTCH THE bathroom vanity and stare into the mirror. The face looking back at me is not mine. I can barely see my blue eyes beyond the bursting balloons of my cheeks. My jaw appears to have been swallowed by skin so swollen it aches.

I wipe away a crust from the slits of my eyes. In the last few days, I can barely see by midday because my swollen cheeks crowd out my eyeballs, leaving my vision blurry. My face is so turgid that today I tried to open my phone, and after multiple failed attempts, I realized that it was no longer recognizing *this* face as *my* face. I had to reset my face ID.

It's three A.M., and I'm far from sleep. So I sit on the toilet and pull out my phone, where one little square on my home screen greets me daily with pictures from my past.

I can barely believe my eyes. The photo album the Algorithm Angels at Apple decided to gift me tonight is all pictures of me and my sister. In the first picture, Kenzie stands next to me, Mom, our brother Tucker, and his wife Melanie. We're all grinning, wearing silly maroon bellhop caps inside the gift shop of Disney World's Tower of Terror, just moments after screaming our heads off on the ride. We went to Disney World together to celebrate that Kenzie had made it through her heart attack just three months before. All week, we took turns rolling her around Disney in a wheelchair, laughing, amazed and grateful that she was *alive*. In the photo, Kenzie's beaming face is nearly as swollen as mine is tonight, her cheeks like puffy clouds, stretched wide from the high-dose steroids that helped *her* survive.

That swollen face means she survived.

I stand up and look into the mirror again. I hold my hands to my missing jaw, fingers cradling my stretched skin, and look myself straight in the eyes.

This shape means you are surviving.

I say it out loud. I say it again.

The medical term for what I see is "moon face." High-dose steroids save lives but stretch both sanity and faces, filling in frowns with retained water and redistributed fat. My face is now a full moon. And it is frightening, to not only be more fatigued than ever, but to no longer recognize myself in the mirror.

But in the moonbeam of my sister's survival, I can better see myself. I cannot be ashamed of this softness, because it is the shape of survival stronger than a heart attack, fiercer than anaphylactic shock, more stunning than a supermodel.

Moon Face. I say it not as a slur but a spell. I decide to let my survival shine for the next person who needs light in their dark.

"LET'S TAKE THE BACKROADS HOME"

RYAN SAYS, LOWERING his sunglasses as he turns toward me in the back seat. "Would that be okay?"

I nod. After that appointment, it's more than okay.

Sarah sits in the front seat next to Ryan, fresh off a plane from San Diego to take over caregiving help from my mom, a distant reality from the trip we took together in June. Sarah just sat with us as we met with Dr. Detective, whirled by what-ifs and whys and white blood cell count alarm. She shakes her head. "That was *a lot.*" She turns to me in the back seat. "I barely could follow that. You basically have a medical degree after all you've been through."

"I know, right?" I laugh. "But I think this was the first time we've had a friend sit *with us* during one of those appointments. And that meant a lot. Thank you for being here."

The appointment was so long that the sun is beginning to set. As Ryan drives away from the clinic, I slump into the pillowed nest we've made for me in the back seat. "Maybe"—I reach for Ryan's shoulder—"maybe if we see any wildflowers on the way home, we can stop? I missed a whole summer of seeing wildflowers. All I want is to see some before the season fully changes to fall."

We exit the highway and pass the suburban sprawl of the south Denver metro before the fields are like lakes of tall sun-gilded grass, open stretches of land with distant mountains instead of steel as far as the eye can see.

"There!" I yell. "There are sunflowers right up there. Pull over!"

Sarah and Ryan glance at each other and laugh at my insistence. But my wish is his command.

Ryan opens my door and puts an arm around me, helping me reach the riot of sunflowers a few feet away from the road. I'm too weak and too stunned to stand, so I sit right in the middle of the flowers. I'm bathed in golden light, buoyed by a small sea of shining faces, and in this moment, I count myself not as cursed but as carried, brought to beauty because my husband took the long way home, just so I could see the light a little longer, just so I could feel something other than sick.

Sarah snaps picture after picture. *This is what I want to re-*

member of this shrouded season: the people who made sure that like these sunflowers, my face kept turning toward the light.

THE VALLEY

THE NEXT MORNING, I wake to my phone ringing. It's Heather from my immunologist's office. "We need you to go to the hospital *right now.* Your counts are too high. We need them to rule out serious infections."

My heart pounds an EDM beat as I tell Sarah we have to head to the hospital. We rush around my bedroom, gathering essentials. Sarah helps me down the stairs and into Reepijeep.

"Well"—I'm terrified, but I laugh—"I guess we get to take a different kind of adventure than the last time it was just the two of us in this car!" Sarah's face is solemn, but I see the edge of a smile.

I was supposed to be in Acadia National Park this week with my best friend from childhood, Dani, not heading back to the hospital. I clutch Richard Roar while Sarah speeds to the ER.

A nurse draws several tubes of blood, and Sarah reads aloud from *Harry Potter and the Sorcerer's Stone* to keep me calm while we wait. After a few hours, a doctor finally arrives. He has white hair and glasses, and appears stoic, but a sobered look of kindness stretches across his face as he shakes my hand. Dr. Swanson pulls a chair beside my bed and points to the embroidered title over the pocket of his white coat.

"It says 'hospital medicine' there, but you should know that I spent the first half of my career practicing immunology. And that's how I know that you are *very* sick."

Dr. Swanson asks questions and listens closely as I retell the strange story of how I got here, a swollen shell of myself, sweating and fevered and scared. I don't stick to the script of what to say in the ER, because I sense he already respects my reality.

He carefully explains that he's had blood cultures drawn that will take a few days to come back, and that it's possible I have a blood infection, an infection in my heart, or maybe even leukemia. I think I see the start of tears behind his glasses.

Dr. Swanson tells us that a year and a half ago, his entire family got Covid, and his daughter, who was just a few years older than me, didn't survive. His face is wet with tears as he tells us that his daughter lived her life full of love.

He folds his arms across his chest and sighs. "If you were forty years older than you are, you would not survive this." He looks me in the eyes. "And, you still might not."

I blink back tears.

"You are living Psalm twenty-three right now. You are walking through the valley of the shadow of death."

Now I'm shivering not just from fever but awe. This doctor has no idea what those words mean to me. He has no idea I've published two books on Psalm 23.

"The Lord is my shepherd." The words rise from my mouth as a reflex. I look Dr. Swanson in the eyes as tears stream down my face. "I lack nothing."

I'm surprised to sense the truth behind my tears and those words. If those words aren't true here in a hospital, they aren't true anywhere.

He grabs my hand and clutches it tight. "May I pray for you?" He pleads for my life and prays for my peace. Sarah joins, pressing a warm hand against my cold shoulder, right above the blood pressure cuff.

THE GREAT IMITATOR

"IT'S MOST LIKELY lupus." Dr. Swanson sits in a chair at the end of my hospital bed, stroking his chin.

I've been in the hospital for a few days. A transesophageal echocardiogram ruled out any heart issues, but I still have a low fever and am so fatigued, I can barely sit up in bed. At night, my bones ache, or at least it seems like it's coming from my bones. It hurts so bad, I wish I could cut off my leg.

"Your blood cultures aren't growing, but it looks like there is what we call a *leukemoid* process going on. It could be acute myeloid leukemia or b-cell lymphoma, but it's looking most like lupus."

"You know about my sister, right? She had a heart attack from lupus."

Dr. Swanson nods. "If your white blood cell count doesn't go down, we'll have to do a bone marrow biopsy. But, yes, my hunch is that we're dealing with lupus here, too, not cancer."

I'm at a loss for words. *This can't be real.* "Okay."

He turns to leave the room and looks back. "I promise that I'm not going to let you leave this hospital sicker than when you came."

When the door closes, I shake with silent sobs.

I'm relieved I probably don't have cancer, but the prospect of leukemia somehow doesn't scare me as much as living with the disease that almost killed my sister and did kill my aunt. I know cancer is a bigger monster, but sometimes the monsters we've met are scarier than the ones we haven't.

Medical professionals have long called lupus "the great imitator," because it is the true chameleon of chronic disease. Lupus can morph to look like almost anything, including, sometimes, leukemia. It can attack any organ in the body, and no two cases look the same. That's probably why it takes on average *six years* after the onset of symptoms for patients to receive a diagnosis of systemic lupus erythematosus.[9] If that's true, I'm once again scoring above average, because I've been dealing with symptoms that we thought were all from Ankylosing Spondylitis for nearly fifteen years.

My autoimmune disease is a shape-shifter that has never fully fit in one box, which has forced me to fight hard for it to be believed and treated. Maybe this is why.

DOCTOR DICK

I'VE HAD LESS than twenty-four hours to be afraid of the diagnosis I've most feared before my fear is engulfed by rage. Once again, the healthcare system has slammed a door on my hopes of being helped.

Dr. Swanson's rotation ended last night, so today a new hospitalist is in charge. I figured one doctor's plan of care would be carried out by the next, but that's clearly not happening. I trusted Dr. Swanson when he said I wouldn't leave here sicker than when I came, only to be dismissed by the next doctor who walked through the door.

Dr. D—let's just call him Dr. Dick—just stood over my bed and coldly informed me that I'll be discharged tomorrow. It's

9 S. Al Sawah et al., "Understanding Delay in Diagnosis, Access to Care, and Satisfaction with Care in Lupus: Findings from a Cross-Sectional Online Survey in the United States," presented at the European League Against Rheumatism (EULAR) 2015 Annual Conference, June 2015, Rome, Italy.

clear that he decided this before he ever even *saw* me. He brushed off my elevated blood counts as my body just "re-adjusting" after so many anaphylactic episodes. One doctor believes I'm in a serious flare of lupus or might even have leukemia, and this doctor thinks I'm fine.

But I know in my body that I'm not. It feels like something is dying inside my leg. I'm constantly drenched in sweat. And I'm so weak I can barely stand without someone holding me up. I also know that outside of the hospital, tests Dr. Swanson said I likely need, like a bone marrow biopsy, will take weeks or months to schedule instead of hours or days. I'm being pushed out the door more perplexed than before, in a body that feels like a giant bruise, with my white blood cell count and neutrophils still soaring. But sure, Dr. Dick, send me home to handle hell on my own.

ASSISTIVE DEVICES

IT'S THE NEXT morning, and I'm about to be sent back home having received no real help to heal. Remember, my immunologist *sent* me to the hospital extremely worried, and now the hospital is just sending me home. I'm a pinball in a medical machine, hit and hit from all sides. Who is winning this game?

Before I'm discharged, an occupational therapist stops by to discuss home healthcare. After she assesses my ambulation, exhaustion and grief tackle me like linebackers. I collapse in a sweaty heap on the bed. We talk about things I need that I've only ever seen my grandpa own—pickers, a travel wheelchair, a seated walker. I need assistive devices, and I have no answers for why I need them.

My eyes can't contain my overwhelm. Tears cascade down my face like creeks onto the sweat-soaked hospital bed. My misery is still a complete mystery, which means there's no clear path out of it.

I am thirty-four years old, and I need home healthcare. I am thirty-four years old, and I need to learn how to walk well again. I am thirty-four years old, and I need a walker and a wheelchair.

I'm heartbroken to be returning home so unwell. I feel abandoned by authorities in the medical system. But I won't let some powerful prick take my peace away.

My recovery may be longer because of him, but I *will* rise.

INDIVISIBLE

SEPTEMBER

MY LEFT SHIN is screaming. When I stand for more than a couple of minutes, it feels like my bone might shatter. The legs that carried me across creeks and up mountains just months ago feel like fables. The body that sweat from hiking now sweats from constant fever and a heart rate so high, you'd think I was sprinting. I'm so woozy and weak that it's hard to believe I'm the same woman who just three months ago drove cross-country alone.

I'm just not getting better. I'm camped out on the border between my bed and being hospitalized again. I keep getting passed from specialist to specialist like some diseased hot potato plucked from the coals of a campfire no one wants to sit near. Each specialist evaluates one group of organs and systems, as though the whole of my body could be split into separate parts. But no singular organ in my body exists autonomously from the rest. My skeletal system is inextricably linked to my circulatory system, and the capillaries that carry oxygen from my lungs to my limbs are no less connected to my immune system than my tongue is to my throat. If screaming would help, I would shout:

My body is not a bag of parts.

SPACESUIT

IT'S BEEN A week and a half since I was discharged. We just left yet another doctor's appointment and decide to stop at Costco with my brand-new blue travel wheelchair. I haven't been inside a store in months. Ryan guides the wheelchair through wide aisles, hunting together for low-cost but moderately cute clothes to fit the new size and shape of my ever-expanding body.

Yesterday at one of my endless specialist appointments, the medical assistant made me stand up from my wheelchair to record my current height and weight. I knew the number would be high. I've sensed the swelling of my stomach. I can't unsee the full moon of my face. But I've felt confused—even dysmorphic—having returned from my first hospital stay and its searing starvation so light, my rings were falling off my hands.

Since I last remember being weighed, just two weeks ago, I have gained fifty-three pounds. In *two weeks,* I have gained more weight than I have in my entire adulthood.

It's hard to describe the disorientation of losing the sense of one's place in space so quickly. I've moved through the world at a size 10 for decades. Now I bump into dressers and walls daily, in part because something's deeply wrong with my left leg and, in part, because my mind has not caught up with my mass.

Ryan pushes my wheelchair down an empty aisle shelved with giant jars of pickles, and I chirp, "Go faster! Faster!" My hair blows behind me like a model in the wind of his sprint. I laugh the whole way down the aisle, cackling at the irrational joy of finding fun in the fury of unwanted change. In my best moments, like this one, I feel like a badass.

We are astronauts of affliction. We are traveling through trauma the other shoppers passing us probably can't imagine. They are on Earth. We are on a shuttle through the space of suffering, amazed at every star, terrified at the distance between ourselves and our desire.

We leave with a stack of soft clothes. My spacesuit is ready. And for this brief moment, I can imagine that the truest thing about my size is not that I needed to buy new XL clothes. The truest thing is that my body holds more within her frame than anyone can fathom. In my needs are nebulas. Look under the layers of my soft stretch-marked skin and you will find the same molecules that make up stars.

FOCAL POINT

I KNOW IF there's anyone who will understand why my body is so swollen, it's my endocrinologist. In the last three weeks, an unpleasant bone marrow biopsy ruled out leukemia, but pain and horrible fatigue are still chaining me to bed.

Ryan wheels me into a tiny exam room and sits in a chair beside me. I attempt to dry my sweaty hands on my black stretch pants. Even though steroids are practically Dr. Traeger's specialty, I'm still a little ashamed to let her see what they've done to me.

Dr. Traeger enters the room with a smile that she immediately swallows. She sits across from us and scoots her stool closer, eyes filling with tears. Even though she already knows the gist of what happened to me over the summer, seeing it is harder than hearing it.

I start to describe my symptoms and realize every symptom needs the full story to make any sense. I launch into the litany and am barely on day two of anaphylaxis before I start sobbing.

Ryan places a hand on my leg. "Will you let me tell the story? Is that okay?"

I nod.

Ever since the summer, more often than not, when I sit across from any specialist—old or new—I try to explain the story of my symptoms and suddenly feel trapped within the pages of my pain. Even though my body is here in a doctor's office, it's like *I* am stuck inside the story. I sit there, shaking, unable to crack the spine with speech.

Ryan is like my librarian. He knows right where the story sits on the shelf. When he tells the story, he tells it steady and true.

After listening to Ryan's recap, Dr. Traeger prescribes a beta blocker to slow my frenzied heart into a steadier rhythm. She writes out a plan to continue my rapid taper off high-dose steroids, followed by a much slower taper to safe, small doses—a process that will take over a year. Then she looks up from her computer, meets my eyes, and ever so tenderly asks how I've been coping with seeing my body so swollen.

I tell her I've been making self-portraits most days, as an artistic practice of not turning away from my own face. "I'm trying to see reality instead of closing my eyes to it," I explain. I know from years of experience that Dr. Traeger holds respect toward how I value embodiment as both a fellow professional and a patient.

She pauses. "A few years ago, I climbed Denali."

I scowl. *In what universe does anyone think it's relatable to tell a woman in a wheelchair about that one time you climbed Denali?* I take a deep breath and remind myself: Dr. Traeger has more than earned the right to be heard.

"For twenty-one days, I didn't look in a mirror," she says, "and it was freeing."

She swallows hard and explains that since my steroid dose was so high for so long, it will likely take at least a year to start looking like myself.

"Right now, your face is so swollen that seeing it *is* traumatic. It happened too fast for anyone's mind to handle, so fast that every time you glimpse your face, you are re-traumatized. I know you don't want to turn away from your own face, but I want you to try only looking in the mirror once a day, if that. Focus instead on what your mind and heart can do. Focus on the strength you are gaining."

MAYBE THE MIRACLE

DECEMBER

RYAN AND I sit across from each other in a booth. Crimson, white, and gold paper snowflakes glitter between twinkle lights from every foot of the restaurant's ceiling. Fake snow-covered Christmas trees line the windows. A black cane rests beside me in the booth next to our thick coats. Outside, the wind howls in the dark of a cold Minnesota night.

I fidget with my fork. "What if being here isn't worth it? What if we leave with no answers?"

Ryan looks up from his spaghetti. His eyes are always a bright ocean. Tonight, they brim with tears.

For fifteen years, we have said that if things ever got really bad—if we ever got to a place with my health where there was no way forward—we would come *here*. This is where you come when your sickness is so strange, your specialists need specialists. This is where you come when your matter is a mystery and your life a misery. This is where I never wanted to be.

My rheumatologist referred me to the Mayo Clinic just one month ago. "I've never had success getting a patient in," he said, cautioning against too much hope, "but I think it's the best next step for you." That day, we had gone through a list of lupus diagnostic criteria, checking off more boxes than not. I remember mindlessly raking a hand through my hair as we spoke, then holding out my full palm to him. "I've already lost my face, my work, and my appetite. Now I'm losing my hair. Send the referral."

We woke before the sun this morning and shuffled through a basement tunnel to a lab appointment where a phlebotomist took fifteen tubes of my blood. Once those tests come in, we'll discuss the results with Dr. Perkins, who happens to be the same world-class rheumatologist my sister saw last year. When we met her earlier, I pushed hard to explore a diagnosis for the pain in my leg.

Across the restaurant, a large table of diners are laughing and toasting, probably a company holiday party. I take another bite of my dinner. I ordered gluten-free ravioli in a mushroom tomato cream sauce, thinking the mushrooms might make me smile. It's the best food I've tasted in nearly six months, but eating is too exhausting to get more than a few bites down. These days, I'm too sick to eat. Even though my stomach is never full, my face still is. Under my thick black sweater, stretch marks zag like an albino zebra's hide. Instead of swelling with new life this fall like I had hoped, I got stretch marks from steroids.

Ryan looks at me tenderly across the table.

"Do you want to go back to the hotel?"

I shake my head no. I want to sit here a little longer. I want the twinkle lights above us to transform this dinner into the celebration today was supposed to be. Instead, I think of mothers in Gaza, wailing for their dead children. I think of Mary, fleeing with a bundled Christ to Egypt to escape genocide, waiting in an unfamiliar land until it was safe to go home. I think of the unnamed woman in the gospels who bled for twelve years straight, who so dared to dream that she was worthy of wellness that even after spending all she had on doctors, she stood in a crowd she wasn't welcome in to reach a hand toward the hem of Jesus's clothes to be healed. Maybe the biggest miracle wasn't that she was healed, but that she never gave up on herself.

My phone buzzes. It's a Mayo Clinic notification. "New test results."

I turn my phone toward Ryan. We both know what I'm not saying. *Should I dare to hope?*

Two more results have returned from this morning's pile of tubes. Both indicate I likely have lupus or mixed connective tissue disease. It's not a diagnosis, but it's likely the beginning of one.

I show Ryan the results. We wipe back tears and clasp our hands together across the table in hope.

"I think it's really courageous of you to come here. It means you are saying your life still matters."

I nod. *It does.*

The waiter comes to box my food and brings a container of chocolate mousse for us to take back to the hotel.

It's my birthday. I turned thirty-five today at the Mayo Clinic. It's the last place I would have chosen to be to celebrate. And this was not a celebration. It was a choice to find a way to live for many more birthdays to come.

CITY OF WHEELCHAIRS

IF MY NATIONAL parks trip was a pilgrimage into my past, this trip to Mayo is a pilgrimage aimed at trusting I have a future. The word *pilgrimage* has its origins in the late thirteenth century word *pelgrimage,* the "act of journey through a strange country to a holy place."[10] Intractable illness is, indeed, a strange country. As fellow Mayo patient and memoirist Nora Gallagher writes, "To pass into this place, you have to not know whether you are going to get out."[11]

Never before have I been among so many fellow pilgrims of pain. I've never visited another place where being too sick to walk is so normal. In my own city, I feel like a citizen of an unnamed, invisible country that no one wants to visit, or worse, inhabit. At Mayo, I am one among many, and even my need for a wheelchair to move through these long hallways to test after test is a need that is centered on rather than treated with contempt.

For days, Ryan has been wheeling me around Mayo in one of the hundreds of navy-blue wheelchairs that line both the clinic's

10 "Origin and History of *Pilgrimage*," etymonline, https://www.etymonline.com/word/pilgrimage.

11 Nora Gallagher, *Moonlight Sonata at the Mayo Clinic* (New York: Vintage Books, 2013), 8.

halls and the sidewalks of downtown Rochester. I wish he didn't have to push me everywhere, but he not only doesn't mind, he makes it fun. We laugh our way down the halls in between nervous waits. Smiling attendants make sure those in wheelchairs get on elevators first, and everyone is glad to oblige. No one bats an eye when we take a wheelchair through the maze of underground tunnels connecting the clinic to our hotel to rest.

When we pass under the sprawling yellow-and-green Chihuly chandeliers in the atrium, I pass other patients in wheelchairs and smile. Everywhere else we go, we are refugees of our preferred realities. But here, we are all citizens of the same strange country. We pass people speaking Farsi and Spanish, but I know we all tremble in the same tongue.

Ryan and I sit in the Skylight Commons, Mayo's cafeteria. All around us are patients and their families—a woman with a bald head, a man who is gaunt, a teenager in a wheelchair with a cast on her leg. I notice an old man in an N95 mask sitting across from us. He resembles the lovable curmudgeon Carl from the movie *Up,* which is fitting, because Ryan and I have started referring to Mayo Clinic as the Disney World of Medicine. Here, efficiency serves compassion. In the lab, conveyor belts whisk tests away, producing results within hours rather than days. Even the cafeteria is innovative. Robots bring your food right to your table. At every reception desk, staff members greet patients with smiles and make it clear that your questions are welcome. It's not the happiest place on earth, but it might be one of the kindest.

So far, I've roamed this place without receiving much clarity. A pilgrimage here requires accepting the uncertainty of what your visit will hold. Schedulers work hard to try to set up as many specialist appointments and tests as they can for you in a one- or two-week span, but there are no guarantees of appointments nor answers. I've been prodded with needles for an EMG, lain still in a cold tube for an MRI of my tibia, had every major joint scanned on a table, filled a whole gallon jug for twenty-four hours with my urine, wore a heart Holter monitor under my clothes for a day, and placed a pulse oximeter on my finger as I slept in bed. *Will I leave here after all of that and still feel stuck?*

I watch as the old man's wife comes up beside him and wraps him in a hug. I look at Ryan and smile a prayer. I want to grow as old and precious as them. The truth of the matter strikes me like a bell. This pilgrimage is not simply about reducing pain but about receiving the love that remains.

TEST RESULTS

"I'M SORRY YOU haven't been able to see immunology yet," Dr. Perkins says, crossing her arms over her white coat. "I will be honest with you, though. I doubt anyone—even here at Mayo—is going to be able to tell you what happened with your port."

I swallow the lump in my throat. If there were anywhere in the world I might get answers for why I almost died, it would have been here. I reach toward Ryan, sitting beside me on a wooden built-in bench beside Dr. Perkins's desk. The exam rooms in rheumatology are vintage, relics of mid-century modern design. I wonder how many patients have sat here before me with secrets that could not be solved.

"However, after getting your test results back, I do believe you are experiencing some form of mixed connective tissue disease, most likely a lupus variant, with some features of Sjögren's syndrome."

I squeeze Ryan's hand in my clammy palm. We're not getting all the answers, but we are gaining *some.*

"That's close to what my rheumatologist at home thinks, too, and one of the doctors who treated me in the hospital. They both thought I probably have lupus."

"Well, I don't want to diagnose you with lupus quite yet, because your case might involve some other features that lupus typically doesn't exhibit. But yes, treatment mostly will be the same."

Dr. Perkins explains that if the biologic medication I'm already on for Ankylosing Spondylitis does not bring major improvement in the next three months, she recommends that my rheumatologist switch me to Benlysta, a biologic that specifically targets lupus. My lips part like an opened window. My sigh is a gust of wind. *At least I'm leaving here with proof for some of my problems and the start of a plan for how to treat them.*

"Now," Dr. Perkins says, glancing at her computer and scrolling through my test results. "Have you seen the reports on the imaging we had done of your tibia?"

"Yes." My heart sprints. "What exactly does 'microfractures' mean? Like, there are tiny breaks in my bone? Does mixed connective tissue disease do *that*?"

Dr. Perkins frowns. "So, these results are beyond the scope of my expertise. This isn't from anything autoimmune." She points at the report on the screen. "Your imaging showed swelling in the bone marrow of your tibia. It also included some views of the knee, and that's where there are tiny breaks in your bone. So, I'd like to get dedicated imaging of your knee, and I'll be referring you to orthopedics for a consult on those results."

"Should I be walking on a bone that has tiny breaks? How did that happen? I never fell. I don't remember hitting anything hard. How does a person just end up with little *breaks* in their bone?"

Dr. Perkins shakes her head. The corners of her mouth are a dipping crescent moon. "I really can't speak to that. I'm so sorry. But we'll try to get you in with ortho ASAP."

WE PRAY

I JUST FINISHED an appointment with a medical geneticist, a kind woman who validated the reality that my family medical history lights up bright as the huge Christmas trees in the lobby, but with diseases and disorders no one can explain. She believes there must be a strong genetic component to our family story of illness and would like to sequence my genome and my sister's—though she warned that few of her autoimmune patients receive answers that way.

When this appointment was added to my schedule, I sent Ryan home without me. He's already had to use so much family medical leave for me, and I figured I could handle a genetics appointment alone. Maybe an ortho appointment will get added, too, but I'm not banking on it.

I step through an automatic door into a quiet, dark room. I clutch my cane for support and glance around Mayo's Center for the Spirit. Beige carpet swirls with tan into a large spiral that meets in a small circular gathering space sheltered by ocean-blue stained-glass panels. I'm pulled like a magnet to the wooden wall on my right, stacked with simple horizontal slats filled with scraps of white paper tucked inside. It's a prayer wall.

I've barely prayed in months. My life seems locked in some liminal phase. Weeks and months pass, but this sickness just hasn't. I am stuck, spending nearly every hour of my life in bed while everyone else gets to have a life. I exist in the dark, shrouded by the disappointment of nearly no improvement. Sometimes, despair is my closest companion. Sometimes, I wish I'd let my throat close. I was afraid of dying, and now I'm afraid of living the life I was left with.

My life and faith have been emptied of everything but rest. I cry to a void I barely can name, a God who has gone silent. And I know God is not some gas that fills our voids nor a genie who grants our wishes. But maybe God is the ground beneath our grief.

I haven't stopped believing in God. I've stopped trying to bud belief in the bitter cold. I haven't forgotten my faith. I'm letting it lie fallow.

For so long, I've felt like a seed trapped in bad soil, but in this dark, womblike room tucked between the hallways of Mayo, I can see that my suffering is shared. Every scrap of paper tucked into this prayer wall is proof of a person like me, planted in pain, connected by sorrow. The wood-paneled wall is a web.

I take out a pen and write a prayer on one of the scraps stacked on the counter.

Breathe life back
into my every bone.
Revive my spirit.
Grant me determination
and courage
for the road ahead.
Sustain and heal me, O God.
Amen.

I fold the small slip of paper in half and place my prayer in the wall, trusting beyond trauma that my separateness is the real illusion.

HOBBLING

TWO DAYS LATER, I sit in a blue armchair on the fourteenth floor of the Gonda Building beside a giant waiting room. My legs rest on the armchair beside me, and I stare out floor-to-ceiling windows at the roofs of hotels against a light blue sky. This morning, I waited in yet another waiting room, trying to get a last-minute appointment in immunology. I left with an appointment scheduled for February. I fly home tonight. I don't want to come back to Minnesota in February, if ever.

Yesterday I got the knee MRI the rheumatologist ordered, and now I'm waiting to see a nurse practitioner in orthopedics to discuss the results. I've pushed for doctors to take the pain seriously, all while struggling more and more to walk. Perhaps in finding microfractures—whatever *that* means—I'll finally know what's going on and what I can do about it.

How can so much go wrong in less than six months? Tears fall down my soft, round face.

A woman from the front desk approaches me. She tells me the provider I was going to see saw my imaging and needs me to see an orthopedic surgeon instead. *Surgeon?* I don't like that word. The woman says they've made another appointment for me, in the sports medicine building on the other side of Mayo's campus, just fifteen minutes from now.

I hobble as fast as I can through the subway tunnel, wishing

I hadn't sent Ryan home. Walking takes so much effort that by the time I reach the waiting room, I'm dripping sweat, even though it's below freezing outside.

Once I'm seated in the exam room, a young doctor pulls up images of my knee on a computer. He turns to me with tense, raised shoulders, like his body is holding the weight of what he just saw.

"I'm so, so sorry."

I hear the words *avascular necrosis* and *decay* but nothing else sticks. The doctor says this is beyond the expertise of his department, and that I'll need to see a different surgeon instead. He sends me back to the main building, back to the fourteenth floor, and I hobble back on a knee I was just told is full of tiny fractures and decay.

Surgeon. Necrosis. The words stab like knives in my mind while I struggle to walk. I don't even have time to google the diagnosis to make it back to the orthopedic surgery department in time.

I'm breathless when I reach the next surgeon's office. A resident enters the exam room, his shoulders yoked with weight. He extends a hand in greeting, and a storm cloud of pity travels across his face. He shakes his head. "You've already been through so much." *Word travels fast here.*

A middle-aged surgeon enters the room and has me lie on an exam table to assess the range of motion in my knees. Thin paper crinkles beneath me. I watch his face for clues. When I sit back up, he says I probably need surgery. He points at images of my knee on the screen, and I listen to what he's saying, but it's like I have earplugs in. Everything is muffled. The words are too sharp to absorb.

NECROTIC

I'M HUNCHED OVER in a metal booth at the Minneapolis airport. The airline counters are all topped with tinsel—Christmas is just a few days away. Most of the people around me seem happy, headed home for the holidays. The seat is hard beneath my throbbing joints, but the booth has a high divider, and I need privacy. After that extra surgeon appointment, I missed my shuttle and had to get an Uber and rush to get to the airport on time. Now that I know I'm not going to miss my flight, I try to recount everything I just learned. I press a palm to my left knee, as though touching it might make it feel real.

Just hours ago, a surgeon held my knee in his hands, moving it back and forth to test its flexion before pulling up images on a computer.

"Do you see this?" He pointed at dark areas, jagged lines, and rubble nestled inside a bone. *My bone. My femur.*

"You have a condition we call avascular necrosis, or osteonecrosis. It most often happens at the top of the femur, in the hip, but more rarely it can happen in the knee, like it has with you."

I looked from the surgeon to the resident, wishing Ryan were with me. I never expected to hear news like this alone.

The surgeon continued. "The high-dose steroids you were prescribed in the hospital cut off blood supply to your distal femur, and large sections of the bone in the lateral and medial condyles have died."

I didn't even know bones could die.

When a body is buried, the one part of a person that remains intact after everything else has decayed in the dirt is their bones. I lived, and a bone died.

The surgeon said he'll be consulting with a colleague who's

an expert in avascular necrosis—AVN—and that someone from that surgeon's office will be calling me to schedule an appointment and surgery.

I was too shocked to even ask what to do while I wait. *Should I be walking? Is my bone going to collapse? Am I damaging my bone every time I take a step?*

I crumple into a heap on the metal table and weep. Recovery already felt too daunting. I don't think I can bear the weight of more bad news. I don't think I can survive this getting harder than it already has been.

How am I supposed to accept that the thing that kept me alive killed part of me?

I'm haunted by what I knew by sensation long before any scan. I've been telling my doctors for *five months* that it feels like something is dying in my leg. *Dying.* It's the best word I've been able to find for how it feels. I don't even know how I recognized the sensation as decay. And I feared that doctors might think I'm either a diva or deranged for calling it that. But if I had not trusted my own perception of reality as reliable and worthy of a response, I would still be suffering in silence, disturbed by pain beyond anyone's capacity to hold, losing my ability to walk with no good reason why.

What would have happened if someone took my sensations seriously five months ago? What would the images of my femur have looked like today if a doctor had trusted my intuition that something was dying inside my leg?

IF SHE CAN SURVIVE THAT

THERE'S STILL TIME before my flight, and I feel too exhausted and alone to keep crying so hard. In the days since Ryan flew home, I've been simultaneously reading and listening to Suleika Jaouad's memoir, *Between Two Kingdoms,* and I'm close to the end.[12] For days, I've found comfort in reading her firsthand account of enduring leukemia and learning to live again after. Even though I don't have cancer, I don't know how to live with so much loss. I crave stories of those who have found a way.

Suleika's soft, strong voice tells me exactly what I need to hear: "I used to think healing meant ridding the body and heart of anything that hurt . . . But I'm learning that's not how that works. Healing is figuring out how to coexist with the pain that will always live inside of you, without pretending it isn't there or allowing it to hijack your day. It is learning to confront ghosts and to carry what lingers."[13]

It's not that I haven't acknowledged this truth of healing before. But truth, like grace, must be gathered. It glints most clearly from a collective. I need to hear this truth in the space between my pain and someone else's. To reach a destination, we need directions. I am alone in an airport far from my husband and home, carrying news and pain that are changing the course of my life, but Suleika's story stands as sturdy as a road sign.

If she can survive that, I can survive this.

I hear Suleika read the final lines of her memoir right as my boarding announcement is called.

12 One of my favorite and perhaps nerdiest ways to *treat myself* is to pair an audiobook with a physical or digital copy, listening and reading simultaneously. It's like a multisensory immersion in someone else's words. 10 out of 10. Highly recommend.

13 Suleika Jaouad, *Between Two Kingdoms: A Memoir of a Life Interrupted* (New York: Random House, 2021), 311–312. Kindle edition.

I PROMISE.

WHEN I GET home, I buy myself a desk for Christmas. Not even really a desk, but a long stretch of pre-cut woodblock countertop from IKEA with a white cabinet and chest of drawers for legs. I want to write on a symbol of space.

Years ago, after a reviewer of one of my books called me "biblical but bitter," I said that as long as people confuse honesty with bitterness, I'll keep fucking writing. A reader named Karis, who lives with chronic pain, cross-stitched *keep fucking writing* onto fabric encircled by a green vine. The hoop has been hanging in my bedroom, willing me to keep journaling, and now it will hang above my massive desk.

Fatigue all but chains me to bed every single day, but I order the desk anyway. The purchase is a promise to myself.

I *will* finish writing the book that has become a story I never would have imagined for myself. I wish this wasn't the story I had to tell. But it's the story that's mine. I will write my way through weakness. I will pen a path to strength. I will stitch something beautiful from my pain.

PART IV

This is what I know: that the small is huge, that the tiny is vast, that pain is part and parcel of the gift of joy, and that this is love, and then there is everything else. You either walk toward love or walk away from it with every breath you draw. Humility is the road to love. Humility, maybe, is love.

BRIAN DOYLE,
One Long River of Song

COMORBIDITIES

JANUARY

THE EXAM ROOM smells faintly of lemon disinfectant. Posters of the pulmonary system and asthma processes line the far wall. Ryan sits beside me, his hand resting on my thigh in a silent bid for strength. I clutch a tissue in my left hand—ready for the tears this conversation could bring—while I anxiously swipe through screenshots of test results from Mayo with my right. I want to be prepared for this conversation with my rheumatologist, whom I jokingly like to think of as Dr. Space, because the genius's other job is working for NASA.

After a twenty-minute wait, Dr. Space knocks at the door.

"KJ! It's so good to see you sitting up!"

I beam. In all our previous appointments, I've been too fatigued to sit in a chair, lying instead in a heap on the exam table or slumped over in my wheelchair. Sometimes I forget that even slow progress is progress.

Dr. Space has dark hair and skin like rich earth. He's always intense—sarcastic, but deeply kind.

"How was Mayo? Was it a complete waste of time?"

I laugh. "No. *You* were right. It's good that we went."

I share the bad news about my knee. Dr. Space holds a hand to his head, face crumpling like the tissue in my hand.

"We did get some clarity on why I'm still so sick, though." I hand over my phone with the test results pulled up and relay what the Mayo rheumatologist said about mixed connective tissue disease.

"Well, I have to say," Dr. Space hands me back the phone, "I disagree slightly with the Mayo rheumatologist. I've been tracking your bloodwork and symptoms, and I believe we have enough evidence to call this lupus." He folds his arms over his white coat and striped button-down.

"Okay . . ." I mumble. "What does this mean? Have I always had lupus, and we just didn't know it? Were my past rheumatologists wrong about me having Ankylosing Spondylitis? Have I been on the wrong treatments all along?"

Dr. Space looks at me squarely. "I believe you've always had lupus, but that it took something this big, this life-threatening, for lupus to show us her whole face."

I swallow back tears. "Well, it definitely was big."

Ryan squeezes my hand.

"It's rare to see them together," Dr. Space continues, "but I believe you have both AS *and* lupus. And we need to more aggressively treat both. You weren't on the wrong treatments; you just weren't on all the treatments you need. I'd like to start Benlysta right away to better target lupus, and I'd like to double your dose of Cosentyx for AS."

I wring my hands. Dr. Space reaches toward them and begins pressing on each knuckle, checking for swelling. I mention a few joints that are tender and then interrupt his exam.

"So, the MRI report on my left knee mentions possible 'infarction' on the right side, too." I gulp. "I've looked it up. AVN most often attacks bilaterally. How do I know that femur isn't dying, too? How do I know I don't have dead bones everywhere?"

Dr. Space inhales like he's about to dive in deep water. He

exhales, leveling with me. "I've had one other patient get AVN after high-dose steroids like you, and she had it in several joints. It's possible that's happened in your case, too."

I bury my head in my hands, wishing I could hide my tears. Ryan rubs my back.

"It's going to be okay, KJ." Dr. Space rests a hand on my shoulder. "Even if you have AVN in multiple joints, you can have surgery one by one and still lead a good life. And with lupus and AS, I really do believe we're going to get this flare under control."

I want to believe him, but I wonder if he gets how much this hurts. I wonder if he understands how heavy hope has become.

VOWS

"I'M SO, SO sorry," the provider on the other end of the phone says, and then pauses. "The MRI showed that it's in your right knee, too."

Ryan's inside Torchy's, picking up tacos for dinner. I'm in the Jeep in the parking lot, clutching my phone in shock. Having AVN in both my knees means my chances of having it in every joint that hurts is high. I could be facing years of surgery. Years of pain beyond description. Dr. Space says it'll be okay with surgery, but I've joined the online support groups. I know it's often not as simple as that.

I stare at my phone, a little metal box of bad news, and glance up at the sky. Pikes Peak is covered in snow and blanketed by clouds. Light leaks through, as though the clouds are crocheted.

I'm not just fighting disease. I'm fighting despair. I didn't get a choice nor a warning in being pumped full of the high-dose steroids that cut off my bones from blood. But I do have a choice in whether I will be crushed by what is crumbling.

I wipe my tears and steel my face to the blue-and-silver sky. I touch my knees and tell them: *We are going to get through this. We are going to hike again.*

Now is the time to grieve, not give up. I grit my teeth and summon new resolve. I speak out loud to my whole self:

No more despair.

I cannot be conquered by this. I have to get stronger. Mentally and physically. I have to practice resurrection until it becomes reality.

We eat our tacos at home, and in between bites, I explain to Ryan how I had to choose—really *choose*—to not despair. It's not as simple as saying it. "I'm so sorry you have to deal with all of this with me, too. It's so much."

Ryan gets up and places his hands on my shoulders. "In sickness and health. You don't just opt out."

I know he means it about himself, but it's about me, too.

We decide to uncork the bottle of champagne Mish bought us for Christmas, and pour it into two vintage pink glasses. Courage always deserves celebration.

I raise my glass toward Ryan and toast. "No more despair."

He clinks his glass to mine and echoes what will save us. "No more despair."

SONDER

I NEED A way to say yes to my life. It's something I've learned as a somatic-oriented trauma therapist: moving the body moves the mind. So, a few weeks ago, I started swimming at the gym directly across the street from the hospital. I still barely have energy to leave bed, and the pain in my knees and shins has become so severe I can barely walk more than a few steps. I mostly use a wheelchair now. But in the water, I briefly become weightless.

I step into crystal-blue water, and its warmth wraps around my aching joints. A sky-blue noodle holds my weight. I lean back as light pours into the pool from windows high above. I let the light linger on my face. The square therapy pool is quiet today, nearly empty, save for me and an older gentleman in the shallow end. He holds water weights in his hands and draws his arms in and out before setting his weights down and beginning what looks like a bicycle motion with his legs, moving toward me and my floatie in the deep end.

I recognize him and wave. I've come to assume that anyone who shows up here as often as I do has a story of why. The poet and novelist Kaveh Akbar calls this sense *sonder,* the awareness that each random person you pass is living a life as complicated and important as your own.[1]

I swim toward the older gentleman. "Hey—what's that motion you're doing?"

"Oh, this? You can pedal your legs like you're riding a bike. And if you want, you can add in your arms, too, kind of like a modified breaststroke."

1 Kaveh Akbar, *Martyr! A Novel* (New York: Alfred A. Knopf, 2024), 176.

"Oh!" I give it a try. "That feels *good*! I've been struggling to figure out what to do that won't hurt my joints too much. Laps hurt way too much, but I have to find a way to move."

"That's how I learned this one!" The man keeps pedaling. "I broke my back one year ago, and swimming is how I've built back up my strength."

My face sparks in a smile. "I had a feeling there was a reason you show up here as much as I do. I'm sorry about your back." I heave out a sigh and decide to tell him about my bones. His eyes are soft with sadness, and he glances down, bowing his head in empathy.

For the next half hour, I pedal across the pool from him, another person who is no stranger to slow recovery, and I feel like a wave in a sea rather than a half-empty glass of water about to be gulped.

Multiple days a week, I swim in the shadow of the hospital where I nearly lost my life. And in every stroke, despair turns into determination.

Don't give up on your life.

PLACES

THE NEXT WEEK while swimming, I think of what Dudley, the Apache elder, told that researcher: *Wisdom sits in places. . . . You must remember everything about them. You must learn their names. You must remember what happened at them long ago.*

Every doctor I have refers to my body as *it*. I'm tempted to do the same. *It* is the thing that broke. *It* is the problem to solve.

But as I move my body, I begin to see the strength I feared I lost. I visit, ever briefly, the joy that is now rare. I glimpse, in flashes, the goodness that has always pulsed through breath and bone. I honor, in how hard it is to move, how much this body has endured. I choose to call my body by name.

"This body is housing—enclosure and infrastructure. Sometimes I wonder," memoirist Jeff Chu writes, "*Can this body also be my home?*"[2]

Wisdom sits in places, and I'm discovering the body is not a thing to possess nor a problem to solve, but a place to love. The body is a place where wisdom sits.

MURMURATION

I HAVE TO go back to Mayo in February after all. On February 22, a surgeon will drill dozens of holes into both of my femurs to give the dead tissue a chance at restored blood flow. He'll also drill into my hips to harvest stem cells, which will then be spun down and injected into the holes in my knees in hope of stimulating new bone growth. Lately, the pain in my legs has been so bad at night that *I scream*. It all seems straight out of a horror film, if you ask me.

And we still don't know if my other major joints are dead, too. I've been fighting insurance to get scans of each one. The faster you find AVN in a bone, the better your chances are at saving it, but the way insurance keeps denying imaging, you'd think I was a kid begging for candy, not an adult asking for the right to stand and walk and work.

2 Jeff Chu, *Good Soil: The Education of an Accidental Farmhand* (New York: Convergent Books, 2025), 156.

We all know someone who can't see past their pain, someone who is so bitter about what their life has become that they can't see through the cloud of their own complaining. I fear becoming *that* friend, slowly sucked away by life's brutalities until I'm just an energy vampire—but that no one will tell me; they'll all just back away slowly until no one is left.

But that's not what has happened.

One of my friends texts me a photo every single day with a glimmer of goodness. She knows I can barely leave the house, so she sends me photos of sunsets and sparkling snow. Yesterday, Dr. Space texted and called colleagues all over the Denver metro to find me more medical support, and then he spent forty minutes on the phone coaching me through what I need to get well. Today, a friend who lives over a thousand miles away texted me a photo of herself in a hospital bed, holding—for the first and last time—her tiny baby girl, who never got to take a first breath.

I've feared being left behind, but lament can locate us, letting others find us with care in the midst of loss.

On the way to the pool today, I saw a murmuration of birds dance across the steel-blue sky above the hospital. Hundreds of starlings swooped and shifted as one, spinning a slice of sky over an ugly road into a stage.

When I got home, I searched online, curious to know the purpose behind the grace of their ballet. I learned that starlings encircle one another, moving forward by moving toward one another at the center, because their collective movement keeps them safer than flying alone.

THE STRONGEST PART

EVEN CONCRETE IS not as strong as the human femur. To break this bone, cars must collide, axes must strike, hammers must fall. Only great force can break a femur, but steroids killed large portions of both of mine.

What happens to the soul of a person when the strongest part of their body dies?

I can't heal the microfractures in my femurs with a little more faith. I can't restore blood flow to the ends of my bones with somatic stretches. I can't, as one commenter on my Instagram suggested, just take more calcium, and suddenly have strong bones again. I need the care of others—a surgeon and my spouse included—to walk again.

In my dying femurs, I encounter the same truth I found in redwood forests. The collective care that healing a bad break or big burn requires exists wherever life does. The tallest trees in the world endure because the smallest filaments of fungi carry nourishment from tree to tree. Through underground fungal friendships more vast than the distance from earth to the moon, redwoods intertwine their roots, holding one another up through fire and storm.

The continuance of life has always been communal. After the Deepwater Horizon oil spill of 2010, oil choked coral forests like lungs sick with pneumonia. Brittle sea stars coiled around as much of the sick coral as they could, cleaning them back to health.[3] Elephants have been observed lifting injured elephants

3 Danielle Olson, "A Brittle Star May Be a Coral's Best Friend," Smithsonian Ocean, August 2017, https://ocean.si.edu/ocean-life/invertebrates/brittle-star-may-be-corals-best-friend.

to safety with their tusks and trunks.[4] Bees learn from other bees to tend the sites of their wounds. Some birds share food and shelter with injured birds, even of different species.[5]

When the strongest part of us breaks or dies, we are repositioned to hear and tell a stronger story. No longer stars nor separate or supreme, we become part of the universe of care, bound up in the innate ecological intelligence of interdependence that could save us from ourselves.

THE GAME

I ARRIVE AT the infusion center in my wheelchair but am given a room that can't fit it. A new nurse awkwardly shifts the chair around the tiny square room like it's a piece of a Rubik's cube. I stand, waiting, hurting. Once my chair is pushed into a corner where I won't even be able to get to it all day, the nurse asks if I have a port. Tears flood my face, and I can't bring myself to explain why.

I carry a super-glued porcelain heart into every room I enter. Sometimes one look or question can crack it right back open.

About five hours into IVIG, Dr. Space knocks on the door. He pulls up a stool beside my IV pole. I tell him about the virtual immunology appointment I had with Mayo last week. "They said their best theory on what happened to me is that I had a rare cytokine storm. Without all the steroids in the hospital, I

4 "Elephant Facts and Statistics," IFAW, April 24, 2024, https://www.ifaw.org/journal/elephant-facts-statistics#:~:text=13.,them%20by%20stroking%20their%20trunk.

5 Alexander F. Skutch, "Helpers Among Birds," *The Condor* 63 (May 1961): 198–226, https://sora.unm.edu/sites/default/files/journals/condor/v063n03/p0198-p0226.pdf.

likely would have had multiple organs shut down." Dr. Space's eyebrows launch like a rocket toward his hairline. "I guess that's the closest thing to an answer we're gonna get," I say.

He agrees with the theory and that this will probably always stay a mystery. "Hey, speaking of steroids, I've got good news!" He shifts on the stool. "There are no signs of AVN in your shoulders or wrists!"

Even though I've already read the reports, hearing it from Dr. Space makes the relief real. He sweeps a chunk of straight black hair out of his eyes. "Your shoulders and wrists all have some minor joint damage from your other conditions, so that's probably what's causing your pain there."

I erupt in laughter. "It's pretty fucked up when damage from disease is good news compared to bone death from your other disease, isn't it?"

We laugh so hard, I have to wipe away tears.

Dr. Space explains he's not surprised I have some new joint damage, considering how active my diseases are right now. I shrug.

"Well, hopefully in a year you'll be doing so much better."

I don't know whether to laugh or cry at that. My doctors don't realize they're playing fast and loose with their timelines—more loose than fast. Four months ago, Dr. Detective predicted I'd be back to working full-time in six months. Now Dr. Space is quoting a year.

He turns to leave and acknowledges my frustration. "You've been dealt a very shitty hand, KJ."

But, fuck, I think, *I'm still playing the game.*

THE RIVER OF TIME

CHRONIC ILLNESS TRANSFORMS our relationship with time. Clocks cannot measure the way illness both swells and stalls time. Symptoms slow me, but the ticking of a clock cannot capture how surrender stretches both my efforts and my attention, turning time into a construct and trust into a wand.

We who are chronically ill might just be the world's most secret magicians, people humbled enough by our limits to trust that time can, indeed, multiply. We lose time to illness, and yet, that loss often compels us to live the time we do have with a fullness few know. When we surrender to the flow of our fragility, we encounter the everlasting.

I belong to a larger river of time now. My hope is not in quick relief but in slow, hard-fought healing.

I must surrender to the river's flow.

I've had to let my life become as small as a drop of water. I swell. I surge. I sink. I am vapor and I am cloud. Every time I fall, I am but rain returning to a river that will never run dry.

BENCHED

FEBRUARY

"WITH LUPUS AND Factor V, you have a lot working against you." Dr. Drill shields his arms over his light gray and blue plaid suit. We're back at Mayo, in a cramped and windowless exam room. "It is very difficult to restore blood flow to a bone that is being assaulted every day."

I clench Ryan's hand. "I understand." Hope creeps from my mouth like vapor, filling the small exam room yet evading my grasp. "I consulted with that coagulation specialist you asked me to—"

"Yes," Dr. Drill interjects. "Those coagulation panels didn't really tell us anything new. The majority of patients who are on high-dose steroids never get AVN, and it usually remains a mystery why some, like you, do."

"What are her chances of success?" my dad growls from the other side of the exam room. He's like a coiled metal spring of stress, about to pounce on my surgeon. Mom's beside him, wringing her hands.

"I can't say that. I can't promise that this will work. At the very least, core decompression *might* reduce some of the pain inside her bones from the pressure that's building up in them. At the very best, we'll see some bone regeneration. But as I said"—he holds up a hand like a stop sign—"with her conditions, there's a lot working against that happening."

Mom has covered the lower half of her face with a hand, trying to hide what remains obvious—fear, and a broken heart. Dad coils forward, jaw clenched.

Dr. Drill adjusts his round, black wire-frame glasses. "Look, it's possible that the surgery won't help at all. But it's the only option we have for her condition. And I wouldn't do it if I didn't think there was a chance it would help."

For a moment, we're all speechless. My surgeon's somber attitude isn't entirely surprising. Over the past month, it's become clear that my case of AVN is, like all of my health issues, *complicated*. One surgeon in Colorado wouldn't even meet me after seeing my scans. "It's good that you are already scheduled for surgery at Mayo," he wrote in an email. "That's the best place for someone like you." *Someone like you.*

I shift from bad odds to preparation. "So, I *really* have to be totally non-weight-bearing for six weeks?"

Dr. Drill's nod is a period. "With the number of holes I need to drill to reach as many necrotic areas as possible, your bones will be very fragile. At six weeks, you can begin to bear weight, but even then, only slowly." He meets my eyes like a laser beam. "It will take time to walk again."

My sigh is a deflating balloon. I knew this already, but I needed to hear it again. Since I'll be fully in a wheelchair, unable to place *any* weight on my legs at any time, I have to recover at my parents' house in Montana while Ryan returns home to work. Our home is two stories, with the bathrooms and bedrooms upstairs. It's been a special kind of cruel to see the dream of owning a home become reality, only to become too sick to enjoy it, and now, too sick to get up and down my own stairs.

"It's good you have your family here," my surgeon says, looking from me to Ryan, Mom, and Dad. "You're going to need their support."

I'm scared about surgery but even more scared at what my life will become if it doesn't help. It has been so hard to hope. But I look at my family, scared alongside me, and I remember: hope is a team sport.

EMPTIED

EARLY-MORNING SUN STRETCHES through the window of my hospital room. Surgery was nearly twenty-four hours ago, and I'm bleary-eyed from barely getting any sleep. Last night, I felt like I was trapped on a bed of fiberglass, itching everywhere but unable to stand or move, my legs swollen, covered in ice packs, and tethered to the bed by pumps meant to prevent blood clots. I haven't been that itchy since anaphylaxis. Apparently, severe itchiness can be a reaction to general anesthesia. For hours, I coached myself to not freak out, and it was during that anxious stretch that I had to learn a whole new life skill: BEDPAN.

At first, when the CNA placed the bedpan under my butt, I couldn't convince my bladder to go. It seemed too gross to pee where I sleep. So the nurse brought in a special tech, whose sole job is bladder ultrasounds, to determine if I needed to be "emptied."

"I'm already emotionally emptied," I quipped, "so I sure hope you don't have to manually empty my bladder, too!"

"We've already done this to you once," the tech replied, shaking her head laughing. Apparently, a catheter was placed in me in the recovery room after surgery, but I only recall a vague and hazy memory of warmth. I woke up wet, and evidently, this is why: the catheter had come undone, which was extra perplexing considering I didn't even know one had been placed.

It's one thing to have a catheter placed when you're semi-unconscious and another to have to remember the experience. So I tried the bedpan again, this time, determined to get over my obviously strong sense of decorum.

I filled that orange baby up to the fucking brim. It felt like I was sitting in a tiny butt-sized bathtub filled with my own urine, but I held myself up, hands on a steel grab bar above the bed, silently praying I wasn't soiling both myself and my sheets.

I thought that was a low moment, but an even lower moment came next when THE NURSE HAD TO WIPE MY BUTT, crotch and all. Thank God—I was so drugged, I barely cared.

But, damn, that kind of medical touch *sticks with you.* I feel like I'm gaining muscle memory for intrusion that I'm powerless to refuse, because it simply has to happen. Butts have to be wiped whether you're a baby or not.

I'm not sure anyone can prepare you for the crude realities of recovery, for the humiliation intrinsic to healing. We all have to learn the hard way that healing can't happen without help.

THE DRILL

I'VE BEEN TOLD my surgeon stopped by the room yesterday before I was fully lucid, so I was too out of it to ask him any questions. I think my family was, too. We were all in some post-surgery stupor. It's still hard for me—really, for any of us—to believe that this is real, that getting a port somehow led me here, to Mayo, where a drill cored my dead bones. The only thing my surgeon said that stuck was that the inside of my knees now look like Swiss cheese.

A surgical resident just stopped by and wrapped my knees with Ace bandages to help my sausages shrink. He said I'll need to keep my knees wrapped until the severe swelling subsides.

Before he wrapped my legs, the resident showed me my incisions for the first time. There are two stitched holes on the sides of each knee, along with two on my hip points where they harvested my bone marrow.

"I'm having a hard time visualizing how that's possible," I said. "How could you drill so many holes through such small incisions? How big was this drill?"

He paused and scratched his head, mussing his blond hair. Then he grabbed a pen from his suit's front pocket. He handed it to me to show me the size of the drill bit that went through my skin, IT band, and outer bone to core the dead tissue at my depths.

It was about the size of the clicker on the pen I am writing with right now.

"IT'S SO SACRIFICIAL OF YOU TO GIVE UP WALKING FOR LENT."

I READ MY friend Ila's text and laugh for a minute straight. Only a fellow sick person could text me that and not get a verbal bitch slap in reply.

I've remained itchy since surgery, so my medical team has me on IV Benadryl, which makes me sleepy but slaphappy. I show the text to Mom, Dad, and Ryan and am doubling over in my hospital bed cackling when there's a knock on the door.

An occupational therapist and a physical therapist introduce themselves, and one steps outside and returns a second later with a wheelchair.

Euphoria crashes down. "How about we start with putting on pants?"

So far, I haven't been allowed to leave bed since surgery, and my post-op pain is so searing that the thought of having to pull on pants sounds like a violation of the Geneva Conventions. Mom grabs a pair of black sweatpants for me from a bag at her side. One of the therapists helps me shift to the edge of the bed, and I find that even just slightly bending my knees over the mattress is torturous. She crouches at my feet, handing me the pants. I groan at the effort of reaching down and realize I don't know how to do this. I don't know how to put on pants without standing.

I drop into a pile of pillows like a turtle retreating into her shell. I hide my face, red with sudden tears, in the pillows. *Why did I think I could handle having major surgery on both my knees at once?*

Mom asks the therapists to give me a minute. They step outside, and she holds me there on the edge of the bed, rubbing my back while I weep.

This is what I have to do, I coach myself. *No one else can do this part for me. I have to learn.*

"Okay." I take a deep breath. "Bring them back in. I'm ready."

I put my heart into the rest of the therapy visit, learning how to slither into my pants like a snake, learning how to shift my weight and use my arms and core to transfer from the bed to the wheelchair and from the wheelchair to the toilet.

I wipe away a bead of sweat from my brow as one therapist mentions she's surprised at how well I'm already transferring. "You must have a lot of upper body strength," she praises.

And I smile at the realization that all the time I've spent in the therapy pool, as feeble and sluggish as it felt, gave me exactly enough strength to make it through what comes next.

DAYDREAM

MARCH

IT'S HARD TO imagine my legs ever feeling good again. Really, it's hard to imagine feeling good at all.

But I've decided that's what I must do.

It's been nine days since surgery, and post-op pain and nausea have been all-consuming. I can't fully bend my knees, but I've started stretching my attention as I work through my range of motion exercises. I slide my heels against the soft brown leather of the outstretched recliner and, in my mind, I'm stepping onto my favorite trails. When I wince, I see aspens and streams. I look out the windows at snow-covered mountains and conjure a future full of wildflowers. I pump my ankles and imagine rivers of red blood returning to marrow that was marred.

Fear paints black over the future. I'm tempted, daily, to swirl the primary colors of pain into one big black blob. But I sense that to give myself a chance at healing, I have to partner with pain as a creative force. I want to close my eyes to this entire brutal season—if I could order a coma on demand, I would. But my body needs me to try believing, even after everything, that the same energy that makes the snow fall and the sun rise is still here, thrumming within my bones.

CAN

I'M HALFWAY THROUGH six weeks of total non-weight-bearing. Halfway through needing my parents' help to even get to the bathroom. Halfway through missing Ryan, who has been back home working while I work on getting well. He's visiting now, here at the halfway mark, and Resa is curled at my feet, snoring as I write.

Surviving life-threatening illness is a gift that comes with so much grief. We get to live, but the life we are left with is altered. Sometimes I think surviving my own survival is harder than it was to hold on in the first place. I've been left with so many losses and limits, and if I'm honest, most of the time I feel sad.

In this season of limits—when I can't walk, can't work, can't drive, and can't even live in my own home—I'm learning to let others love me, not in the way I wish they could, but the way they *can*.

My whole life, I've wished my dad could welcome more of me, that he could be soft when I sting. One night during the first week of staying here in Montana, I burst into tears over how much pain I was in and how much I missed Ryan, and Dad—for real—roared back, "I can't handle your emotions!"

My dad might not know what to do with my tears, but he does know how to creatively turn problems into possibilities. He's always been an innovator. Every December, our Christmas tree outlasts the season thanks to a self-watering stand Dad made when I was little, before anything like it existed in stores. Around the same time, he welded rebar into a collapsible, adjustable grill for our summer campfires, so that even if our campsite only had a ring of stones, we could still cook anything over flames. The man hasn't met a problem he can't solve. Except for the illnesses that have taken his daughters to hell and back.

When my dad learned I'd be recovering from surgery for a long stretch at his house, he instantly went to work getting it ready for me. He built a huge ramp so I could get in the front door and a small ramp into my makeshift bedroom. Then he started plotting a plan to create a motorized lift system so I could access his hot tub as soon as my surgeon let me back into water. While I was in surgery, Dad was brainstorming and ordering parts.

Last night, snow fell softly as I sat shivering in my wheelchair, wearing only a black swimsuit, excited to get back in water for the first time in weeks. Dad helped me wriggle a blue sling under my legs, then fastened its straps onto a white frame he had specially welded for me by a friend. The hoist *click click click*ed me up above my wheelchair, and though I have never weighed more, I laughed like I weighed nothing. Ryan and Kenzie grinned next to Mom as she held up her phone, capturing the whole wild debacle on video. "I should send this to your surgeon!" Dad pushed the hoist along its track, and we all roared with laughter as I dangled above the steaming water.

Dad lowered me in, and hot water instantly enveloped my hurting bones with relief. As he helped me out of the sling, I grabbed his arm, tears filling my eyes. "Thank you for making this possible for me."

He smiled and shrugged. "It was the only way I could think of to show you I love you."

And in a new way, while I can't stand or walk or work, now I can see. Limits can become the land where we encounter just how loved we already are.

BUOYANT

ABOUT A WEEK later, I started swimming again. The Bozeman Hot Springs is the only pool I've found in town that is currently open and has a lift for wheelchair users to access the water. Even so, the staff had to scramble to find someone who knew how to use it, which didn't exactly inspire the same confidence I had using my dad's lift. But it works.

My first time back in a pool, Mom swam at my side for moral support, trying out my special bicycle-breaststroke combo, complete with a pool noodle, even though we both felt self-conscious. I lasted for about ten minutes before it hurt too much, and we spent the rest of the time soaking in the heat. Mom helped me get dressed afterward and told me she was proud of me for trying.

But I miss Ryan. It's his voice I want most. To be so far apart after being so dependent on him these last several months is heavy and disorienting, like I'm sinking.

Today, I swim alone. I float on my back in warm aquamarine water that smells faintly of sulfur. The sun shines bright through a skylight high above, and I bask. I close my eyes and angel my arms and legs, stretching out on the surface of the water as though my fingertips and toes could trickle out all the grief I've been holding. My therapist recommended letting the water hold the weight of everything that feels wrong, and as I float, I feel it—not leaving, but lifted.

I turn over and begin moving toward the far end of the pool, noticing an older man with goggles swimming freestyle a few feet away. When I reach the tiles at the end of the pool, I set my noodle on the edge and follow his lead. It's my first true lap since I started swimming months ago.

It's uncomfortable but not unpleasant, and when I reach the

rectangle of light streaming through the skylight again, I flip onto my back and smile soft and wide, surprised at the return of a feeling I recognize as joy.

I'VE GOT BIG BROWS AND I CANNOT LIE

YESTERDAY I WAS supposed to get my hair cut. I've lost about half of my hair's thickness to lupus, hair that took several years to grow thick and long. Now, only a scraggly rat-tail's thickness reaches past my sternum. I think it only makes me look sicker.

Hair has long been an indicator of health for me. The first year I was on methotrexate—at just twenty years old—I lost my hair in clumps. It's never grown at a normal rate since. To lose it again, and so much worse than before, feels cruel.

When the hairstylist canceled last second with an infection, I cried for more than a minute. It's silly, right? It's just a hair appointment. But with so much loss, it was one thing I was looking forward to, one way I could start to see myself as strong again instead of simply sick. It took longer to be okay with my canceled plans than I care to write down.

So today, I got my eyebrows laminated. It's a thing. Look it up. I sent a selfie of my newly bold, big brows to friends in an ever-running old-roommate text thread.

My friend Jess's reply was fire: "I love seeing this. Every act of kindness to your body is a fist of defiance to the darkness."

And that is exactly what it was. Framing my face to fight instead of freeze.

P.S.: Moment of silence for sixth-grade me, who was bullied by a boy about her thick eyebrows AND SHAVED THEM OFF.

WHEN DO GIRLS STOP GROWING?

APRIL

PROBABLY ABOUT A year after I sacrificed my eyebrows on the altar of being accepted by a cute boy, my mom took me to see our family doctor for my annual sports physical. His nurse measured me at five feet, five and a half inches tall. Minutes later, the doctor came into the exam room and announced that I was done growing. Being me, I shed a tear, mostly because I wanted a few more inches to better my chances at becoming my basketball team's starting forward. I looked back at the doctor and declared *No*. I told him that I wasn't done growing and that he was wrong.

I grew another half inch that year, and I've still never let a doctor determine the limits of my growth.

Today was my first time walking in six weeks, right after over a week of fighting the flu while still fully in my wheelchair. Zero of five stars experience. Do not recommend.

Only time will tell if my bones will regrow or my pain will worsen, but today the best part of walking is that I suddenly feel *tall*. I guess I got so used to being under everyone's eye level in my wheelchair that standing on my own two feet feels like soaring.

When do girls stop growing?

Today I feel tall enough to bet that we never have to stop.

THE HAPPIEST PLACE ON EARTH

WE REUNITED IN the airport. When I saw Ryan at the end of the jet bridge, I leaped from my wheelchair to my feet, almost equally as proud to show him I can stand again as I was overjoyed to be together.

I didn't think I'd make it here. This trip was planned months before my medical crisis, back when planning felt possible. And the improbability of it is only adding to the magic.

Today we strolled hand-in-hand down Main Street, USA, with the scent of buttered popcorn and baked goods wafting in the air. Ryan walked while I rolled in the red electric scooter Dad rented to help make our family Disney trip accessible for my baby post-op legs. It's a strange choice to visit what is basically the capital of walking at just five days into learning how to walk again, but Disney World has long been the place where my family celebrates surviving hard things.

I kept looking from Cinderella's Castle to Ryan, my smile unstoppable. As we wove through the thick crowd, it parted while everyone paused to watch a twentysomething, bent down on one knee, proposing to his mouse-eared girlfriend in the shadow of the castle. I squeezed Ryan's hand three times, the way I have for nearly fifteen years since he bent his own knee on the edge of an Alabama canyon to ask the question that carried us here. *I. Love. You.*

I never expected Prince Charming. I expected adventure. The moment Ryan popped the question, hawks swooped over the canyon toward the river far below. We've always joked that it was like a Disney movie, that a director must have ordered right at the perfect moment: *Release the hawks!* Ryan had brought me there, to Little River Canyon, on the far south end of the mountain where we met, on the pretext of bringing me to beauty. I was hobbling around that month, arthritis flaring from a nameless disease I was just starting to accept, and Ryan convinced me to go on a day trip drive, so I could take in a beautiful place even if I couldn't do what I would have preferred—climbing or hiking. Even though that flare became embers, and I've hiked more miles than I can count in the span of between then and now, I count the birthplace of our commitment as more beautiful because Ryan accommodated—and even more important, *accepted*—grief as our companion.

I held Ryan's hand tight as we passed the newly engaged couple and turned along with my family toward Tomorrowland, where we celebrated my mom's sixtieth birthday with the backdrop of fireworks over the castle. Before the light faded, I stood beside her for a photo. I blinked back tears both to be standing and to be there, by my mom's side for a milestone moment I now know as a gift instead of a given.

We're back in bed now. My knees ache, even though I'm basically only standing to get on rides from my scooter. I fear what the pain means. I anecdotally know from my online support group that the patients with successful core decompression surgeries don't feel *any* bone pain once they start standing. Ryan just brought me ice packs from my parents' freezer in the hotel suite across the hall, and I strap them around my slightly swollen knees.

The longer I live, the more I realize that grief serves almost as the skeleton that makes joy sturdy enough to stand.

BLAME

WE'RE IN THE air over the rolling hills of Arkansas. Finally, Ryan and I get to go home *together.* Clouds fleck the hills like the last bits of cotton candy our niece and nephew couldn't finish yesterday as we wandered across EPCOT. I just watched an in-flight movie, Dan Hartley's documentary *David Holmes: The Boy Who Lived.* David was the stunt double for Daniel Radcliffe for most of the *Harry Potter* films before a spine injury on set changed the course of his life.

David's mom confessed her temptation to blame someone for her son's paralysis. "I was very angry with those who were involved. . . ." she said. "And *I* wanted someone to blame." One day while visiting David at the hospital during his initial recovery, she asked him if he'd be taking legal action against anyone for his injury. And David replied, "Why, Mum? My life's been ruined. Why would I want to ruin anyone else's life?"

Weight left my body when I heard those words. Recently I searched my online AVN support group to see if anyone had sued for the damage high-dose steroids had caused them. No one had any success. None of us were handed a specific steroid consent form in the hospital that said a doctor could choose life over limb, and many of us have struggled with our lack of choice. The main population of people who get avascular necrosis are like me, patients who have survived life-threatening autoimmune disease or patients who have survived cancer. No expert can say why some of us develop AVN and others don't. Horrific pain is the price we pay for surviving.

The damage done in my body is significant, but far less so than David's. Even so, he incurred his injuries doing a job he knew was incredibly risky. I was just trying to survive life with a special immune system; I didn't have a choice.

But the same choice remains about what to do with the blame for everything that broke.

I recall sitting in a community development class in college about cultural differences. The professor held a textbook up high. "Pretend this is a plate." He then dropped the book on the ground. "Some might say, *You broke the plate!* But in a more collectivist culture, a person would say, *The plate broke!*"

The observation captivated me. Somewhere in my childhood, I'd internalized a script where any mistake or spill of emotions meant I had ruined the day. In fact, *I ruined everything* was probably one of the phrases that most populated both my mental landscape and my mouth's vocabulary. The first twenty years of my life stung with an interior salty voice of shame, directing blame right onto myself. I broke the plate, and I knew it. The passive-voice description from another culture where society is not ordered around individual success but mutual honor blew my tortured mind. The plate broke. It just *is*.

When I heard David's mom share her son's words from the spinal cord injury hospital, I felt the blame of my brokenness shatter on the floor of this plane. All that's left in my hands is honor. And the choice of what to make with these shards.

THE ARM OF THE STARFISH

MAY

YESTERDAY MY LEFT knee gave out while swimming. It seems that even near weightlessness is no match for the might of pain in my bones. I swam the remainder of my laps dragging my left leg like a big barnacle on my body that technically is living but mostly is clinging. I'm still limping today.

I have a date set for my next surgery. August 22. It's marked on my calendar as *Maybe—Surgery at Mayo,* but the maybe only exists because the probably does.

Photos just popped up on my phone from the Redwoods: me, standing in hiking boots on a beach, orange starfish on a big black rock, the ocean an expanse in the distance. *Starfish.* I can't help but think of Sarah's silly nickname for me.

Growing into a life again doesn't happen overnight. It takes patience and persistence to tolerate being in between sickness and health. To tolerate yourself, still weaker than you wish you were. To tolerate pain, more present than you'd like. And most of all, to tolerate hope: the terrifying energy that keeps rising within you to want and seek more life and more joy.

Trying to live again feels like a risky dare. *What if I work so hard to rebuild my strength only to lose it again?*

Five days a week, I get up to work on this book, slowly rebuilding my endurance from thirty minutes of writing to a few hours. Five days a week, I show up at the pool, slowly strengthening my legs and lungs. I don't quite feel like a sea creature, but Sarah's nickname for me speaks to the place self-affirmations can't reach.

Sylvia Plath once wrote, "Sometimes I nursed starfish alive in jam jars of seawater and watched them grow back lost arms.

On this day, this awful birthday of otherness, my rival, someone else, I flung the starfish against a stone. Let it perish."[6]

I can look at my life like Sarah or Sylvia. I can nurse my soft body like a brittle starfish, trusting the cells in my limbs still carry the code for coming back to life. Or, I can let the rival inside me fling hope against a stone.

Fucking starfish. I laugh at myself and stretch out my sore legs like a star, believing again that surely if my body can do scary things, she can do stunning things, as well.

CROWN SHYNESS

"TO YOUR NEW job!"

We clink glasses, frozen mango margaritas almost spilling over their Tajín- and salt-rimmed edges. I raise a second cheers, eyes brimming with tears of pride and gratitude. "And, to *you*—to your endurance!"

Today was Ryan's first day at a new job as a hospice chaplain. He finally gets to work in our own city rather than commuting to Denver.

"I can't believe you did it. I can't believe you carried on with that commute *and* being my caregiver for a whole year."

We've both done a very hard thing in surviving this year, but it's Ryan's love that made my endurance possible. He's driven me to hundreds of medical appointments, spent his commutes fielding endless medical calls, and made sure we both stayed fed. He's held me through tears countless times, and somehow,

6 Sylvia Plath, *Johnny Panic and the Bible of Dreams: Short Stories, Prose, and Diary Entries* (New York: HarperPerennial Modern Classics, 2008), 24. Kindle edition.

he still smiles at me like he's actually glad to be with me. In my field of trauma therapy, we present nervous system regulation like a rule for relationships, but in my own dysregulation—in my inability to perform my pain more pleasantly or to always smile instead of shout—I've received love that doesn't simply regulate but restores. I've always known Ryan loves me, but now I believe it in a way I never have been able to before.

"How did you do it?" I ask.

"What choice did I have? There are some seasons when you have to live beyond your capacity because the person you love needs you. I was so tired—I *am* so tired—but I kept going because I love you."

I move aside a bowl of tortilla chips and red salsa so I can hold his hand across the table. "I don't understand how, but you've never treated me like *I* am the bad thing that happened to us."

He squeezes my hand. "Because you're not."

Somehow, as we've faced the bad thing side by side, the bitter has become sweet. In giving each other room to be less than our best selves, we've become best friends. We've chosen to be present to each other while pain changes us. We've held space for hurt—including how Ryan has been hurt by my rage—and that honesty has made us grow.

Our tacos arrive, and I take a big bite of carne asada as Ryan tells me all about his first day. He likes his new coworkers and learned a lot in a training on supporting patients with dementia. I beam. If anyone deserves to love their job, it's Ryan.

We both dig into our tacos and laugh when Ryan drips hot green salsa on his button-down.

"Hey, remember how I needed to write that affidavit?" I spent half of yesterday writing a character statement for a close friend in a court battle with her ex.

"I hate knowing J has had such a bitter taste on her tongue for years in her marriage while we're tasting such sweetness."

I eat another chip. "Do you think this is how most of my friends feel about me—with my health? Feeling an ache they've never felt?"

For a decade, I've watched my friend's partner refuse to give her room to change and grow almost as equally as he has refused to tend to his own inner health. *Why and how do some of us grow while others refuse to let things go?*

Ryan's shoulders sag. He releases a sigh like a gust of wind through the last leaves of fall. "It's wild how many couples in our lives are getting divorced right now." We counted earlier this week. At least four couples we know are in the process of getting divorced. Some are a searing surprise, some a massive relief.

I look up at Ryan as he finishes his tacos. I want a love like ours for every person in my life. We are not heroes, and our friends are not villains. We are vulnerable, every single one of us. Love is a forest, and life can bring fire. A million little things and decisions determine what breathes and what burns.

I think of my time in the Redwoods, probably because it's what I wrote about all day. I can almost hear that father's voice again, teaching his kids to look up to the crowns of the trees to learn an eternal lesson: the space between our solitudes is where the sun falls. Joy depends on holding space for one another to grow.

IN THE MOUTH OF THE MOUNTAIN

BEFORE ALL THE Awful, on days that felt dark, I would drive straight to a trail and set off without premonition or plan. Even though it stings that seeking the solace of nature has to look different for me now, I drive to Garden of the Gods in search of a bench with a good view.

I quickly realize I parked far from the most accessible benches, so I decide to try walking. Cane in hand, I step onto gravel and dirt toward a spot I love. It's my first time back on a trail, my first time walking farther than the width of my house or the length of the track at my physical therapist's office. I make it farther than I have walked in months and find a boulder where I can rest.

Here, at the foot of massive mountains, red sandstone juts from the earth like jagged teeth. You can hide yourself in the mountain's mouth.

I lean against cool sandstone, journal open, trying to be with my sadness and pain. A gentle breeze graces my bare arms, and I close my eyes, imagining my pain is a petal. I let the wind carry away the weight of wondering whether pain will keep taking up more space in my story than I want.

As I open my eyes, I see a woman, around my age, with dark brown hair. She helps her two small children scramble over the boulders beneath me. *I might never get to do that.* I sigh. *But I love that they are.*

I move a few feet lower, and just as I begin writing again, the woman approaches me.

"Hiiiiii," she says, then pauses, clearly not wanting to interrupt. "Are you . . . an author?"

I nod.

"KJ, right?"

I learn that her name is Jen, and she's a therapist in North Carolina. She's here with her family on vacation, and she wanted me to know that she recommends my books to many of her clients. I tell her that today is my first time on a trail in almost a year since having a medical crisis.

"Oh, I know," she interjects. "I've been following your story on social media. You know—I saw you scramble down that ledge with your cane. Your legs looked so stable!"

I nearly cry at the glimpse of growth.

There are tears in Jen's eyes, too. Before she walks away, she tells me thank you for writing, that the words I write matter so much.

I'm speechless.

Pain brought me here, and peace met me here. I am not comforted in seeing the purpose in my pain. I am comforted by how pain calls out for connection. I'm consoled by the curious way that choosing to be *with* ourselves in pain reestablishes a sense of kinship within and through us, sometimes to people we may never meet.

I open my hands and place them back on the cool stability of the sandstone beneath and behind me and let all of this pain pulse back into the mouth of the mountain that will outlive us all.

PRAYER IN THE PARAMOUNT THEATER

JUNE

I DON'T REALLY know what prayer is anymore. I know pulse sprinting, hand wringing, head falling. I know hope is a hammer and I am the nail, pounded into place.

Today I had a virtual doctor's appointment that ended with a flash flood on my face. We love Ryan's new job, but changing health insurance is more than a challenge when you have chronic illness. Today we found out that our new insurance is denying the IVIG treatment I've been on for two years. I've been fighting this denial for nearly a month, but today's news meant we are nearly out of options to appeal. I know how sick I will get without IVIG. Within moments, my mouth sputtered into a loop of *I can't go back. I can't go back. I can't go back.*

I drove to Nicole's terrified and tear-stained, still mumbling my mantra as I passed the hospital on the way to her house. I stepped inside, and her presence gouged around the grief wedging me to fear.

Afterward, I drove to the pool to swim out my rage at the reality that insurance companies can discontinue care whether your life has recently been on the line or not. As I dried off, I saw a message from a reader with the contact information for a dear friend who happens to be an executive with our insurance company. *Is this prayer?*

Three days ago, we sat with Nicole and Alex near the top of a sold-out theater in downtown Denver, spellbound by the joy pulsing from the stage to every seat. We watched as our state's poet laureate, Andrea Gibson, gave grief a voice so lovely that for those few hours, it was as though every loss in the room levitated. During intermission, I complimented the mushroom tattoos adorning the arms of the woman sitting in front of us, ten years my junior, and found out she flew all the way from Canada to Colorado for the chance to feel encompassed, not just by Andrea's words, but by the community they have formed. The crowd was a choir as potent as the poetry. Twelve hundred people, all gathered to revel in the joy of being human, the birthright of every kind of body.[7]

Three weeks earlier, the scheduler for my IVIG treatments had made a mistake, and I had to decide whether I would attend Andrea's show or get treatment that same day. For the first time in a year, I was healthy enough to postpone treatment instead of poetry. For the first time in a year, I got to make a medical decision aimed at enjoying my life, not just surviving it. All night, I shimmered with the electricity of being alive.

If anything is prayer, that was.

Here where the hammer falls, I know that prayer is presence that pulls us from the wall. Metallic misery, ringing out for a hand to reach us. A request for prayer is a request for presence.

Bombs still drop. Bones still die. Babies are still born breathless.

And every heart still beats to be beloved.

Maybe the miracle of prayer is not the removal of disease or the bypassing of discomfort, but an assent to undo the aloneness at the center of our ache.

7 Andrea's performance that night was filmed for a special that became part of the documentary *Come See Me in the Good Light*. We had no idea the luminosity of that night would be Andrea's last public performance before dying of ovarian cancer in July 2025. Their light lives on—a legacy of kind words to reclaim the joy of being human, including in our deaths.

THEY SAY IT'S THE IVORY ANNIVERSARY

AND TO THAT, *Good Housekeeping* and I say, "No thank you."[8] This year took its tusks to our life and held us down on the ground so long that even if we gave each other ivory towels, we'd have to throw them right out after wiping off all the mud.

Even so, we are celebrating. We've been seated outside, and the air is that perfect dry-warm-cool that makes Colorado summer evenings a dessert you crave all winter. We order drinks. I choose a lemon-forward gimlet called Jim's New Knees, because I can't resist sipping my prayers. Ryan picks the Via Ferrata, which arrives topped with a slice of candied lemon. Union Station is steps beyond the restaurant's patio, and I watch as passengers load the silver train to the airport flying to who knows where. *I'm glad to be here. Not going anywhere.*

The sky peeking through Union Station's white canopy is a perfect shade of baby blue with fluffy clouds floating in its sea. We're dining two blocks from one of our old apartments, a glass-and-chrome high-rise where we brought home both Merton as a puppy and each of our graduate degrees. The sidewalks here in lower downtown Denver stretch us back in time: walking to get soup dumplings on frigid evenings, grabbing the 16th Street MallRide to the church where Ryan worked, biking across the Platte to REI, and walking tiny Merton to the farmer's market for flowers and food (and no small amount of compliments on his cuteness). Today, we realized that though we've lived in Colorado Springs for just over a year, Denver still holds so much of our story. We don't know

8 Marisa Lascala, "Every Wedding Anniversary Gift Theme by Year," *Good Housekeeping*, updated July 10, 2024, https://www.goodhousekeeping.com/holidays/gift-ideas/g38388235/traditional-anniversary-gifts-by-year/.

how we feel about that, except that you can have a home and still feel homesick.

Back at our house, I've moved the slice of ash tree from our wedding reception to the desk in my study to remind me of what is important as I write. The rings are even and thick growing out from her core, until you reach year thirty. That year, the tree's rings became small. I don't know the exact stories behind that smallness, but I can imagine the cold and the droughts, the challenges beyond her crown of a climate ever changing in ways she was powerless to stop. Every thin ring is a sign of stress, but also survival.

Ryan and I savor each bite of crispy risotto and pancetta. I crunch crudités in whipped lemon herb feta. I'm not sure I'll ever get over the goodness of being able to eat without fear of anaphylaxis. Before our entrees arrive, we toast to our love, and I pull out a crimson box from the leather backpack at my feet.

This is not a milestone anniversary. It isn't our tenth or our twentieth. It's just our fourteenth. Most wouldn't call that special, but we know the story we survived. If we were a tree, this would be the year the rings changed.

So we give each other symbols of our survival. I hold out Ryan's new ring, hammered rose gold with a sliver of inlaid moss agate, and tell him the truest words I can find.

Mostly, I tell him thank you for loving me back to life.

Mostly, I make clear my commitment to always do the same for him.

PROPRIOCEPTION

MY HANDS LEAVE the metal stability of the balance bars on my left and right. I step with one leg onto a bouncy blue half-moon while my hands hover over the bars.

"They are there if you need them. It's okay to hold on."

My physical therapist, Ann, is always reminding me this, probably because she knows I'm stubborn. We've been building my strength to lunge like this for over a month, and I know it's the stubborn in me that's gotten me this far.

I hold my lunge, leaning into the miniature earthquake in my ankle, knee, and quad before switching to the other side.

"This is way harder than you made it look!" I laugh. Ann runs marathons for fun. A little lunge isn't going to make her shake.

"Of course it is!" Ann validates. "When the body is injured or extremely ill like yours was, it loses its sense of space. That sense is called proprioception." She pauses. "But—of course, as a trauma therapist, you already knew that."

"I did. But knowing something in theory and feeling it in your body are two different things."

I keep lunging, breathing deep and scrunching my face through the pain. I stare at the blank space beneath the clock on the white wall for steadiness. It takes all my strength to balance for five-second increments.

I step off the BOSU and wipe sweat from my face.

"It's like after all that time in the hospital, my body lost her place in space." I take a long drink of water. "It was the weirdest thing. Like my body lost track of the ground, lost trust that it would hold me. And now—" I pause to focus on stepping back on the ball. "Now, I'm finding my feet again."

THE IMPEDED STREAM

"YOU KNOW HOW you can make your wife a happy woman?" I turn to Ryan as we drive away from lunch at the Broadmoor with Mish and her boyfriend. I wag my left eyebrow up and down like it's a tail. He can't say no to that cuteness.

"North Cheyenne Cañon is just a few minutes away. I really want to see some wildflowers."

Ryan turns left instead of right. No words, just a silent yes and a smile. We open Reepijeep's windows, faces bright in the summer sun, breeze cool on our skin. The road curves and ascends. The forest becomes full.

"This is a good spot." I motion to a small opening in the pines on the right. Ryan parks on the side of the road, and I open the door. He grabs my hand. "Please be careful." I smile my yes and step toward the creek, cane in hand for support.

When I first left the hospital for home all those months ago—gosh, almost one *year* ago—my body was a felled forest. I will never forget the feeling of dragging my leg like a log. Like a tree without roots, my foot could barely feel the floor. Now I step down stone steps slowly, cautious and conscious where the old me would have leaped.

I set my cane against the steps and sit down on a rock, glad that I've finally regained the ability to crouch this low. I dip my feet into the frigid water and sigh. Light glistens off the stream's surface, brighter where the water is blocked by rocks. I step into the stream, and the cold stinging my calves is like a song, because *I can stand.* I hold my hand out to cup tall fringed bluebells at the water's edge. Their rhizomes reach beneath the surface of the soil, growing horizontally in the dark long before they bloom in lavender-tinged blue.

For months, I lay in bed, wondering if my legs would ever be strong enough to stand in the forest again. They will never be the same. My bones are forever changed. But the joy of standing in a creek surrounded by trees remains constant. And for a few brief moments, I am a rock in this stream. My body is not a set of bars blocking me from walking any farther into the forest. She is simply a note in a song no one could grow sick of hearing.

ABIDE WITH ME

WE ARRIVE TWO minutes into the liturgy and slip into a wooden pew near the back of the cathedral. I will never make a church building or institution the axis of my world again, but we like to come to the Episcopal church sometimes. Without thinking or grabbing a hymnal, I start singing the right verse and stanza with the rest of the congregation. To let my voice join a collective is a comfort. I'm glad we came today.

Until I'm not. One more verse into the hymn, I hear a woman directly behind me coughing. My shoulders turn to steel. The woman begins to sneeze large, personal thunderclaps from her nose. I try to breathe through the scripture readings, but really, I'm pointing daggers out the back of my head. *Welcome to church, where we pass germs right with the peace. Grrrr.* I imagine droplets from the woman's snot-storm drifting through the air like dust, settling in my hair and invading my face the next time I tuck a piece behind my ear. An image of my bedroom overshadows the stone and stained glass in front of me. *I can't get stuck in bed again.*

Ryan leans toward me. "You're back on IVIG," he whispers. "You'll be okay."

Ryan's right. I have protection against infections again. The insurance executive I got connected to recently ended up being a decisive force in winning my fight to continue IVIG. I'm almost certain that without her kindness, I'd still be fighting that battle and definitely wouldn't be able to risk being inside a crowded church. I long for a world where it doesn't take personal connections and privilege to access the healthcare each body needs.

The priest begins a sermon. But I'm lost in thought, trudging through my nightmares. Last night, I thrashed and screamed while I slept, trapped in the terror of being back in the hospital, with Dr. Dick looming over my bed, about to be sent home sicker than when I came. When I woke, it took a while for the safety of home to feel realer than the nightmare. Another night earlier in the week, I dreamed I was wheeled into an operating room, but the anesthesia never bloomed, and I woke up drenched in sweat right before the surgeon's drill touched my skin. Surviving our scariest stories doesn't mean we aren't scarred by them.

This week marks one year since a vein burst and everything changed, and I hear the story my sleep is telling. I hear the story my body is telling today. I'm not listening to the sermon. I'm listening to the lump in my throat and the butterflies in my chest. I want this fear to be the flutter of new wings, not caged dreams.

Cough. Cough. The lady's hacking again, and I'm out of the cathedral so fast, it's like someone yelled "Fire." I step into the sun gasping for air, face wet with tears. *Breathe.* I slow down my exhale. *You're okay.* Whether I am among people who call themselves the body of Christ or not, I will abide with my body first.

I return to the cathedral, this time in a new pew out of cough range, and slather my hands with sanitizer. I rise when Ryan does, bowing in the aisle before heading toward the altar.

Hands reach toward mine, and I lift a dipped wafer to my lips. *The body of Christ, the bread of heaven. The blood of Christ, the cup of salvation.* My body has lost her sense of place in space, but maybe this body and blood can still find me.

FREE THE FUPAS!

I CHANGE IN the locker room, stripping out of sweatpants and grabbing my swimsuit before swimming my laps. A couple of thin women in their early twenties stand across the bench from me, changing out of their sweaty workout clothes and talking about meeting their weight loss goals. I almost move to the other side of the room, because they are young and beautiful and I am scarred and sagging.

But then, I think about what their futures might hold. They might look at the zebra stripes on my sides and judge me for "letting myself go." But maybe, someday, their bodies will stretch for sickness or sadness or growing a human, and somewhere in the folds of their gray matter, a memory will tell them the truth about the goodness of the body they see staring back at them in the mirror. I know to hold this hope, because it's happening for me now. As I pull out my swimsuit, *I'm* remembering the old woman at the hot springs in Oregon who cannonballed without a care of whether her skin flapped and flopped while she jumped. She was clearly more focused on the joy of moving her body than what anyone else thought about her shape or size.

So I don't move to the other side of the room. I don't hide behind my thin white towel. I quietly pull my black one-piece over my stretch-marked fatty upper pubic area and stand back up with shoulders squared and head held high.

I want my body to be a beacon of belonging.

I smile toward the younger women as I grab my gym bag with my swim cap, goggles, and snorkel and walk with my cane to the pool.

TERRITORIAL WATERS

EVERYWHERE I GO, stories are stuck on me. They name me by my needs. They call me what they curse. They define me by my disability. I am a living reminder of the rare. I am the shattered illusion of our self-determination. I am one small representation of what sinks in this society.

But when I swim, I spring headfirst into a better story. Cold water lights each limb electric, a shock I choose instead of one I can't refuse. And the choice changes how the charge is carried.

The story's theme is strength, and it can only be told beyond the limits of language. Arm over head. Each hand, a propeller. Each leg, a fin. Each pain, a prompt. Stroke after stroke, I learn how to live with my limits without limiting myself.

No one else can tell me this story to make it true.

At the bottom of each lane is a line. The lift of each limb writes a sentence. The end of each lap turns a page. Follow the line, and you'll find the story of strength.

Tell it over weeks, and it seems possible. Tell it over months, and it starts to feel real. Tell it and tell it, until your tissues feel it's true. Let your body tell a better story until strength becomes you.

SEISMIC

BEEP. BEEP. BEEP. BEEP.

I straighten my wrist, attempting to silence the IV pump's alarm. My IV keeps occluding, since my wrist was the only vein we could get to work today.

I'm passing the time at treatment by following the switchback trail of my curiosities around Mount Rainier. I wrote the heart of this book by hand while living it, and since the middle of March, I've been giving that heart a body. Nearly every day, I open my stack of journals and decide what to tell and how I want to tell it. Above all, I'm letting the self of one year ago speak the truth of her life as she experienced it, even though how I speak of the sacred keeps quieting and changing.

I've been writing in the order of what I lived. Right now, that means writing a story I know is about to hurt. The me who explored redwoods and mountains had no idea what was coming, even though I've been surprised to find that she wrote things that were eerily prescient—like "hope lives in my bones." Lady had no idea her actual bones were about to die.

I am comforted by the coherence writing this book is giving me. As I tell myself my own story, I'm afraid to relive my own near demise. But the closer I get to those journal entries, the more comforted I am by getting a glimpse of what my soul sensed before my mind did.

One of the cruelest parts of trauma is feeling robbed of the right to choose the direction our lives will head. I was entirely blindsided when my body fell apart right after feeling her strongest. But in the pages of that first journal, in the prologue to the pain, I can see that some small and wise part of myself sensed what was to come. Every time I find sentences describing knowing things "in my bones" or moments like when I felt the urge to run feral into the sea to bless the body I had, the divide between my before and after is bridged. Writing this book is giving me room and resources to move forward into the future, not as two severed selves, but one whole.

When I was on my national parks trip, I wrote down as much as I could of what I saw and sensed. And now I get to situate some of those sensory details in the context of history and ecology.

I'm currently ignoring the beeping of my IV pump by listening to a podcast interview with a researcher from the US Geological Survey about seismic activity deep in the gut of Mount Rainier. Kate Allstadt's job is to record the voice of the volcano. Low scratchy sounds from Allstadt's recordings are spliced into the interview, which carry some of the same harmonic qualities of whale song. The mountain is always singing, but at lower frequencies than most of us can hear.[9] I learn that by listening, researchers like Kate can predict when Rainier might blow.

One year ago, I sat in another infusion suite in this building, and the blowout in one vein changed the course of my life.

I wonder what would have happened if I had been able to really hear the seismic shifts singing out from the deepest parts of me. I *was* listening. But there are some frequencies we can't

9 Kate Allstadt, interviewee, *Crosscut Escapes with Ted Alvarez*, podcast, season 1, episode 1, "Volcano Songs," Cascade PBS, January 4, 2021, https://www.cascadepbs.org/podcasts/crosscut-escapes/2021/01/volcano-songs/.

fully detect. There are some explosions we can't predict. There are some disasters we can't save ourselves from.

BEEP. BEEP.

My eighth and final bottle of Octagam is done, and now my nurse is switching me to saline before I leave. I haven't seen her since I was brand new to IVIG two years ago. Sophia nurses full-time at a local hospital and picks up shifts here every great now and then. I just gave her the brief overview of what's happened since we last saw each other.

In response to me very likely having to have a brutal bilateral knee surgery again, instead of telling me some bright-eyed bullshit like *be positive* or *I'm sure your bones will grow,* Sophia says, "No one talks about how hard it is to be a survivor."

I sit up straight in my armchair, shook awake by solidarity. Almost no one calls it like it is.

Sophia tells me that she survived cancer, but chemotherapy damaged her liver so badly, she'll have to have a liver transplant someday. Now it makes sense why she always looks a little tan, with a hint of yellow. I sit in quiet gratitude to have been nursed all day by someone who understands the cost of keeping your life.

Twenty minutes later, my bag of saline is almost empty, and Sophia sets down gauze and Coban on the table beside me. I look up from typing.

"Surviving sure has costly consequences," I say.

Sophia leans against the doorframe, waiting for the pump to beep. She nods in agreement. "I wouldn't change it, though. I wouldn't unlive it, because it changed *how* I live."

LEAP

JULY

THE WATER OF the Frio River is both cool and warm, and I swim my laps through waves of light. The sun is high, slanting through the water, shimmering over sunfish and catfish as they dart past. I look down at the light on my legs, patching them like the hide of a glimmering giraffe. I bend my knees back and forth, and for a few moments, they are painless in the sparkling light.

A friend invited me here, to a retreat at Laity Lodge in the hill country of Texas, all expenses paid. When I realized the retreat fell right before my first Anniversary of Awfulness, I almost didn't come. I didn't know what these days might dredge up or whether I was healthy enough to travel alone, hours from a hospital. But Ryan and I decided together: we'd rather approach the anniversary of me almost dying choosing to enjoy our lives rather than fearing the bad that could still happen.

The river is a thin emerald ribbon held up on either side by jagged limestone cliffs. I swim for a while with my snorkel, following the underwater cut where these cliffs once crumbled into one another, forming a crack in the earth. When I surface to rest, I watch as others from the retreat climb the highest cliff and jump off into the river.

I'm already in pain from descending the steep steps down to the river earlier, and I'm not sure if my knees can handle the climb. But I want to try. Surgery looms, along with a lack of options for my legs to reach places like this long-term. But pain grates against the potential of the moment. I feel separate from everyone else at the swimming hole, envying them for seeming so carefree. There may be no lasting remedy nor relief for me, and I realize I need a story I can live with about the pain that remains. I need a story I can tell and retell to pry myself out of self-pity, so I can show up as much as possible and enjoy my life, even while in pain.

The medicine that kept me alive killed the bones in my knees. And I could focus on the death and how much harder things might become—I already have—or I can reclaim the breath it bought me.

This pain means I did not die.
This pain means I'm alive.

I scramble up the cliff, gripping chalky rocks, breathing hard as pain stabs in my knees like knives. And I reach the top. The river reflects the bright blue sky, and I leap in, screaming, *I am alive!*

APOPHASIS

I HAVEN'T BEEN around this many Christians since before my medical crisis, and I keep needing to step out during the retreat's teaching sessions, because it all just feels *too loud*.

Being surrounded by evangelical Christians feels like coming home to a place where my native language is spoken but is no longer mine. Like a visitor from a distant country, I strain to make sense of all the sounds. My mouth can't quite form syllables that used to be second nature.

It's not that I've lost my faith. I've lost the language, or at least, this dialect.

Somewhere over the course of the last year, spirituality changed for me. I didn't stop believing in God. I stopped trying to understand all the absurdity I was plunged into. I was simply too tired, treading water, trying not to drown.

There was a time in the not-too-distant past when I shared about God's kindness and nearness and will straight from my heart, but now I struggle to speak of the sacred with any certainty. I'm not sure most of us know what we mean when we do. I was plunged into a place where words themselves become quieted by the primal presence of Love. And now, when it comes to faith, I need fewer words.

Just because I no longer experience and articulate my faith in heavily coded Christian language does not mean it is dead. Like the poet Christian Wiman writes, "I'm a Christian. Which means that I have faith. Or had it once, and with such enlivening force that to deny it now would be a denial of life itself."[10] I can't deny that the Source I've encountered at my best and at my bottom is real.

I trace the transformation of my faith to the moment one year ago when I fell into the river of time. I fell far and fast and deep, and what I witnessed in the water showed me a whole wide world, more vast than the vocabulary my brain had previously held. My lungs filled with water in the turquoise deep, and I came up gasping, lips forever changed by their brief blueness. What I saw in the water unleashed my tongue and swirled the labyrinth at the center of my ears, unhinging sound itself from speech. I came up a creature from the womb of the world, and my second first breath was belonging.

We are brief and beautiful, and every plant and fish and tree—and yes, person—speaks in a language as sentient as

10 Christian Wiman, *Zero at the Bone: Fifty Entries Against Despair* (New York: Farrar, Straus and Giroux, 2023), 92.

mine. And I know my near breathlessness was a new beginning, an implosion of the star of separation, the first sound of a kinship that is unbound.

MADAM POMFREY ENTERS THE PHYSICAL THERAPY CLINIC

A COUPLE OF WEEKS later, I stand between the balance bars, stepping up and down on the BOSU ball. My coordination and balance are so much better than when I first started PT. I can do these exercises without gripping the bars now. I pause between sets, reaching toward Ann for my water bottle.

"Well, we're finally going to see what my knees look like inside since surgery." I raise my shoulders in a shrug, but really, I'm nervous and hopeful and curious all at once. "I'm finally getting my MRIs done tonight."

I've gotten x-rays of my knees every month or two since surgery, but they can't really show bone death or growth. They're just checks to make sure the joints haven't collapsed. The real reveal will happen tonight.

Ann pauses typing into my chart and stands back from her rolling desk, crossing her arms. "I can't believe it's been almost six months since your surgery. I'm so curious to read these radiology reports."

I step back on the BOSU and hold a lunge. "What if . . ." I turn my head toward Ann in sudden alarm. "What happens if the scans show that more bone has actually regrown than we thought, but I'm still in so much pain?"

No matter how much I reframe the story in my mind about

my knee pain, it's so searing that I do struggle to imagine a life where it does not stop.

"Well"—she steps toward me at the bars—"when I've had patients who, say, had the end of their collarbone shaved off, the pain of that bone healing can be immense."

"What if . . ." I'm pondering the pages of a book I've read on repeat. She finishes my exact thought for me.

"What if it's like Harry Potter? Like Skele-Gro?"

My eyes gleam with mischief. I envision the nurse at Hogwarts, Madam Pomfrey, shuffling over to Harry's bed in the hospital wing after falling playing Quidditch and having the asshat fraud Defense Against the Dark Arts professor Gilderoy Lockhart "heal" his broken arm—by stupidly removing all the bones. Madam Pomfrey set a skeleton-shaped bottle beside Harry's hospital bed and declared, "You're in for a rough night." She then poured the steaming magic medicine into a beaker and handed it to Harry with caution and said, "Regrowing bones is a nasty business."[11]

"Maybe." I look back at Ann with eyebrows raised. "Maybe I'll get my very own Harry Potter moment." We both laugh hard, but in the way that only the desperate do. We aren't laughing because it's insane to pull medical hope from the pages of a children's fantasy novel.

We're laughing because it's the last place left to look.

11 J.K. Rowling, *Harry Potter and the Chamber of Secrets* (New York: Scholastic, MinaLima Edition, 2021), 195.

MY BONE THUGS

RYAN SITS IN the driver's seat next to me, wearing a berry-colored flatbill cap and his running clothes. He's going to work out while I get my scans. We jammed to our nineties and noughties playlist on the way here, like a weird medical pregame pump-up. Sometimes I like to shake off my stress by dancing like a total fool in the car. I give myself bonus style points anytime I can get the driver next to me to make eye contact.

Ryan just parked at the imaging center, acting as my chauffeur yet again, since I'll be drugged for this test. I've had too many panic attacks inside MRI machines to pretend they don't scare me. I feel too trapped in that tunnel of noise to not help myself through it with a little pill and a little weed. I take off my seat belt and pop both.

Suddenly, I'm scared. My left knee is aching, and I'm anxious about lying still through the entire hour exam. But more than that, I'm afraid—terrified—of seeing more necrosis on the scans. I'm afraid this ache might never go away. I place my hands on my knees, breathe a deep sigh, and turn to Ryan.

"Well, it's time for the state of our union!" I glance at my knees and then grin up at him.

He deadpans, "Let's see if your Bone Thugs are in Harmony!"

Our laughter steels me just enough to walk inside.

I check in and am shown back to a changing room, where I slip off my rings, watch, and nose ring and lock up my backpack. I wait in a chair in my socked feet and start to shake. I've waited so long for this day. I still wish I wasn't here at all.

Shit. I forgot to bring something to hold on to. I was just here Monday for an MRI of my cervical spine and clutched my holding cross the whole time. *Why didn't I bring that?* I jump up and unlock the locker, rifling through my backpack for something nonmetal to hold. I only find my journal, a pen, and my leather pouch of emergency shots. I see a pile of plastic-packed hospital socks in a bin on the floor, the scratchy kind with grippy dots on both sides.

I guess a sock can stand in for a cross. I pull one flimsy tan sock out of its package and throw the other in a bin full of used scrubs. I clutch the sock tight.

A radiology technician arrives carrying a clipboard of forms filled with my medical information. She sits down beside me, tucking back a piece of her long brown hair before picking up a pen.

"Any surgeries on the area we're examining today?"

I stifle a laugh. "Yes. Bilateral core decompression with stem cells February twenty-second."

"Of *this* year?"

"Yes. Just this year."

Her eyebrows climb an inch before she looks back to the clipboard. "Any underlying medical conditions?"

Now I'm fisting the sock. "Um . . . a lot? Do you *really* want me to list all of them?"

"Yes. I do need them all. Sorry."

I recite them, trying not to sound too annoyed. "Ankylosing Spondylitis. Lupus. Avascular necrosis . . ." She has to flip the paper over to fit everything else. The technician stands and motions for me to follow her.

She looks up, brown eyes clear. "How did this happen to you?"

I try to explain the shortest version of the story I can as we step into the cold scan room, where the white abominable snowman of a medical machine hulks, ready to growl at me for an hour straight.

"What music would you like?"

"Brandi Carlile, please." Brandi's voice has been the one barrier between me and the monster machine's howls for as long as I can remember. Earlier, I tried to count how many MRIs I've had in the past year and lost track after fourteen. *When does one become radioactive? Often, when I'm around others, I feel like I already am.*

I climb onto the table, extend my left knee into the brace for the first scan, and look up at the tech to ask for an extra blanket. I'm still shaking from fear, even with anti-anxiety meds and half a gummy on board, and this room is an icebox.

Suddenly, I recognize her. "I can't believe it! You did my last knee MRI before I had surgery! It's time to see if I have to do it all over again."

My face is approximately one-third smaller than the last time she saw me, but she recognizes me now, too. We're both amazed. The last time I saw her, she shared that her brother had AVN in his hip. Tonight, she tells me the disease that necessitated the steroids that killed the top of *his* femur is one that we share, AS. I can't believe I've been given a tech who happens to really *get* what I'm going through.

She covers me with an extra warm blanket, wishes me luck, and hands me huge headphones, which I place over my ears as the table inches into the tube. Brandi's voice comes through, quieting the machine's cacophony with song. And I start to cry. Not because I'm scared, nor because I'm sad, but because I am surrounded.

These scans will show what the next season of my life will hold. I grasp my stolen sock while the machine roars, no longer shaking, but smiling. Minutes ago, this was another shitty thing I just had to get through, but now it's yet another moment in which I've been supported.

SO MANY RAINBOWS

WE TURN TOWARD the gym. It's been two days since my scans, and I was just telling Ryan about my wish for Harry Potter magic in my bones. I began wishing it long before my PT made the connection, secretly hoping for months that the pain I've felt is not more decay, but growth. I know my sensations like a potions master knows lacewings and bat spleen. That is, rather well. It's challenging to trust your own perception of pain while remaining open to a more positive story about that pain.

I glance at Ryan as he drives. "I'd love to be wrong."

I check my phone one more time, even though the radiology tech said the results of my scans probably wouldn't be posted until Monday.

"Whoa." I'm a block of ice. "The reports are in."

Ryan parks in a handicapped spot while I read with breath knotted in my chest. My brain cross-references every term against the ones already inked in the dark dictionary housed in the stacks of my mind. *Subchondral T2 signal abnormality. Bone marrow edema. Geographic area of avascular necrosis extending from the anterior to posterior weightbearing aspect.*

I look from my phone to Ryan. "I didn't get my Harry Potter moment." My face is a wilting flower. "I'll have to wait for my surgeon to really explain, but I'm pretty sure there's still a lot of dead bone in both knees. And it sounds like there's more than before."

Even though surgery has been on the books for two or three months, I haven't bought plane tickets or purchased the forearm crutches Dr. Drill recommended for my recovery. A small part of me believed I wouldn't have to do this all over again. I love that part of me. I need that part of me.

Ryan and I hug for longer than it took to read the reports and then walk into the gym. We part at the locker rooms. He's heading to the free weights and machines. I walk to the water.

On the way to the pool, I pass every previous iteration of my mobility. In a full-length mirror, I see one self in two postures. The woman in the wheelchair is just as fierce as the one standing with her shoulders rolled back and head held high. I have come so far to remain so tender.

I reach the lap pool on my own legs and pull a pink swim cap over my hair. I step into the water, place goggles over my eyes, and push off into the lane. The cool water wakes me up to my own determination. When I reach the center of the pool, I notice rainbows radiating beneath me. Sunlight stretches through the window above, casting the lane in radiant light.

With every lap, I let lament drain from my fingers and toes. Defeat rolls out like waves from my heavy heart and head. I let the water hold what is too heavy for me.

As I reach the center on each lap, I wiggle my fingers through prisms as I pull my body forward. I sense the growing strength in my propeller legs. For thirty minutes straight, I chase rainbows. I carry the dark at my depths into the light.

When I finish my laps, I grab my phone and carefully walk it to the slab of light at the center of the pool. I take a video of myself walking into the sun. Rainbows stretch over my knees.

This is what I want to remember about the day I found out more inside me has died: I kept walking toward the light.

WE CAN DO HARD THINGS

AUGUST

BUT WE DON'T have to make them harder.

As I write, a man in a ball cap and a navy-blue collared shirt is downstairs loading our house full of parts to install a stairlift, an addition to our home that I have stubbornly resisted for an entire year, much to my friends' and family's annoyance. *Dear God, are you there? It's me, Mad Woman. I'd love to be choosing tiles for a new bathroom on our main floor, not installing a Grandma Chairiot for my dead bones.*[12]

My original plan for the surgery I secretly hoped I could cancel was that I would have one leg drilled into at a time, so then I'd at least have one literal leg to stand on while recovering. Total non-weight-bearing is a task of enormous commitment, requiring ramps and help bathing and problems one only gains enough imagination to solve after their geometry becomes enfleshed.

I thought by operating on one knee at a time, I'd be able to recover at home, hopping up and down our stairs on one leg with the forearm crutches Dr. Drill recommended I purchase long before surgery "to practice." I'd have fourteen weeks of recovery rather than six, but at least I'd be with Ryan and our dogs. It only took one long attempt at that Hopscotch from Hell to realize my surgeon's recommendation of "practicing" on my crutches was probably just a sneaky way of getting me to accept reality. Could I technically scooch up and down my stairs on my ass for fourteen weeks? Sure. But *should* I do that to myself? No.

With my best crutched plans crushed just two weeks before

12 I have nothing against grandmas; I just haven't lived long enough to be one.

having major surgery again, I pivoted hard and fast. Within minutes, I figured, if we have to go as far as renting a fucking stairlift, I might as well get the hell of recovery over faster and do both surgeries again at the same time. Within two days, our feisty little family unit figured out how to make our two-story, all-bathrooms-on-the-second-floor home temporarily wheelchair accessible. The day after my declaration, a stairlift company assessed our house and put today's installation on the books. Thanks to the wizardry of the web and the kindness of some friends, a foldable metal wheelchair ramp arrived on our doorstep just two days later. Yesterday I constructed a shower bench that doubles as my landing strip from the hallway to the toilet, since my wheelchair won't fit through the door.

Never underestimate the creative power of a woman in pain who values her wholeness.

For so long, the idea of a stairlift has felt like a symbol of struggle. And, it is. I won't pretend the reason I need a stairlift at thirty-five isn't sad. But it's also a symbol of self-compassion.

The Good Witch Glennon wrote wisdom in *Untamed* that I've carried with me ever since reading it:

> "We can do hard things" becomes my hourly mantra. It is my affirmation that living life on life's own absurd terms is hard. It isn't hard because I'm weak or flawed or because I made a wrong turn somewhere, it is hard because life is just hard for humans and I am a human who is finally doing life right. "We can do hard things" insists that I can, and should, stay in the hard because there is some kind of reward for staying.[13]

13 Glennon Doyle, *Untamed* (New York: Dial Press, 2020), 85.

That advice has carried me far. But just because we *can* do hard things doesn't mean we have to do them the hardest way. Evangelicalism steeped me in a spirituality of sacrifice; the harder something was, the holier it was, too. What if self-care and true spirituality include recognizing not just what our bodies *can* do, but what our minds and hearts need to endure hard things without becoming hardened?

THE TELLING

I HAVE FILLED six journals since the day I drove away from home with a tent on my roof and Crater Lake set as my destination. The first half of that first journal is my favorite. It is the story I prefer, the story I wish this book could have held. But every page that follows is proof of a possibility that exists for us all.

The Gospel of Thomas claims to share the secret sayings of Jesus, and one of those sayings is indicative of why I kept writing: "*If you bring forth what is within you, what you bring forth will save you. If you do not bring forth what is within you, what you do not bring forth will destroy you.*"[14]

Stories are shovels. They can dig a grave or plant a garden. The stories we are told about our pain and problems *and* the stories we tell ourselves can bury us in despair or move us into life.

When something horrible happens to us, whether suddenly or slowly, it disrupts our sense of agency. Trauma tries to bury us in believing we are too broken to even try to redirect our

14 Gospel of Thomas, verse 70, http://sites.utoronto.ca/religion/synopsis/gth.htm.

lives back into goodness. In my therapeutic work, I offer clients tools for externalization, containment, and grounding to rebuild their sense of agency.

We must give overwhelming pain a place to live outside of our bodies. A journal can be a container we come to with all that is too heavy for us to keep carrying. A journal can be a safe place to hold our hardest memories and to let our honest fear, rage, and shame be heard without judgment. The blank pages of an open journal offer us power to perceive our lives as places already brimming with more kindness and humor and beauty than we can see when we are overwhelmed by pain. It's a practice of paying attention, a practice that reconnects us to our own power to keep moving forward in lives we would not have imagined for ourselves. We may feel stuck—in bed, in a hospital, in debt, in discouragement—but the slow movement of a pen across a page can help rebuild our trust that we can rise, even with pain.

Choosing to count my worst days as worthy of documentation changed how I experienced them. Telling myself my own story changed the way I lived it.

For months now, I have sat down every day at the spacious desk in my study, sandwiched between two major surgeries, showing up hour after hour with my journals to rewrite the raw material of a story that nearly ended short. Writing this book pulled me out of bed and back into my life instead of waiting for everything to get better first. The untold story could have killed me—if not my body, then my spirit. Instead, retelling my story has given me a refuge to survive it.

Writing this book has not redeemed the pain. It has given me a way to reclaim parts of myself I lost to ruin. Sentence after sentence, I have shoveled away the shame of living in a body that struggles. I have grieved at the bottom of my own grave. I have kneeled in the dirt and asked myself: *What will you plant from your pain?*

"Even when the truth isn't hopeful," Andrea Gibson writes, "the telling of it is."[15] You don't have to write a memoir for it to matter. The very parts of your life you wish you could escape are the parts that are waiting to be witnessed, ready to save you.

Tell yourself your own story. The telling strips trauma of its power to hold you back from joy.

ON THE MOST APTLY NAMED TRAIL IN COLORADO SPRINGS

I SIT IN Reepijeep at the end of the Contemplative Trail in Red Rock Canyon. My knees throb from the short distance I hiked. Cool air dries my sweat and tears. I came to the trail today because I am tender.

In a few days, we'll fly to Minnesota again for my second bilateral knee surgery. That is, *if* insurance approves it. They've denied both the surgery and more of the specialty medications I need to protect my life. And while I have people working to overturn those denials, I don't need the stress of having to fight to receive the only help I have available to maintain my mobility. Our flight leaves on Tuesday, and I'll need an approval before then to go.

In an appointment last week, I found out I've had zero bone growth since my last surgery. I also learned I'm only the third patient my surgeon has done this major surgery on back-to-back, not because he doesn't operate much, but because my

15 Andrea Gibson, *Take Me With You* (New York: Plume, 2018), 107.

condition is that bad and that rare. "Yours is the hardest and most frustrating condition to treat in all of orthopedics," Dr. Drill said. *That's not the kind of special I'd like to be.*

The most common place to get AVN is in the hips, and replacing that joint is often a simple, though painful, fix. But knees are not hips, and repair is far from simple. Even when I do eventually get knee replacements, they won't be able to remove all the areas of dead, aching bone.

Soon, the scars that have healed will open again. My feet will forget the feeling of sole against ground. My legs will miss standing on their own strength. My mind will wonder if we'll reach mountains again. And so I came to the trail today, even though I knew it would be hard, because I need to stock a storehouse of memories to sustain me for whatever comes next.

To even be on a trail tells a truth I must hold like an arrow against my jaw. I have always aimed my life at joy. I have always arched my attention toward aliveness.

Whether I lose the still-painful mobility I've regained or not, I will not lose my resolve.

I hiked even though it hurts. I made my way through a crevice of rock formations far taller than my body. And the body of the land mirrored my life. The trail between health and illness is thin, and the only way home is through.

After resting with my back flat on a cool rock in the shade of a ponderosa pine, I got a phone call from a Minnesota area code and was glad I had cell service to answer. I stared at a cerulean-blue sky dotted with clouds while fielding questions from a surgical resident at Mayo about my various risk factors and specialty medications. After hanging up, I walked through the crevice again, hands against lime-green moss-covered giant slabs on either side so that their permanence could pulse into the parts of me that are shifting. I wept there, surrounded by sandstone.

Desire dripped from my lips. I found myself praying in a way that is now rare. "God, I want to be able to do this for many more decades."

I savored every step. I reveled in every ridge. I knew in my aching bones that seeing beauty is a gift.

When I reached the bottom of the hill near the trailhead, I saw an elderly couple beginning their hike. Gray hair, hands held, ascending steps side by side.

Did they know their bodies were prayers?

PRAYER

FOR A LONG time, I wasn't sure I could say *I'm praying for you* and mean it.

An astounding number of people have prayed for me during my descent into medical hell and in the year since. But some of those prayers have brought more pain than peace, more collision than connection.

Something like the seventy-eighth person just told me they are praying Ezekiel 37 for me. "Just like God made those dry bones come back to life, I'm praying that God will breathe life back into your dead bones again."

Honestly, I've actually lost count of how many people have texted, called, or commented saying the same thing, as though they were the first to discover that the bible does, indeed, have something to say about dead bones. They care. They really do. But right now, I don't need dozens upon dozens of people to draw a direct line between an ancient prophet's vision about a whole people group living in oppressive exile and my literal bones.

Rather than hearing my reality, many people want to rush right past it to the first related comfort they can find. It seems that many folks can't tolerate their own anxiety about the fact that absurd and awful things can happen to any of us at any time.

I am not rejecting prayer, nor am I rejecting the possibility that dead things can come back to life. I'm remembering the God I met in the river of time—the cosmic Christ who breathed life into me when I couldn't, the love that connects me to all that lives and will continue to even when every bone in my body has died. I'm returning to a faith that doesn't make God into either a magic surgeon or nothing at all.

For a long time, I secretly wondered if prayer was a possession I lost, a relic of a reality that made more sense. I stopped trying to pray and started watching for love.

The longer I lean toward my pain, the more prayer is coming to mean noticing the love that is present. Prayer is paying attention to life as though we are all inextricably bound up in one another's flourishing. Prayer is participation in the joy that threads us together, weaving grief and goodness into one indestructible love. Surprise of all surprises, prayer now means more than pleading for the removal of pain.

When I say *I'm praying for you,* what I mean is, I'm imagining you standing in the light of a setting sun, smile stretched across your face. I'm visualizing love like a mycelial web, threaded beneath you in joy and in sorrow, pulsing electric with kindness and strength you couldn't create. I'm gathering up the grace that has carried me through my hardest griefs and letting it travel from my lungs to my lips, breath deep and slow, bridging the miles between us. I'm picturing the pain in my body and soul like a storm, lightning splintering energy across a giant sky, and hoping you, too, will face your squalls with feral awe. I'm naming the reality of evil and naming you as good. I'm saying your name aloud multiple times a day—with a huge smile, and sometimes, with tears. I'm stopping to smell the lilacs, pressing my face into their soft mounded petals, willing you to pause. I'm chopping green onions and popping in a bite, blessing what is sharp as the bringer of flavor, trusting you will taste it. Now, when I say *I'm praying for you,* what I mean is, I'm holding you as beloved in the hidden imagination of my heart.

SILLINESS IS A SUPERPOWER

ALL SUMMER, AS I've translated my stack of journals into something resembling a memoir you might not throw in the trash, I've been most surprised by laughter. Horrible things have happened to me, but in rewriting these stories, I can't deny that hilarious things have, too.

I've found ridiculousness scrawled across the pages of my journals, and the humor has served like helium, turning something bleak into a balloon. I've wept at my desk writing this book more times than I can count, but, fuck me, I've also had a riot.

Neither Ryan nor I want to go through yet another hard thing. But, if I'm going to walk through the next decade and beyond on my own legs, we have to give surgery one more shot. So, as we approached surgery and another hard recovery, we decided to take a page out of my own book. We decided to bring some mirth to the misery.

A week ago, a new friend told me about his favorite video game, and I noticed he was talking about it with the same awe that I feel foraging and hiking. I haven't played video games since I was a lonely kid enduring endless miles across America from the couch of our RV on my purple Game Boy. It beat asking *Are we there yet?* as many times as I thought it. But in the years since, I slated video games in the same category as sugar: not nearly as good for you as the substance you could find in a forest or in reading a book. But as I listened to my friend, I realized he was describing an adventure that could be accessible to me in yet another six post-op weeks of not being able to touch grass. He was showing me a way to inject play into pain.

Ryan and I drove to a store the next night and purchased a Nintendo Switch. It took over an hour for us Great Recession Millennials to comprehend that you can purchase games digitally as well as on cartridges. Our Sega Genesis and Super Nintendo cartridge–shaped minds struggled to grasp that this could work just like streaming Netflix on our Apple TV. And that's where the laughter started—in feeling old and inept. And it just never stopped.

I've learned this year that if you can bring silliness to a sad thing, it can't stay just sad.

My new mobility scooter arrived right before we left for the airport this afternoon. Since I need to leave a wheelchair at the top of our stairs, I need a second wheelchair to get around. I chose a lightweight scooter as an act of self-compassion toward my aching wrists and shoulders, so I can hurt less while helping my legs heal.

When the scooter arrived, I propped my phone on a table and filmed myself zooming through the frame, grinning. I dropped *that* utter delight into a text to several friends with no explanation except "Making assistive devices racy since 2024."

On the way to the airport, we named the scooter Toots. Because Toots scoots. And I am a creature who tells people she loves them by sending poop emojis with laser effects, so this way, every time I think of my scooter—which I would much rather not need—I get to smile about a steady stream of fart jokes.

At the Denver airport, Ryan filmed me speeding on Toots through a frame of departure times, and instead of lamenting having to leave home for surgery, we boarded the plane laughing.

We then spent the entire flight to Minneapolis playing Mario Kart. I raced to Mayo fueled by gallows humor and glee, dueling against Ryan's Donkey Kong as Dry Bones, for obvious reasons. Instead of steeling ourselves for the hard weeks ahead, we are leaning hard into happiness.

SUPER BLUE MOON

IT'S NEARLY MIDNIGHT, and Toots is loaded in the back of the rental car beside our suitcases. She's already giving us so much laughter. I figured out how to hold a suitcase *and* my handlebars to scoot to the rental car, even though Ryan was more than happy to wheel both. The quizzical looks I got while driving like that were pure gold.

We drive the hour and a half to Mayo in Rochester under the light of a super blue moon. She glows large overhead, lighting our way south through a blanket of thin, sheared clouds like a kid reading a book far past bedtime, hidden beneath a comforter with a flashlight her parents definitely still see. Astronomers say we won't see another super blue moon until 2037. She stretches in our eyes like a dime turned nickel here at her nearest to Earth. This month, she has come this close twice, her perigee pulling our tides higher along with our eyes.

In the light of this rare moon, I see more than the grief darkening our days. I see silliness. I see patience. I see a spouse who brings me halfway across the country for specialized medical care with no questions asked nor complaints lodged. I have fallen farther than I thought possible when I started writing this book, but the net of love has held me up. The threads of joy cannot be cut. Tomorrow we'll navigate the halls of Mayo for a full day of pre-op appointments. Tonight, we hold hands under the bright light of the rarest moon.

Ryan puts on an album I haven't heard in years. It's Midlake's *The Trials of Van Occupanther,* an album we adored in our earliest years together. The beat takes me straight to the roots of our relationship, falling in love to indie music on a road trip to a conference in Minneapolis, no less, driving the other direction on this same highway.

The track "Young Bride" comes on—Ryan's favorite—and our clasped hands are a portal to the past. I see our younger selves sitting in a similar—though much more janky—sedan nearly two decades ago, before sickness showed up as the background music to our lives. Those two kids had no clue what was coming.

I look at Ryan, his red hair catching the moonlight as he yawns. I am his young bride and he is my steady love—vowed for life at twenty-one and twenty-four, just a year and a half after that road trip, with lips that already knew *in sickness and health* wasn't a suggestion. I would not wish our vulnerabilities on anyone, but I can't deny the beauty of a vow kept. Ryan smiles at the song and then at me as he exits toward Mayo.

DRESS

NEARLY EVERY CHAIR in the giant waiting room is filled. Adults accompany their aged parents, sighing at what has clearly already been a long day. The room is full, but I don't see anyone my age. I pass the chair where I sat alone last December waiting for the appointment that changed my life. I squeeze Ryan's hand three times before sitting down. We get to face this together.

I smooth my clammy hands over small pink flowers on my blue dress. Both times I have come to Mayo, I've worn sweatpants every day, simply because I've been too sick and swollen to stand long days of appointments and testing in something nicer. But today I chose to wear a dress as a small symbol of my slow but substantial recovery. Its side slits are a bonus, since I'll have to show Dr. Drill my legs for his pre-op exam of my knees. I may be having surgery once again, but that fact does not undo the progress I have made. The dress helps me believe it.

I left Toots at our hotel room and walked here instead, because I want my surgeon to see me walk into his office. The last time I entered his exam room, Ryan wheeled me in. I was too sick and in too much pain to stand. Tomorrow, I'll let him drill once more into the necrotic tissue in my femurs and into my hips to harvest stem cells.

Today, I'll show him how hard I've worked to walk.

I CAN'T BELIEVE SHE'S TELLING US ABOUT HER BUTT AGAIN

IT'S 11:18 P.M. in Room 8-225 at Mayo Clinic's Methodist Hospital. Surgery and steroids sure do bring out the silliness in me. I've started to tell friends that writing this book has turned me into an amateur sit-down comic. Apparently, I've now reached the She-Lie-Down Era of post-op comedy. Everything—and I do mean *everything*—is hilarious to me right now. So naturally, I'm writing it all down while drugged. You're welcome!

Once I finally got out of surgery and post-op and was brought up to my hospital room, I met my nurse for the day. Sally is a no-nonsense middle-aged Minnesotan with hair like the sun and a smirking face framed by perfect bangs and cute glasses. I told Sally I needed to pee like a hose about to burst, and since I'm not allowed to "touch the ground" or "leave bed," Sally handed me my old friend, Bedpan.

"Do you know how to use this?"

"Oh, I sure do!" I declared, already quite proud of the Sick Skills I have acquired this year alone. "But here's what I want to avoid." I wagged my finger. "Last time I had this surgery, in February, my catheter came undone, and I woke up in a puddle of pee." I paused for dramatic effect. "It was one of the lowest and wettest points of my life."

I broke out in a series of snort-laughs I couldn't contain.

Sally was, thankfully, also amused. "Well, let's make sure that doesn't happen, shall we?"

We planned to count to three for our team maneuver. I did a pull-up on the metal rod hanging above my bed while Sally shoved an orange bedpan under my butt.

I lifed my bodweight with ease. *Oops I left out some letters. Damn drugs.*

"Wow! You are *strong*!"

"Thanks for noticing!" I laughed my ass off while she wiped it. "I've been swimming five days a week! So I'm glad to hear all that work is paying off!"

Later, Chandler, a kind-faced, maybe twenty-year-old nursing student, got to take his turn assisting with the evacuation of the massive amount of fluids I've been drinking. I taught Chandler how to do the derrière dance. "I'll grab here, and you place that beneath my butt."

The baby nurse-to-be stood at my bedside, arms crossed over his chest. "Are you *sure*?"

The choice was easy. I could either become a stinky human waterfall or let this twenty-year-old dude see my bare butt. "Very sure."

I achieved bladder bliss and, thankfully, Sally returned in time to wipe my ass while I stayed in pull-up position. On her way up from my butt, Sally hit her head on the metal rod so hard, neither of us could pretend it didn't happen, and somehow—perhaps angelic intervention—she didn't spill the nearly overflowing contents of my special orange seat, even though we both were cackling.

Chandler returned once my bottom was covered and declared, "That was the best bedpan usage I've ever seen on this unit! You *are* strong!"

My smile was supercharged. I told Sally and Chandler how sick I was before my last surgery, and how swimming got me here—stronger—how it has become a way to show up for myself, to commit to moving into life, even if that life is challenging.

Sally looked from Chandler and Ryan to me. "Well, you're definitely strong now."

And I have to tell you, I didn't expect joy to come from a bedpan, but here we are.

APPALOOSA BONES

SEPTEMBER

GREGORY ALAN ISAKOV's newest album in five years released the day after I got my port removed last August. I played *Appaloosa Bones* on repeat like it was compounded medicine made with exactly what I needed to get well. It became the soundtrack to this book, the soundtrack to survival.

So I was especially surprised when I got a text from my friend Meredith while flying home from surgery. "I have two tickets to see Gregory Alan Isakov at Red Rocks, and I just realized my seats are handicapped . . . seems like they are meant for you two! IF your body is up for it!"

I showed Ryan and said yes, knowing it would be a stretch.

It's been ten days since surgery. I'm seated on Toots beside Ryan in Row 70 at Red Rocks. This is my first time out in public for something nonmedical since surgery. The air is cool, but the warmth of the day still lingers. We sit in front of a railing, facing the distant-but-clear stage. To our left and right, the vermilion giants of Creation Rock and Ship Rock stand guard, encircling everyone in sound. Beneath us, the amphitheater is packed. Seated beside us are other couples and groups with people in wheelchairs or with canes propped against the long railing. I know gratitude is not a tax that disabled people must pay for getting to participate in life. I know I don't have to feel thankful for a seat I can reach, but I am.

A few days ago at IVIG, I was roomed upstairs. Halfway through treatment, I learned that the elevator had broken. *The wheelchair isn't a prop,* I tried to joke to my nurse. But by the time my last bottle of Octagam was empty, the elevator was still broken, and I found myself having to be rescued by a team of firefighters. I knew there wouldn't be a silver lining to the situation, but I was hoping for at least a smoky one. I regret to inform you that none of the firefighters was even hot. At least I got one more ridiculous story to tell.

This year has given me a crash course in how inaccessible so much of the world is, and it's part of why I am grateful tonight. In many places, I feel like an afterthought. Here, I am included.

Gregory takes the stage against the backdrop of a navy-blue star-studded sky and begins to perform several songs from *Appaloosa Bones,* a title that refers to the many-spotted Appaloosa horse whose bones are uniquely strong.[16]

Isakov recorded the album in a barn on his farm just a little north of here in Boulder County, which he bought after losing almost everything he owned in a flood that he considers the messenger of change he needed most. Isakov had been having panic attacks while touring, but after the flood, he quit drinking and started healing.[17] I read that when creating a new album, he writes dozens of songs before whittling the wood of each album into its final shape.[18]

I hold Ryan's hand as the night grows cooler, spellbound by

16 Chris Young, "From Farm to Stage: A Q/A with Gregory Alan Isakov," *The Source,* August 28, 2024, https://www.bendsource.com/music/from-farm-to-stage-a-q-a-with-gregory-alan-isakov-21754527?media=AMP+HTML.

17 John Wenzel, "Acclaimed Colorado Musician Gregory Alan Isakov Lost Everything, Then Found It Again on a Boulder Farm," *Denver Post,* updated November 17, 2021, https://www.denverpost.com/2018/09/20/acclaimed-colorado-musician-gregory-alan-isakov-lost-everything-then-found-it-again-on-a-boulder-farm/amp/.

18 Ibid.

lullabies formed in loss. I look from the stage to my still-swollen knees. My bones might not be appaloosa strong, but I'm learning to trust the truth that tenacity lives inside me. Like Isakov, I am slowly rewriting a story that speaks to the strength hidden deep within us, a strength we often cannot find without a fall.

TETRIS TRUTHS

I'VE SPENT THE last two weeks filling literal and figurative holes. I've been hard-dropping tetrominoes on a matrix, spinning shapes into submission, letting the little wins of lines cleared light me up. This is not a joke, though I have been making many. I am a video-game person now.

Moment of silence, please.

Most humble apologies to the vast gathering of gamers around the globe. May every book-exalting past version of myself fall prostrate on the ground in repentance at your feet. Forgive her, for she knew not what she did, looking down her nose from the pages of her precious books in silent judgment on you, *wasting your lives.* You've known all along. Play has always been a powerful way of disarming pain.

Fourteen days ago, I was on the receiving end of a power tool, and I am happy to report I am now hole-ier than thou. There are approximately forty new holes in my already Swiss Cheese Knees. I like to imagine myself a medical Leonard Cohen: the holes are where the humor gets in.

Ryan and I have spent the last two weeks treating my post-op pain with play. I've napped more hours than I have in my entire type-A non-napping life, and during my waking hours, we almost beat the entire beginner's level of *Tetris Effect*. That last level is currently kicking our asses, but like despair, I shall beat it.

It turns out, there are nerve endings inside our bones, and they get rather grouchy when someone drills into them. But as I played Tetris, I noticed I was in less pain. I did a little Google Scholar geeking, as one does, and lo and behold: Tetris has been found to improve brain efficiency,[19] reduce intrusive memories of trauma,[20] reduce stress,[21] increase healthy gray matter in the brain in PTSD survivors,[22] and lower levels of anxiety.[23]

It turns out, play is the polar opposite of trauma.[24] While I cannot control my circumstances, I *can* choose the posture I take toward pain. Play is one way to soften what is sharp so that it doesn't pierce the most tender parts of you.

19 Rui Nouchi et al., "Dorsolateral Prefrontal Cortex Activity During a Brain Training Game Predicts Cognitive Improvements After Four Weeks' Brain Training Game Intervention: Evidence from a Randomized Controlled Trial," *Brain Sciences* 10, no. 8 (2020): 560, https://doi.org/10.3390/brainsci10080560.

20 L. Iyadurai et al., "Preventing Intrusive Memories After Trauma Via a Brief Intervention Involving Tetris Computer Game Play in the Emergency Department: A Proof-Of-Concept Randomized Controlled Trial," *Molecular Psychiatry* 23 (2018): 674–682, https://www.nature.com/articles/mp201723.

21 Shruti Rajan Kappil and Anuradha Sathiyaseelan, "Tetris: A Next Generation Stress Buster?," *Research Journal of Social Science and Management* 5, no. 3 (July 2015): 41–46, https://www.researchgate.net/profile/Anuradha-Sathiyaseelan/publication/314239176_Tetris_A_Next_Generation_Stressbuster/links/5c6b74d8a6fdcc404ebae318/Tetris-A-Next-Generation-Stressbuster.pdf.

22 Oisin Butler, "The Brain at War: Stress-Related Losses and Recovery-Related Gains" (PhD diss., Humboldt-Universität zu Berlin, 2018), https://edoc.hu-berlin.de/bitstream/handle/18452/20742/dissertation_butler_oisin.pdf?sequence=3.

23 Jannika Baltes, "Cognitive Resilience in Trauma: Exploring the Impact of Mood and Tetris on Intrusion Development" (master's thesis, University of Groningen, June 2023), https://gmwpublic.studenttheses.ub.rug.nl/2614/1/Revised%20Master%20Thesis%20Jannika%20Baltes.pdf.

24 Breanne E. Kearney and Ruth A. Lanius, "The Brain-Body Disconnect: A Somatic Sensory Basis for Trauma-Related Disorders," *Frontiers of Neuroscience,* November 21, 2022: 16, https://pmc.ncbi.nlm.nih.gov/articles/PMC9720153/; Michael D. De Bellis and Abigail Zisk, "The Biological Effects of Childhood Trauma," *Child and Adolescent Psychiatric Clinics of North America* 23, no. 2 (April 2014): 185–222, https://pmc.ncbi.nlm.nih.gov/articles/PMC3968319/.

Pain has a way of yanking back the curtain on the places where we still believe our personhood is chained to what we produce. Day after ouchie post-op day, I've found myself reaching for my phone to type up some fragment of an Instagram caption or pretty little poem wrested from my still-healing wounds. I've been noticing my penchant to stitch each and every hard day into a doily for your darkness.

Sure, part of my soul says, *I can turn surgery into something stunning.*

Here, the little performer inside me announces, *I will make us potpourri from pain!*

The thing I might love most about Tetris is that when I am playing it, I cannot play performer or poet. When I'm searching for spots to place a shape, I cannot search for the meaning in my misfortune. In Tetris, there is only room for the happy delight of filling in holes.

Ryan went back to work yesterday after two weeks straight of bringing me ice packs and drinks and little treats like it was his purpose in life. Alas, his purpose extends beyond keeping me comfortable, and he's back to seeing his hospice patients. But in these hard days of feeling approximately like a steaming turd, the best things have happened. *Togetherness. Tenderness. Laughter.*

As the day drew closer for Ryan to return to work, my attention became more focused. I relinquished my reflex to turn my pain into inspiration porn. The time was too precious for that. Somewhere along the way, I realized that getting all of this uninterrupted time together was a gift, full of joy. And a present cloaked in pain is still a gift. I guess you could say Tetris taught me that.

ECOTONE

THE STARS ARE a cup of sugar spilt over a blackberry sky. I open the window from the back seat and breathe in cool, clean air carrying the scent of pine. It is a moonless early morning, and we are fifth in line to drive up the alpine road to the summit of Pikes Peak to watch the sunrise.

The road is only open this early four days a year, to a small number of vehicles, and when Tara asked me to join her, I said yes, knowing I'd be seeing the sunrise from a wheelchair beside a friend who knows bodily weakness well. I pinned the date like a pennant to my calendar, announcing to myself that adventure is still possible in a body altered by disease. I don't have to be able to stand to love the land or my life.

This morning's adventure was going to be just the two of us, but Tara's seventysomething British-Canadian dad is visiting and came along as our gruff-but-lovable chauffeur. The gates open, and Bob begins our dark, curving ascent to the top of what the original people of this land named Tava, meaning "Mountain of the Sun."

The thick pine and aspen forests thin as we ascend—an ecotone into the alpine tundra. I'm quiet—listening to Bob and Tara talking in the front seats, smiling as I picture my dad at the wheel of our motorhome or the old Ford diesel truck we always towed, driving our family up more mountains than I can name. It dawns on me that the last time I was on this mountain was with them, on one of our national parks trips.

"You okay back there?" Tara turns to me. "Is it coffee withdrawals or pain?"

"Neither." I smile. "I'm just feeling grateful."

I point back at the red emergency "stop here when flashing"

sign at the hairpin curve we just passed. "For so long, my range was the radius determined by my EpiPen. One year ago, it would not have been safe for me to drive this far from a hospital." My habitat has expanded.

I look out the window at the sheer drop beside us and the city of Colorado Springs in the distance. Bob glances at Tara. "You *will* let me know if you have any chest pains, right?"

She places a hand on his shoulder. "Of course I will, Dad. I brought nitroglycerin with me as a backup."

I blink back small but sudden tears, thinking of my own dad, of both my parents, who, like Bob, have had to watch their daughter, my sister, suffer her own heart attack and all the pain and surgeries and procedures since. I think of them sitting at my bedside, praying my anaphylaxis would stop. There is an unequal distribution of pain in some families, Tara's and mine included. I look from Tara to Bob with tenderness. Our parents love us in ways I can't fully comprehend.

We arrive at the massive concrete and stone visitor center on the summit while it's still dark. Tara retrieves my scooter from the trunk, and I lean out the car door to unfold it. I transfer to the chair and introduce Bob to Toots.

He smiles slyly and wisecracks, "Well, I'm already suffering from Altitoots."

I face-palm, giggling into the freezing cold air before accelerating upwind from him. "What?!" he calls out. "That's what we call it! I'm from sea level!"

Bob opens the door to the summit house, and I scoot in behind Tara.

THE ESSENCE OF ALIVENESS

INSIDE, WE GET the sorriest attempt at a cup of coffee I've maybe ever had—more accurately, hot brown water with a hint of the extract of coffee—and head outside. The light has just begun to turn over the curve of the earth in a line of salmon red topped with tiger orange. The blackberry sky has brightened to lilac and amethyst. A low row of stratus clouds separates the yawning dawn from the night.

I hand Tara my phone while we wait for the full sunrise to film me on Toots zooming through the frame, as is now my chronically silly custom. The light is growing, and I notice a thin layer of frost and snow on the railing and rocks. The foothills beneath us glow, their canyons and saddles sharpened by shadows. Yellow lights dot the land far in the distance as our city begins to wake. It's almost time.

Tara digs into her tan leather crossbody. "I want to anoint you before the sun rises. Would that be okay?"

"Of course." I tear up. "It's more than okay."

Tara stands back against the stone building and rifles through her purse while I take photos of the sky. I turn back to her. "You okay over there?"

"Yeah," she says, "just frustrated. I usually carry anointing oil in my purse—"

"For such a time as this, right?" I smirk. *Of course Tara carries anointing oil in her purse, like all women do.* I can't contain my giggles.

"Well, I can't find it. But I did find eye drops, so I guess that could work."

"That's actually even more perfect," I say, chortling. "It just feels right that you would anoint me with something medical." We both laugh, and a snort sneaks out my nose.

Tara stands next to me, her blond hair covered by a huge black Roots toque, complete with a red maple leaf—ever the Canuck. The sky slowly ripens like fruit, and Tara takes off her gloves and holds my freezing hands in hers.

"There is a lot of essence that carries us, and the same word that means 'essence' in Hebrew also means 'bones.' *Estem*. Sometimes we must have skeletal systems of shared essence. And the reality is that the essence of *you* is already healing bones for other people."

I gasp.

"And that," she continues, "is unfortunately the shitty journey we can't not do as writers. We would do anything else if we could. I don't want the story to hurt in the end, but we both know we can't promise, nor are we promised, what it's going to be. But this kind of thing"—she grasps my hands together, shaking them in hers—"it always will be. And so, no matter what, I anoint you with never losing this moment—not because you won't forget, but because it's shared. Because anointing is never something we give ourselves. And not because I'm special. Okay"—she smirks—"maybe a little—"

"You are," I interject.

"I forgot my fucking anointing oil, but you know—it's fine."

I grin. "This is better."

Tara laughs before continuing, wiping a tear from her eye. "You are anointed and known and loved. And that will never let you go." She uncaps the eye drops, drips them onto her cold fingers, and touches my forehead in the sign of the cross.

"In the name of the Father, and the Son, and of the Holy

Spirit, One God and Mother of us all, I anoint you up here for every mountain you will climb from now on."

Bob wanders up behind us. "May I join in?"

I tear up even more. "Of course."

Bob places a hand on my shoulder and takes a deep breath. "May all the breath in my body join you in healing your body."

They wrap me in a hug, and I stare into the glowing panorama—now neon pink dotted with cumulus clouds against an orangesicle sky. *It is so good to be alive.*

Seated between these two precious humans, anointed by my friend's hands, I realize that aliveness is carried between us, in the place between our pains, not solely on the strength of our own bones. Like this moment, it is always shared.

A PILGRIM

I AM ON the top of the mountain I stared at from my hospital bed day after day for strength. For so long, I dreamed of finishing this book from a national park to close the circle where the story began. But this—this is better.

The distance between that hospital bed and my seat on this mountain has shown me that somehow, joy can meet us anywhere we are willing to be present.

Joy is a feeling we want and a presence we pursue, but even more, it is a thread that finds us. Like cloth that has been cut, we must let our lives be held and stitched back together. Every place of piercing is a prompt to be sewn, from loneliness to love.

When everything in my life changed, joy didn't. I have not journeyed into a new understanding of joy. I've crashed so hard and so often that I'm starting to trust the net laced beneath me is stronger than any fall.

From the forest to my own fragility, I have been shown that love is like mycelium, the web beneath all we see, and joy is simply the sense that we are woven, never truly isolated but ever interdependent. Joy is not the opposite of sorrow nor the absence of grief, but the surprise, sensed over and over, that the truest fact about who we are is that we are connected. Joy is the feeling of finding that underneath your life, no matter how far you've fallen nor how much you hurt, the web of love still holds.

I think I'll spend my whole life sticking a spade into that soil.

A red cog railway train *click-clack*s in front of us, interrupting my reverie, and a crowd of fellow beauty hunters spills out its doors. Tara and I move farther down, past the train, right as the orb of the sun peeks over the plains.

My jaw drops at the sight. Freezing air stings against my tongue. The entire horizon is hot pink contrasted against a low, dark cloud cutting the horizon in two. We get a double scoop of sunrise today, two chances to savor every drip of peach into strawberry light.

I open the camera on my phone again and notice I've gotten a few texts from my best friend. I haven't had service all morning, but I guess we're high enough up to catch a signal. Three weeks ago, I left for Mayo in hopes of holding on to my ability to walk, while Mish flew to Europe on a sabbatical from her job to walk a stretch of the Camino—something we've both separately wanted to do for over a decade. Mish has been texting me pictures along the way of trees tunneling over the trail, small stone chapels filled with light, and her standing beside fellow pilgrims she's met along the way. It's stung to see her walk a trail I may never be able to travel by foot. But I've also smiled, so much, seeing her take a pilgrimage in solitude to better befriend herself.

I open the texts. In a photo, Mish stands with her backpack in front of the towering Santiago de Compostela Cathedral. I laugh. Of course my best friend has finished her pilgrimage in the same hour that I sit on this summit watching a double sunrise, closing the chapter of writing this stretch of my story. The next text from Mish is a screenshot of a tattoo she wants to get, a quote from Meredith on *Grey's Anatomy:* "And the sun still rises on my life."

And it does. The sun still rises on my life.

I do not know if lupus will threaten my life again. I do not know what the coming months will bring. I don't know whether my bones will regrow, or whether the knives in my knees will keep stabbing, cutting off my ability to walk well. The most likely scenario is that they will. When I started writing this book, I thought I was on a pilgrimage into my past to find the good I overlooked, but now I know it was always a pilgrimage into the present, to greet the good that coexists with grief.

I ask Tara to take a picture of me on an overlook as the sun stretches over the last low-hanging cloud. I press myself up with my arms in the corner on the cold railing, hovering above my chair so that my face is suspended against the orange-and-yellow sky.

I smile—free and easy and wide—because no matter what the next chapter of my story holds, I will welcome it.

ACKNOWLEDGMENTS

How we carry the scars of our stories depends on who surrounds them. In *The Wild Edge of Sorrow,* therapist and soul activist Francis Weller tells the story of a young woman in Burkina Faso whose face was scarred in a violent attack by her own mother. Her village immediately surrounded her with care, transforming what could have been carried as shame into support and a deepened sense of her worth and welcome. "In other words," Weller writes, "what occurred to her remained superficial; it did not penetrate beyond the skin and become part of her story. She carries a scar, but her soul is intact. Her village could see her value and helped her remember her essence."[25] I both survived the story of this book and grew

25 Francis Weller, *The Wild Edge of Sorrow: Rituals of Renewal and the Sacred Work of Grief* (Berkeley, CA: North Atlantic Books, 2015), 55–56. Kindle edition.

strong enough to tell it because my own community of witnesses surrounded me with enough kindness to remember my essence will always outlast pain. To them, I now turn with thanks. To Ryan, your love is the purest beauty I have ever seen. I am here because *you* have held me. Mom, sorry not sorry that the soap backfired. Thank you for filling my childhood with curiosity, for loving me as I change, and for daring to choose your own wholeness even though it hurts. By the way, I can trace the imagery of joy being a thread back to you and your love of sewing beautiful clothes for us kids. Dad, the truth is *you* taught me how to work hard, and because of that inheritance, illness does not get to limit my imagination of what is possible to create and achieve in the body I have. Thank you both for all the national parks trips; you laid the foundation for me to live with adventure and awe. To my sister, Kenzie, I hate that we share the same disease, but I thank God I get to endure alongside you. You are going to be a remarkable doctor. To Mom Ramsey, thank you is not enough. Your care in those horrible days kept *me* intact. To Mish, your friendship will always be one of the greatest gifts in my life. To my literary agent, Alex Field, so often you have believed in me and in this book more than I have. I couldn't have written my first memoir, nor found my way through all the stress, without you. To Sarah Southern, thank you for taking the risk of adventure with me, loving me when my light faded, and letting me see the fierce and holy human you are becoming. Don't ever stop writing, my friend. To Sarah Harrison, you see me in a way few ever have; thank you for showing me how to unapologetically be myself. To Sarah Ocando, your friendship through our shared experiences of chronic illness gives me strength to keep showing up in my story; this book is especially dedicated to *you*. To Alexis de Weese, you've basically been my book doula; thank you for always offering me hard wisdom and deep kindness. To Tara Owens, it is a gift to create both friendship and books by your side. To Meredith McDaniel, thank you for singing over the bones and running with the wolves with me from afar. To the many friends who brought us meals, took rides on my Chairiot, laughed—and cried—in my bed with me, and just kept checking in, thank you for showing me I am loved as I change. To all the doctors who ever dismissed me and my symptoms, thank you for giving me the gift of rage to believe my body more than your prejudice and to devote my gifts to the dignity of patients in pain. To Dr. M (Dr. Detective), thank you for dedicating your career to complex patients. To Dr. P (Dr. Space), thank you for honoring the uniqueness of my body. To the many nurses and providers who were present on my worst days, thank you; your kindness made more of a difference than you know. To the team at Convergent, thank you for giving me freedom to write as my feral, feisty self. To my long-standing readers, thank you for supporting me through sickness. I'm still stunned at your generosity. And to all my readers, old and new, thank you for the honor of letting my words keep you company. Here, in the place between my pain and yours, may this book be received as one reminder that your life is worthy of being witnessed, your story deserves to be heard, and your joy will survive.

ABOUT THE AUTHOR

K.J. RAMSEY is increasingly feral and utterly devoted to the joy of being alive. She is a disabled mystic, a body-centered licensed professional counselor specializing in trauma recovery, and an acclaimed author of prose and poetry, including *The Book of Common Courage, The Lord Is My Courage,* and *This Too Shall Last,* as well as the bestselling Substack *Embodied*. *The Place Between Our Pains* is her first memoir. Ramsey advocates for fellow autoimmune patients and lives in Colorado with her husband Ryan, a hospice chaplain, and their two wildly cuddly velcro dogs.

ABOUT THE TYPE

This book was set in Scala, a typeface designed by Martin Majoor in 1991. It was originally designed for a music company in the Netherlands and then was published by the international type house FSI FontShop. Its distinctive extended serifs add to the articulation of the letterforms to make it a very readable typeface.